BYZANTINE CHRISTIANITY

EMPEROR, CHURCH AND THE WEST

HARRY J. MAGOULIAS
WAYNE STATE UNIVERSITY

BYZANTINE CHRISTIANITY

EMPEROR, CHURCH AND THE WEST

WAYNE STATE UNIVERSITY PRESS, DETROIT   1982

Waynebook 48

Library of Congress Cataloging in Publication Data

Magoulias, Harry J.
    Byzantine Christianity.
    (Waynebook; 48)
    Reprint. Chicago: Rand McNally, 1970. (The
Rand McNally European history series)
    Bibliography: p.
    Includes index.
    1. Orthodox Eastern Church—History. I. Title.
II. Series: Rand McNally European history series.
BX290.M3 1982   281.9′3   81-13089
ISBN 0-8143-1704-9   AACR2
ISBN 0-8143-1705-7 (pbk.)

With filial devotion
I dedicate this book
to my parents,
The Reverend Father John Eustratios Magoulias
and Constantina Dounias Magoulias.

Contents

Preface

Byzantine studies in the United States are just now coming into their own. Countless numbers of Americans have never heard of Byzantium, and those who have frequently use the adjective Byzantine to connote intrigue of the worst and most sinister kind. When I went to high school no history teacher ever spoke of Byzantine culture and civilization. Indeed, they seemed to be as ignorant of the Byzantine empire as their students. Perhaps they had read Gibbon's *Decline and Fall of the Roman Empire,* but they were convinced that in an empire of despotic and cruel emperors, corrupt eunuchs, benighted monks and cantankerous theologians forever engaged in abstruse religious controversies much too subtle to be useful, there was nothing that merited serious historical study. Even Byzantine art, with its blatant disregard of the most elementary principles of classical composition and perspective, only confirmed the general estimate of Byzantine civilization. It is now admitted that perhaps no other religious art in history has so well portrayed the miracle of the incarnation of the spiritual and the divine in material form.

In this work I have not tried to enumerate all the major contributions of Byzantium to the course of Western civilization. I have limited myself instead to a survey of Byzantine Christianity, Byzantium's greatest creative contribution to mankind. The final chapter attempts to show how the fortuitous fusion of opposing religious, political, cultural and economic aims culminated in the destruction, by the Fourth Crusade in 1204, of the Byzantine state, the greatest and most enduring Christian empire the world has known.

In an age suddenly and rudely awakened to the need for ecumenism in political as well as religious affairs there is, I believe, a lesson to be learned from the mistakes and the successes of societies that, although separated from us in time and space, are still akin to twentieth-century society in the crucial problems posed by "alien" ideologies and in the desperate search to find the necessary conditions of coexistence. The failure to solve this problem has led, as this text shows, to the murder of some societies.

It is my hope that students of medieval history, political science and theology, as well as those hosts of students in the nation's colleges of liberal arts, will find something of value here to enable them to better understand the world in which they live.

The extensive quotations of the Byzantine historian Niketas Choniates, as well as the briefer portions of the historian Doukas and the mystics, St. Symeon the New Theologian and Nikolaos Kabasilas, have been translated by me. The sources of all other direct quotes can be found in the bibliography.

HARRY J. MAGOULIAS

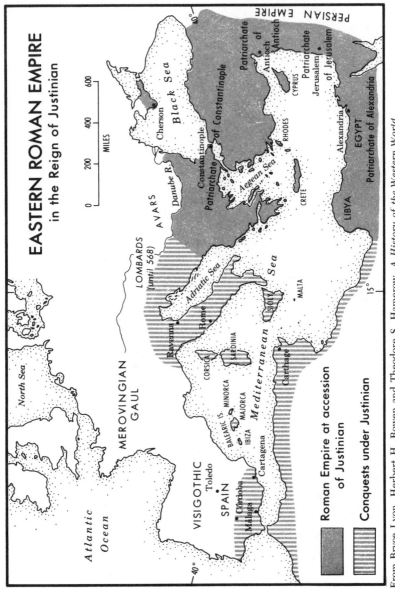

EASTERN ROMAN EMPIRE
in the Reign of Justinian

MILES

0   200   400   600

Roman Empire at accession of Justinian

Conquests under Justinian

Atlantic Ocean

North Sea

MEROVINGIAN GAUL

VISIGOTHIC SPAIN

Toledo

Córdoba

Málaga

Cartagena

BALEARIC IS.

MINORCA

MAJORCA

IBIZA

CORSICA

SARDINIA

Mediterranean Sea

MALTA

SICILY

Rome

Ravenna

Carthage

LOMBARDS (until 568)

AVARS

Adriatic Sea

Danube R.

Black Sea

Cherson

Constantinople

Patriarchate of Constantinople

Aegean Sea

RHODES

CRETE

CYPRUS

Patriarchate of Antioch

Antioch

Patriarchate of Jerusalem

Jerusalem

Alexandria

EGYPT

Patriarchate of Alexandria

LIBYA

PERSIAN EMPIRE

40°

15°

40°

From Bryce Lyon, Herbert H. Rowen and Theodore S. Hamerow, *A History of the Western World*
(Chicago: Rand McNally & Company, 1969), p. 88.

(© Copyright by Rand McNally & Company, R. L. 81-S-56)

Chapter 1

Byzantine Christianity and The Imperial Cult

And thus, by the express appointment of the same God, two roots of blessing, the Roman empire, and the doctrine of Christian piety, sprang up together for the benefit of men.
Eusebius of Caesarea, *Tridecennial Oration* (A.D. 335)

In the fourth century of our era Christian theology was to transform the pagan Roman empire into the Christian state of Byzantium. It was not only that the church was favored by the Emperor, Constantine the Great (324–337), but the imperial ideology itself was consciously Christianized and, consequently, Christianity soon became the official state religion. Byzantine theology, as it evolved, was all-embracing; the state and the church were wedded in Christ. As a result, the imperial cult had its own theology, ritual and iconography. In fact, it formed a close parallel to the divine cult of Christ, and in discussing their respective institutions it is often difficult to tell which came first. In any case, they mutually influenced each other. Therefore, a discussion of the Christian emperor is a must if we are to have an adequate understanding of Byzantine Christianity, one of the most remarkable and unique religious systems in history.

If one were to ask what was the cornerstone of the Byzantine state, the dominant element that set it apart in world history, the answer would be the role of the Christian emperor. To early and medieval Christians he was the central and harmonizing source of law, order, power and civilized life. Byzantium had no written constitution, and the special fascination of the study of its history is how this complex society adapted itself to ever-changing conditions while remaining in essence unchanged.

But to begin: How does a pagan empire become Christian? Unlike Islam, whose founder created a new society under Allah's law, Christianity emerged in a Greco-Roman world with extremely sophisticated legal, social and cultural institutions. If its political framework was Greek and Roman, its unique religious life was rooted in Palestine. With the conversion of Constantine the Great, the Greco-Roman and Jewish tradition had to be somehow amalgamated, a task successfully undertaken by Constantine's contemporary, Eusebius.

PRE-CHRISTIAN BACKGROUND

Actually, the Roman emperors assimilated and developed ideas taken from the Hellenistic kings of the Near East, who in turn were influenced by Hellenic and Asiatic concepts. The Egyptians, the Mesopotamians and their successors the Persians had, from ancient times, looked upon the ruler as a father and shepherd to his people. For Homer, the king was a demigod, standing midway between gods and men. The Greeks had deified their heroes also, considering them to be godly men since one of their parents was a god; as demigods they were worshipped, and statues were erected as a part of their cult. Many of them were honored as founders of city-states.

When Alexander the Great conquered Greece, the Near East and parts of India, thereby creating a universal empire, it was natural for him and his successors to combine these ideas and to introduce the deification of the ruler as a political instrument aiming at the unification of such diverse subjects as Greeks, Persians, Syrians, Egyptians and Indians. Alexander was proclaimed by the Greek philosopher Callisthenes as the son of Zeus. Not only did the priest of the oracle of Ammon, god of Cyrene, announce at Siwah that

Alexander was Ammon's son, but as he had been crowned pharaoh in Egypt he was believed by the Egyptians to be the incarnation of Amon-Re, or Horus. If in Persia the king was not a god incarnate he was nonetheless endowed with the radiant spirit of Ahura-Mazda, the supreme God of Light whose indwelling brilliance dazzled ordinary men.

In the autonomous Greek city-states the critical problem was how to find a legal basis for the monarch's exercise of extraconstitutional authority. As kings the Hellenistic rulers had no such authority, but as gods they had to be obeyed. Thus deification was the answer to the question of how to legalize absolutism. Democracy was feasible in the small, circumscribed, self-sufficient Greek polis, but no form of government other than an absolute monarchy could control vast territories whose populations were so heterogeneous and dissimilar. It was Ptolemy II (273–270 B.C.) who proclaimed himself and his consort Arsinoe gods and demanded worship from his subjects. While the ancient Greeks had declared deserving heroes gods after their death, the Hellenistic monarchs demanded deification in their lifetime. Aristotle, Alexander's teacher, gave support to this practice by claiming that that individual in the state who is incomparably preeminent in virtue and political capacity "should be rated as a god among men."

Plato's ideal ruler was the philosopher-king, who would be both an original scientific thinker of the first order and a moral saint whose personal life would set the standard for the rest of society. Succeeding Greek scholars of the Hellenistic period further developed the theory that the king is to his people as the supreme deity is to the world. To them, the king was also the incarnation of the Logos, the divine spirit of universal reason, and consequently had the unique power to become mankind's benefactor, shepherd, savior, preserver, god-manifest, father. If the king is a god he is also animate law (*empsychos nomos*), the source of all law in the state. As the animate constitution, the king was the unifying and binding element of the state.

The Stoics also supported the idea that monarchy is the best form of government and that the ideal monarch is he who rules in accordance with the Logos. They believed that such a king would rule in accordance with law for the benefit of all men as common citizens in an ecumenical state.

The Old Testament view of kingship is expressed in the Biblical verse, "I will declare the decree: the Lord hath said unto me, Thou art my Son; this day have I begotten thee" (Ps. 2:7). The king is the "anointed of God" (Christos) and God is his father because the ruler personifies the Jewish nation. The New Testament picture of Christ as the king of all men reflects that view and those held by Jewish and Greco-Roman society at that time. Christ, as the anointed of God, is also god-manifest, savior and shepherd of his flock.

The position of the pagan Roman emperor as first developed by Augustus (27 B.C.–A.D. 14) was also subject to evolution. Because of Julius Caesar's tragic failure to make himself a monarch, Augustus was compelled to maintain the fiction that he was preserving the Roman republic. His constitution was based on the sovereignty of the Roman people, which was then delegated to two agents, the princeps (Augustus as the first citizen) and the senate. The princeps was constitutionally a magistrate despite the extent of the dictatorial powers and divine honors accorded him. His dignity was for life and was not hereditary. Not only could it be revoked by the senate, he could theoretically be put to death and subjected to a *damnatio memoriae*, in which case his name would be effaced from all public monuments.

Legally, the princeps' authority was based on the combination of the several magistracies he held: The imperium, bestowed either by the army by acclamation or by the senate by decree, made him imperator, the supreme commander of the army. Tribunician power, conferred by senatorial decree and confirmed by the assembly of the people in Rome, enabled the princeps to convoke and preside over the senate and to veto its decisions. As censor he could modify the membership of the senate to his liking, and as *pontifex maximus* he presided over the official cult. Since theoretically the princeps' power was transmitted to him by the people, he also became the source of law.

Once again deification became an instrument of political expediency. Augustus had the assassinated Julius Caesar proclaimed divine. Tiberius (14–37) did the same for Augustus after his death, and this remained the custom until Domitian (81–96) assumed the title of lord and god in his own lifetime.

By the third century one disaster after another overtook the Roman empire, and almost by necessity the Augustan principate evolved into a military despotism. Civil wars convulsed the empire, and its once vaunted unity was lost temporarily. Invaders swarmed over the defenseless frontiers along the Rhine, the Danube and the Euphrates. As if this were not enough, plague decimated the empire's population from seventy to fifty million. Only a thoroughly militarized state with absolute authority could save the empire. Recovery finally began during the reign of Aurelian (270–275) who was justly called "Restorer of the World" because he defeated the barbarian Germanic tribes along the northern frontiers, recovered Gaul and reconquered the East. Aurelian attributed his victories to the invincible sun-god (Sol Invictus) and erected a temple to this supreme god, the new "lord of the Roman empire." Sol Invictus, believed to have given military victories to the Roman troops, was now claimed to be the source of the emperor's authority and his divine protector. Coins were minted with an inscription declaring Aurelian "born lord and god." The doctrine of the divine right of kings had come into being.

The idea that the emperor had a divine companion (*comes*) was a traditional element of great importance. Those mortals whom the Greek gods in Homer favored were protected and guided, but the emperors of the third century claimed to have come to power in the first place through the providence of a god. Diocletian (284–305) adopted Zeus as his guardian deity, while Constantine, before his conversion, claimed Apollo.

THE CHRISTIAN EMPEROR

One of the most momentous events in history was the conversion of Constantine to Christianity. Although it has been argued that the Roman empire had to become Christian and some emperor had to be converted, no historical law admits to such a necessity. In the empire of Persia Christian churches were established. There, as in the Roman empire, persecutions provided the same opportunity of increasing rather than diminishing the number of the faithful. Yet no Persian king was ever converted. Without royal favor the Christians remained a small minority, and Persia never became Christian although it turned Muslim as the result of Arab military conquest. Within three to four hundred years after the Christian lands of Syria, Egypt, Palestine and North Africa fell under Muslim domination in the seventh century, Christians had become an insignificant minority once more (merely by social pressure, for persecution was rare in Muslim lands). Moreover, when Constantine chose Christianity the Roman senate, the army, and the vast majority of the population in the western parts of the empire were devoted pagans. To the title Peer of the Apostles (Isapostolos), which the Greek Orthodox Church has bestowed upon him, Constantine had a certain claim, for his career profoundly influenced the history of the church and the future of Christianity.

Obviously, the conversion of the pagan emperor Constantine to Christianity posed a peculiar problem to Christian political theorists. The pagan emperor, as we have seen, was finally regarded as one more deity in the pantheon, but one who ruled under the special auspices of the supreme god. What was to be the role of the Christian emperor in this scheme? Christians worshipped only one God, the supreme ruler of the universe, whose kingdom extended over both heaven and earth. The conversion of the Roman emperor required a new definition of his position and function as the ruler of the state. Only a Christian scholar who had studied the pagan philosophers and who, as a result of personal experience, had valuable insight into political questions could provide this definition. Such a man was Eusebius, the metropolitan bishop of Caesarea in Palestine and a close friend and adviser of Constantine. Fortunately, the oration Eusebius composed on the occasion of Constantine's thirtieth anniversary as emperor was preserved for therein we find the fullest and most important single statement of the new Christian political theory. By Christianizing pagan political concepts Eusebius created a unique ideology.

The Platonic ideal, the Hellenistic Logos and the Roman comes were all fused with the concept of the Christian God. In the theory of Hellenistic kingship, the ruler was both an imitation of the supreme deity and the incarnation of that deity's guiding spirit. If the supreme deity was the archetype of the true king, the Logos was the ruler's necessary guide. It is not at all difficult to adapt this Hellenistic framework to Christian political ideology. The Christian God simply replaced the pagan supreme deity as the ruler of the universe; as such he was regarded as the source of imperial power. The Stoic Logos had already been adapted in the Gospel of St. John to designate Christ as the Word (Logos), the second person of the Holy Trinity. The Logos of the Christian Trinity was equated with the comes, the emperor's divine companion who gives him both power and responsibility.

Eusebius next resorted to the Platonic world of ideas to establish the proper relationship between the Kingdom of Heaven and the earthly kingdom and between the King of Heaven and the earthly king. Thus the earthly kingdom is but the mirror-reflection of the Platonic reality, which is the divine kingdom in heaven. The function of the Christian emperor is to prepare his subjects on earth and then to lead them into the Kingdom of God. "And so adorned with the image of the kingdom of heaven, Constantine looks up at the archetypal form [in heaven] and governs those below in accord with it. He is strong in his conformity to the divine monarchical power," writes Eusebius in his *Oration*.

Eusebius then goes on to delineate the emperor's function from the perspective of the divine. God, he maintains, directly teaches and discloses to Constantine the mysteries of His sacred truths and secret wonders. It is true that God alone is perfectly good and strong, "the begetter of justice, the father of reason and wisdom, the spring of light and life, the treasurer of truth and virtue, and the author of kingship itself and of all rule and authority." Since the emperor, however, is the mediator between God and man, he possesses all these virtues automatically. Eusebius stresses that the emperor "moulds his soul by means of royal virtues to a representation of the kingdom above." What Eusebius is saying is that the emperor, as vicegerent of God, has universal power and universal responsibility. The earthly ruler, beloved of God, "bears the image of the highest kingdom. By imitation of the greater king [God], he steers in a straight course all things on earth." Almost a Messiah figure, the emperor singlehandedly defeats the earthly forces of evil. The emperor is the elect of God because the empire represents the divine plan, God's ultimate victory over evil. Theoretically, the Christian empire is coextensive with the inhabited civilized world (*oikoumene*); outside the empire there is nothing but disorder, chaos and barbarism.

The Kingdom of Heaven, like its counterpart on earth, is governed by the supreme monarch, God "the Almighty King," and has a pyramidal, hierarchical structure. Outside it is the chaotic domain of Satan and his demons. Monarchy, consequently, is the ideal form of government. A democratic government on earth would be as unthinkable as a heaven governed not by God but by a parliament of angels. Democracy, in these terms, represents anarchy and chaos.

ATTRIBUTES OF THE CHRISTIAN EMPEROR

After the extinction of the Theodosian dynasty in the fifth century a religious coronation was introduced to enhance the prestige and legitimacy of the emperor. The first instance of a religious coronation recorded is that of Leo I (457–474) who was crowned by the patriarch of Constantinople in 457. Following the outdoor military ceremony during which Leo received the diadem from the hands of a representative of the army, the new emperor proceeded to the Great Church of Hagia Sophia (Holy Wisdom). Taking the diadem from his head he placed it on the holy altar; after a passage from the Holy Gospels was read, Patriarch Anatolios (449–458) placed the diadem back on the emperor's head. In Byzantium, it should be noted, ecclesiastical consecration, a usage that became sanctified by custom, followed the assumption of full imperial power by the emperor.

Whatever the means of access to the throne, whether by election, association or revolution, the emperor was elevated infinitely higher than simple mortals. In acclaiming him the army, senate and people were merely ratifying the divine will; the emperor was "crowned by God." This superhuman relationship of the emperor to God, his divine election, is no better expressed than in the preface of the *De administrando imperio*, written by the Emperor Constantine VII (913–959) for the instruction of his son Romanos II (959–963):

And the Almighty shall cover thee with His shield. . . . Thy throne shall be as the sun before Him, and His eyes shall be looking towards thee, and naught of harm shall touch thee, for He hath chosen thee and set thee apart from thy mother's womb, and hath given unto thee His rule as unto one excellent above all men, and hath set thee as a refuge upon a hill and a statue of gold upon a high place, and as a city upon a mountain hath He raised thee up, that the nations may bring to thee their gifts and thou mayest be adored of them that dwell upon the earth.

The Byzantine conviction of the interpenetration between heaven and earth was so profound that acclamations frequently stated that the emperor reigned jointly with Christ. Also the emperor occupied only the left side of his throne, as the right was left empty for Christ, his co-ruler. Because of the emperor's unique relation to God, with whom he shared the government of the world, the emperor was described as sacred and divine. Everything connected with his person partook of this sanctity—the palace, his vestments, the imperial properties. Those persons who received gifts or insignia of office from the emperor had to do so with covered hands (a custom borrowed from the Persians) to avoid imperial contact with the hands of ordinary mortals. With Diocletian it became obligatory for all persons approaching the sacred emperor to kneel in adoration before him. It was Justinian, however, who insisted on prostration and kissing of the feet. At the same time he required for himself the title of despot which denoted the relationship of master to slave as did the physical act of prostration.

It was Emperor Heraclius (610–641) who first adopted officially the Greek title of basileus to designate emperor. The only other sovereign who was allowed the title of basileus was the king of Persia. However, after the Muslim conquest and the disappearance of the last Persian monarch, the Byzantine emperor remained the only basileus on earth. In general the Byzantine chancellory refused to use this form of address for any foreign prince, preferring in its relations with the West to use the neutral title rex while all other rulers were styled archon or governor. The Greek titles basileus, despot and autokrator all point to the autocratic and absolute power of the Byzantine monarch.

Constantine the Great called himself the "bishop (episkopos) of those outside the Church" while other emperors were honored with the liturgical titles of priest and high-priest. Indeed, the Byzantine emperor had certain liturgical privileges. He had the right to enter the sanctuary reserved for the clergy and for those in minor orders; he could preach to the congregation; he gave himself communion in the manner of the clergy; he censed the icons and the congregation with the censer and blessed the congregation with the three-candle and two-candle candelabra (symbolizing the Holy Trinity and the two natures of Christ), a prerogative of bishops. However, it must be remembered that the emperor was not ordained to the priesthood. Only priests and bishops could celebrate the sacraments of the church. The boundary was clearly defined and could not be crossed: although the emperor was not an ordinary layman, he was also not a priest.

Thus the conviction in the interpenetration of the heavenly and earthly kingdoms, the joint reign of emperor and Christ, the indivisibility of empire and church assured the emperor that in his struggle to defend the Christian state against the barbarian enemy divine assistance would never be lacking. On his way to give battle to the usurper Maxentius in 312 at the Milvian bridge, Constantine was promised victory as the result of a divine vision. Eusebius, who records this famous incident in the *Life of Constantine,* assures us that he heard this story from Constantine himself.

> He said that about noon, when the day was already beginning to decline, he saw with his own eyes the trophy of a cross of light in the heavens against the sun and bearing the inscription "In this sign conquer." At this sight he himself was struck with amazement, and his whole army also, which followed him on this expedition, and witnessed the miracle.

This is a most revealing passage. The cross is called a trophy, a monument or military symbol of victory, and the emperor is promised victory if he uses the symbol of the cross. Constantine also told Eusebius that the same night of the miraculous vision "the Christ of God appeared to him with the same sign he had seen in the heavens, and commanded him to make a likeness of that sign which he had seen in the heavens, and to use it as a safeguard in all engagements with his enemies." The cross was called the victory-giving symbol. If the cross symbolized Christ's victory over death, the prince of darkness, it also signified the emperor's triumph over the barbarian enemy. This idea was also conveyed in the many representations of the emperor showing him holding the orb of the earth surmounted by the cross.

By Christianizing another pagan principle the Byzantine emperor was to secure added assistance on his military campaigns. The pagan Roman emperor was always accompanied by Victoria, the goddess of victory; Victoria was merged with Venus Victrix. These feminine principles were easily replaced by the Virgin Mary, the Mother of God (Theotokos), who became associated with the imperial victories. In 610 when Heraclius appeared before Constantinople at the head of a fleet determined to overthrow the tyrant Phokas (602–610), he had attached icons of the Virgin Mary to the masts of his warships. Henceforth, the Theotokos became the patroness and protectress of Constantinople. All subsequent victories were attributed to the Blessed Virgin who, it was believed, would never abandon the city of Constantinople in which she actually dwelled. Together with the cross, the holy icon of Theotokos called the Hodegetria, meaning the leader, became the trophy of victory par excellence. Thus the pagan Roman belief in the emperor's divinely predestined victory was Christianized and remained an essential aspect of the imperial mystique.

When the Emperor John II Komnenos (1118–1143) returned victorious from his campaign in Anatolia against the Turks, he decided to celebrate his victory with a triumphal procession into Constantinople. He ordered a chariot fashioned of silver and embellished with semiprecious stones. This historic event is described by Byzantine historian Niketas Choniates.

On the day that the triumph was to take place, purple-bordered and gold-embroidered veils adorned the boulevards. Nor were the likenesses of Christ and the saints, as many as were embroidered by the hand of the loom on frames which, as it was said, appeared to be alive and not inwoven, missing from these places. These things were worthy of wonderment as were the wooden scaffolds and platforms set up on either side of the triumphal way. The regions of the city, prepared in this fashion, extended from the eastern gates of the city to the Great Palace itself. And indeed the exquisitely fashioned chariot was pulled by four beautifully maned horses whiter than snow. Having given up his own place on the chariot the Emperor mounted on it the icon of the Theometor [God's Mother] in which he rejoiced . . . and ascribing the victories to her as the unconquerable general, and having given the reins to be held by his most powerful officials. And having directed his relatives to attend the chariot on either side, he himself preceded, holding in his hands the Crucifix and travelling over the route on foot; and having entered the Church named for the Wisdom of God [Hagia Sophia] and having rendered thanks to the Lord God before all the people for his achievements he thus directed himself to the palace.

The festivities were then continued with chariot races in the hippodrome. The hippodrome was actually the center of the imperial cult. All public life, in fact, gravitated here. The Blue, Green, White and Red stable factions, called *demes* and representing the popular parties of Byzantium up to the ninth century, were officially incorporated by the imperial government to participate in all state ceremonies, and their stations and functions in the hippodrome were spelled out in detail in the Byzantine ceremonial code. In the ritual of the imperial cult they chanted special hymns on behalf of the emperors.

Whether it was an audience for foreign ambassadors, a procession to the Great Church of Hagia Sophia and the celebration of a special feast day, a magnificent banquet given in the Hall of the Nineteen Couches or games in the hippodrome, every gesture of the emperor was minutely prescribed, as were those of all who participated.

The intricate, complex, colorful and magnificent court ritual was the externalization of the imperial majesty and served as a propaganda mechanism. The emperor's daily life had to conform to the strictest regimen. "For just as a body that is not elegantly formed but consists of disproportionate members may be justly described as disorderly, so the emperor's conduct, if it is not carried out in an orderly fashion, will not differ at all from the life of a private individual," writes the Emperor Constantine VII in the preface of the *De ceremoniis* (*Le Livre des Cérémonies*), his compilation of court ceremonies. By collecting the proper rituals, he goes on, we may "represent the harmonious motion of the Creator's universe; the imperial dignity will appear nobler to the subjects and therefore sweeter and more admirable."

There was a prescribed ceremony for every important event in the life of the imperial family from birth to death. For example, on the birth of a son and successor in the purple chamber of accouchement, special prayers of thanksgiving were offered. Eight days later, when the newborn infant received his Christian name, the imperial couple sent blossoming branches to the nobility as a special invitation to attend the solemn occasion and the banquet that followed.

The sanctuary of the imperial cult, of course, was the sacred palace. The main audience hall, the Chrysotriklinos, was built exactly like a church, with a cupola over a cross-in-square foundation. Instead of an altar in the east end (apse), there stood the emperor's throne. In the case of an audience meant to impress and awe foreign ambassadors, the emperor was enthroned under a canopy like the ciborium standing over the altar of a church. It is worthwhile to cite here the description of such an audience granted to Liutprant, Bishop of Cremona (described in his *Works*), who came to Constantinople in 949 as the envoy of Berengar II:

> Before the emperor's seat stood a tree, made of bronze gilded over, whose branches were filled with birds, also made of gilded bronze, which uttered different cries, each according to its varying species. The throne itself was so marvellously fashioned that at one moment it seemed a low structure, and at another it rose high into the air. It was of immense size and guarded by lions, made either of bronze or of wood covered over with gold, who beat the ground with their tails and gave a dreadful roar with open mouth and quivering tongue. Leaning upon the shoulders of two eunuchs I was brought into the emperor's presence. At my approach the lions began to roar and the birds to cry out, each according to its kind. . . . So after I had three times made obeisance to the emperor with my face upon the ground, I lifted my head, and behold! the man whom just before I had seen sitting on a moderately elevated seat had now changed his raiment and was sitting on the level of the ceiling.

The splendor and opulence of the imperial palaces, the awesome imperial audience, the colorful processions and impressive and complicated church ceremonies, the hippodrome games, the lavish imperial banquets, the exquisite beauty of official costumes and the refinement and sophistication of Byzantine etiquette all had but one end: to demonstrate the superiority of Byzantine civilization to the rest of the world, to show that the emperor, God's vicegerent on earth and the sun around which Byzantium revolved, was far superior to all the other kings and rulers of the civilized world.

THE PROBLEM OF CAESAROPAPISM

As a Christian emperor Constantine believed himself responsible for keeping the peace within the church; perversion in doctrine might lead to God's wrath and result in the physical ruin of the state. This was a problem with which the pagan emperors never had to deal.

Christians were periodically persecuted by pagan authorities, but this was because their refusal to accept the political ideology of the Roman state by recognizing the emperor as a deity was construed to be an act of treason. The revolutionary introduction of the concept of orthodoxy, the insistence on the "correct" and "true" faith as opposed to all other "corrupt" faiths made the state vulnerable to the disrupting ills of heresy. Although the Roman pantheon had no difficulty welcoming and including one more god, the exclusion of all deities but the one true God created new problems and required a radically new attitude toward the world and man's role in history.

Constantine was soon made aware of the new ramifications of his function as a Christian emperor. In a letter concerning the Donatist controversy in North Africa, a dispute over the validity of the sacraments of those clerics who had surrendered church books and holy vessels to the pagan authorities during the persecutions, Constantine wrote:

> And all these quarrels and wrangles might well rouse God not only against the human race, but also against me, to whose rule and care his holy will has committed all earthly things. . . . I shall never rest content or expect prosperity and happiness from the Almighty's merciful power until I feel that all men offer to the All Holy the right worship.

The pagan Roman emperor also had been both the chief religious functionary of the state (pontifex maximus) and the secular ruler, but there had been no question of a pagan church and pagan orthodox doctrine. The Constantinian Peace, however, brought with it a new dimension to the supreme responsibility of the emperor on earth. The Christian monarch, as Constantine clearly understood, was also responsible for the well-being of the Christian church; and the welfare of the church was viewed as inextricably bound to the destiny of the state.

Heretofore, Christian society had been alienated from the Roman state—at best ignored and at worst persecuted for treason. With Constantine's conversion, Christianity became the norm, a unity embracing all aspects of Greco-Roman civilization. The tables had been turned and paganism was on the defensive.

As vicegerent of God, if no longer a deity himself, Constantine looked upon his function vis-à-vis the church as comparable to that of the bishop; he was charged with the conversion of non-Christians in the empire. This new Christian political ideology was to have far-reaching consequences for the future development of church-state relations. The point here is that the fourth-century church, emancipated and favored by the emperor, officially recognized his responsibility in church affairs. The Christian Roman empire was a unity, and no firm division between church and state was conceived. The church was bound by its great debt to the emperor and honored him for his great services to the Christian cause.

This brings us to one of the most controversial topics of medieval history. Some Western scholars, whose attitudes have been colored by their Latin, Anglo-Saxon and Germanic backgrounds, have accused the Byzantine emperors of being guilty of Caesaropapism. The term itself was coined in the West and discloses a special bias, implying that the Byzantine emperor exercised absolute control over the church, even in matters of doctrine. The claim that the Byzantine emperor was both Caesar and pope is misleading. No pope, in the course of Byzantine history, had the authority, outside an ecumenical council, to pronounce alone on dogma. When certain emperors did interfere in church affairs they did so because they conceived such action to be their prerogative as supreme ruler and vicegerent of God, and not because their authority usurped that of any pope. The foremost duty of the Byzantine emperor, as we have seen, was to lead his subjects to God and to guard the purity of the true faith.

It is undeniable that the emperor appointed and deposed patriarchs, altered the boundaries of ecclesiastical jurisdictions and legislated on behalf of good order and discipline concerning clerics, monks and church institutions. But could the emperor, on his own authority, pronounce on dogmatic truths? This alone is the crucial issue because the church accepted his power to do all the rest.

Dogma is based on what the Greek church calls Holy Tradition. Holy Tradition, as distinct from the many and varied local traditions, includes the Holy Scriptures, the authoritative theological writings of the great church fathers, and the elements of faith set down and formulated by the first seven ecumenical councils. In this crucial sphere of the formulation of dogma, it was not the emperor who was charged with this prerogative but the bishops in ecumenical councils under the infallible guidance and inspiration of the Holy Spirit. Even the despotic Justinian, when trying to formulate dogma on his own, was finally compelled to convoke the Fifth Ecumenical Council to confirm his pronouncements. "It has always been the practice of our orthodox and imperial forefathers," he writes in a letter to the Ecumenical Council of 553, "to counter every heresy as it arose through the instrumentality of the most zealous priests assembled in councils and to keep the Holy Church of God in peace by sincere preaching of the true faith." The authoritarian iconoclast emperors also felt the need to convoke councils (albeit packed) to give the semblance of official sanction to their dogmatic views.

The first seven ecumenical councils, it must be understood, were convoked neither by the pope nor by the eastern patriarchs but by the Byzantine emperors. The emperor or his representative, in fact, presided over the proceedings, a usage inaugurated by Constantine himself. These councils of bishops were regarded as a kind of ecclesiastical senate, and the same procedure was applied to them as was followed in the Roman senate. It should be recalled that the emperor did not vote with the senators and that it was this limitation that saved the principle that the definition of faith, the formulation of dogma, is solely the prerogative of bishops. The emperors, however, signed the decisions of the councils and proclaimed them law binding on every Christian throughout the empire. Again, the validity of the ecumenical council depended upon the presence of the patriarchs of Rome, Constantinople, Alexandria, Antioch and Jerusalem or their representatives.

The emperor, it is true, might exercise undue influence and pressure on the bishops who sat in the church councils. But the views of the majority of both clergy and laity could not be defied by even the most authoritarian emperor, and more than once the will of the people overturned the decisions reached by the bishops. When at the end of the empire's life two emperors packed the Council of Lyons in 1274 and the Council of Ferrara-Florence in 1439 with Greek bishops who agreed to vote on union with Rome, the masses in Byzantium, both churchmen and laymen, refused to accept the councils' decisions subjecting the Greek church to the papacy. In the fifteenth century the true defenders of the faith, the repository of orthodoxy, proved to be neither the emperor nor the bishops, but the laity and the clergy, who together constituted the conscience of the church. The emperor, we may conclude, could not formulate dogma *ex cathedra*.

Chapter 2

Byzantine Christianity and The Heresies

In the Greco-Roman world, the problem of how best to rule an extensive empire, composed of heterogeneous populations, was finally resolved in favor of divine monarchy. In the fourth century, as we have seen, the role of the Christian emperor was conceived as a mirror image reflecting God in the Kingdom of Heaven. On earth, the Christian basileus was God's vicar.

The idea of a universal government appointed by God for the benefit of all men was paralleled by the concept of one church and one faith established by Christ for the salvation of all mankind. In other words, the church and the empire were coextensive. If the empire had to defend itself against its external foes, the barbarians, the church also had to deal effectively with her enemies, the heretics, the dissenters or sectarians. Should the purity of the faith be jeopardized, the consequences would be fateful for the destiny of the empire. As Constantine I was soon to learn, the question what constitutes "right worship" had no easy answer. The heated political controversies of the classical Greeks were succeeded by incandescent theological disputes in the Greek East.

A true or correct opinion had always been the ideal of the ancient Greeks. They were the first people on the stage of history to use reason (dialectic) to scrutinize, classify, criticize and evaluate all existing political and ethical systems. From the Greek *ortha dokein* comes the concept orthodox, all-important to the Christian empire. To transgress the proper limits of anything was considered to be the sin of hubris for the ancient Greeks, and nemesis, its punishment, was sure to follow. For the church, theological hubris became heresy, transgression against the true faith, which was punished by anathematization or excommunication in church councils. For the Christian empire whose material well-being depended on orthodoxy, heresy was tantamount to treason.

Latin and Greek Christians, however, began early to diverge in matters of theological emphasis, customs and usages. The critical question was soon raised: What is the exact relationship between Christian faith and Greek reason? The Latin Tertullian (ca. 160–230) had asked rhetorically: "What does Athens have to do with Jerusalem?" Evidently, he thought, nothing. The fathers of the Greek East thought differently. They contended that the divine revelations unfolded in Holy Scripture needed to be probed and interpreted in order to give them their full meaning. The monumental task set before the church was to define clearly the limits bounding the essence of the Christian message within which reasoning may move freely without ceasing to be Christian. This is what the Greek fathers accomplished.

Indeed they sought to raise faith to knowledge with the use of Greek philosophy. A valuable source for this attitude is St. Basil's short treatise, *How the Young Can Profit from Greek Literature.* "Just as we avoid the thorns when we cut the flower of the rosebush," he writes, "in like manner we must protect ourselves from that which is damaging, picking only the beneficial fruit of Greek literature." St. Gregory of Nazianzos adds:

> Thus we have retained from pagan culture whatever is the study and theory of truth; whatever, however, leads to demons, to deceit and the abyss of destruction we have repelled. But all, even their deceits, are useful to our piety, for they make us know the good by antithesis with evil, for with their weakness they strengthen our teaching. We must not condemn knowledge, therefore, because some would have us do so.

Thus, in the Greek East from the fourth century on, the classics became the possession of both pagans and Christians.

Two important theological schools had very early emerged: one in Alexandria and the other in Antioch. The question on which they were most divided was: "Where ought we to seek the essence of religious faith—in the spirit or the letter of Scriptures?" Alexandria opted for the spirit and Antioch for the letter.

The Catechetical School of Alexandria, which was elevated to a theological school by Pantainos (died 202) at the end of the second century, was characterized by freedom in thought, the elevation of faith to knowledge through philosophy and use of the allegorical method in the study of Scriptures. These methods, of course, were not new; the Stoics had used them in interpreting Homer, and Philo of Alexandria (30 B.C.–A.D. 50) had employed them in his attempt to use Greek philosophy to interpret Judaism to his contemporaries.

Allegory, one of this group's major tools, goes beyond the immediate meaning of a word to its deeper, hidden meaning. This comprehension of Holy Scriptures in their "ineffable and mystical and difficult meaning" is no easy matter. Origen (died 254), a successor of Pantainos, concluded that there are three levels of meaning in the Bible: first, the *somatic* or literal (this is the body, so to speak, of Holy Scriptures); second, the *psychical* or ethical; third, the *pneumatic* or mystical and prophetic. These levels can also be used to represent the three categories of Christians, proceeding from the simple believer to the perfect Christian who fully comprehends the spirit of scripture. To understand fully both somatic and psychical levels, however, one must work back from the highest (pneumatic) stage. Here is an example of how Greek philosophy is used to give a Christian interpretation to an Old Testament text. Clement of Alexandria (died 220), who also followed Pantainos, writes: "Moses, certain that it will never be possible to know God through human wisdom, cries out, 'Appear unto me my God,' and the Divine Voice is quickly lost in the darkness from whence it came." But what is this darkness? Clement says, "It is the ineffable and formless idea of being, for indeed God is not found in darkness or in space but beyond space and time and the quality of things." Thus does Clement describe the appearance of God to Moses in the burning bush.

As opposed to the theological school of Alexandria, which favored the interpretative method, the School of Antioch, founded in 260, adopted the grammatico-historical approach. Staying as close as possible to the letter of the text, the followers of this school rejected allegorical meanings and concerned themselves with the immediate meaning of words. They sought the moral, historical and human elements in Holy Scripture, preferring to eschew the mystical aspects of the Christian faith. Their methodology, in fact, led to rationalism. It is important to note that with the exception of the Alexandrian Origen, all the great heretics of the church came from the theological school of Antioch. The most complete interpretation of Scriptures, one might add, requires the combination of both methods, textual criticism and allegory.

The originality of Byzantine culture is that it gave a new content to every element borrowed from Greek philosophy. There was a mutual influence: the Christian chose certain propositions from Greek philosophy, and these acquired a new content in their Christian synthesis. At the same time, these propositions opened new horizons of thought.

The pivotal issue of Byzantine Christianity was the person of Christ. All the major Christian heresies dealt with by the first seven ecumenical councils centered on the second person of the Holy Trinity, the Logos, or the Word, that became incarnate as Jesus Christ. What was the exact relationship between Christ's humanity and his divinity? Was Jesus a deified man, a humanized god or perfect God and perfect man at the same time? For several centuries this cardinal problem of definition convulsed the church. Consequently, the one church was fragmented.

Sectarians, it must be remembered, are always "orthodox" in their own eyes. And when emperors joined them and gave them their official support and delivered over to them the major episcopal sees, they constituted, for a time, the established church. To avoid misunderstanding, however, by "orthodox" we shall mean that party which adhered to the definitions and doctrines formulated by the seven ecumenical councils beginning in 325 and ending in 787. Thereafter, we shall distinguish between the Greek (Orthodox) Church of the Byzantine empire and the Roman or Latin Church of the West.

ARIANISM

The first great religious crisis in the fourth century was initiated by a priest in Alexandria whose name was Arius (256–336). His doctrine was therefore called Arianism. A speculative thinker, Arius put forward a teaching that led to a quarrel with his bishop, Alexander. If God is a divine unity with no parts, no passions and emotions, how can Christ be divine also? If Christ is the incarnate Word of God, argued Arius, he must be a radiation from God— divine, in a sense, but not as divine as God. Christ must be subordinate to God since his nature must of necessity differ from the nature of God.

Arius was a well-trained theologian; he had been the student of the founder of the theological school of Antioch, St. Lucian, a martyr in the persecution of 312. His doctrine caused rioting in the streets, and the brilliant Athanasius (ca. 293–373), Bishop Alexander's archdeacon and protégé, opposed Arius by contending that Christ's nature is the same as God's. God is man (Christ) who is fully God. Compromising his former position, Arius emphasized not the differences in the natures of Christ and God but their similarity. Arius introduced the term *homoiousion,* meaning that Christ is of like essence or substance with the Father. The Athanasians used the term *homoousion,* meaning that Christ is of the very same essence or substance as the Father.

Constantine I was scandalized by the quarrel; the unity of the church was too important to allow this division to continue. The emperor dispatched his personal chaplain, Hosius, Bishop of Cordova in Spain, to Alexandria with a letter exhorting both parties to become reconciled for the sake of church unity. After all, or so thought the emperor, it was only a minor matter. It is all right for philosophers to discuss such issues, but they should not introduce them to the public. Constantine, no theologian himself, could not understand the issue's implications, and his advice was rejected by both sides.

Let us now take a closer look at Arius's teachings. Arius contended that "there was a time when Christ was not." In other words, Christ was not eternal. Christ, he explains, was created out of nothing but before time. Since this is so, he was subsequent and inferior to God the Father; thus God was not always the Father. God cannot be a progenitor, said Arius, since this involves passion; God is impassible. Arius preferred, therefore, to think of God as a creator who brought Christ into being out of nothing as the first fruit of all creation. Christ was made of matter and consequently could not be of the same nature or essence as God. Such a Christ, who was not of the same substance as the Father but created out of nothing, could never know God perfectly. Jesus is only figuratively "the son of God." Christ can be thought of as God only by participation and as such he can be worshipped, but the essence of divinity Arius reserved for God alone.

The Athanasian party contended that Arius's teachings were inconsistent and illogical. If Christ were a created being, then the Arians, by according him worship, were guilty of idolatry. If Christ is not of the same essence as God, then the Arians were guilty of destroying monotheism by worshipping him. By claiming that at the Incarnation Christ had assumed a human body and soul and that the place of human reason was taken instead by the Divine Logos, the Arians had, in effect, repudiated the belief that the second person of the Holy Trinity had truly become man. The Arian Christ was neither perfect God nor perfect man. The emperor insisted on conciliation and wanted unanimous approval of the council's decision. He himself put forward the homoousion formula, supporting thereby the Athanasian party as orthodox. The doctrine that Christ is of the same essence as the Father preserved monotheism by declaring that the persons of the Holy Trinity shared in the divine essence. The bishops of the Council of Nicaea drew up a creed repudiating Arius's propositions and stating the orthodox teaching of the church concerning the person of Christ. Those who refused to sign the Creed were exiled, and Arius's books were ordered burned. The decisions of the Council were confirmed by the imperial signature and became a part of imperial legislation; heresy was now treason to the state.

Eusebius, a moderate Arian, described the Council as a unique episode in the history of the church. The Council of Nicaea, he claimed, was the work of God; it was a new Pentecost.

Unfortunately, the problem of Arianism was not definitively resolved at Nicaea. Constantine himself fell under the influence of the Arian bishop of Nicomedia. The emperor believed that peace could be restored to the church only if Arius were reinstated; it seemed as though Arius was finally to triumph. But while on his way to his acquittal, he died in a latrine from an intestinal rupture—a death, say his detractors, befitting his foul teaching! Paradoxically, Constantine, "Peer of the Apostles," a saint of the Greek church, was baptized on his deathbed by Eusebius, the Arian bishop of Nicomedia.

Thanks to the Cappadocian Fathers—St. Basil the Great (ca. 330–

379), Archbishop of Caesarea in Cappadocia, St. Gregory of Nyssa (ca. 332–398), his eminent philosopher brother, and St. Gregory of Nazianzos (ca. 329–390), also called "the Theologian"—the orthodox finally won out. The Cappadocian Fathers, as they are known, used the "club of Greek philosophy" to beat down the Arians.

St. Gregory of Nyssa put a series of paradoxes before Arius's successor, Eunomios (died ca. 393), Bishop of Cyzicus. The paradoxes are an example of St. Gregory's extremely sophisticated logic. The Arians, as we have seen, claimed that God, as Father, must be prior to the Son who must logically come after; the Son cannot exist before the Father. In other words, there must be an interval of time between the two, Father and Son. The paradox then is this: if there is an interval of time between Father and Son, then God as Father must have a beginning in time and cannot be eternal. For example, if man was created five days after the creation of heaven, then five days prior, heaven did not exist; or again, if two roads are unequal and we place one on top of the other it becomes clear that one is longer than the other; the longer one has a beginning at a certain point and therefore must have a beginning in time. To maintain the eternity of the Father, however, we must eschew the idea of a beginning for the Son. In eternity, as in the Holy Trinity, there can be no beginning or end; there is no time in eternity; ideas of before and after are contingent upon time. Time and space, the created world, all came into existence simultaneously; there was no space or time prior to creation. Eternity is uncircumscribed, unlimited and not subject to the categories of space and time. In eternity all things are equally present, coeval. The Father, Son and Holy Spirit cannot be divided by time and space. The Arians, however, admitted that Christ was not created in time but before all other creatures. They fell into irrationality, and Gregory won on a point of logic.

Eunomios also claimed that God, being unbegotten (ungenerate), could never be of the same essence as that which is begotten. St. Gregory replied: Adam was unbegotten since he was created; Abel was born of Eve and yet both Adam and Abel were men of the same essence or substance; hence, the Father is of the same substance as his only-begotten son Christ. Again, Eunomios was defeated by a master of logic.

Arianism did not have either social or nationalist overtones, but it did kindle, even in popular circles, this keen and almost all-consuming interest in theological subtleties that was to persist throughout Byzantine history. St. Gregory of Nyssa refers tartly to how the controversy of Arianism permeated all levels of Byzantine life: "If you ask how much something costs, they tell you about the Begotten or the Unbegotten. If you ask the price of bread, they reply, 'The Father is greater and the Son is subordinate to Him.' If you ask, 'Is the bath ready?' they reply, 'The Son was made of nothing.' "

MACEDONIANISM

The Arian party next shifted its attack to the Holy Spirit. Macedonius, Patriarch of Constantinople (342–346; 351–360), whose heresy was called Macedonianism, challenged the orthodox regarding the third person of the Trinity. Is the Holy Spirit begotten or unbegotten? If either, how does he differ from the Father or the Son? To resolve this problem the orthodox resorted to the scriptural text: "But when the Comforter is come, whom I will send unto you from the Father, even the Spirit of truth, which proceedeth from the Father, he shall testify of me" (John 15:26). Thus the Holy Spirit is neither a creature nor a son, since he is neither fashioned nor begotten. The Holy Spirit's mark of distinction is procession, which in itself is incomprehensible since it defies human thought. To use an inadequate simile, the Holy Spirit is comparable to the rays emanating from the sun. Travelling to earth they give off heat and promote life. At the same time, the rays are distinct from the sun, yet they are one in essence with it. So does the life-giving Spirit proceed from God the Father. The inter-relationship between the persons of the Trinity have now been defined. The Father is ungenerate or unbegotten and proceeds from no other source; he begets the Son before all ages and the Holy Spirit proceeds from him eternally. The paradox is that each of the three persons is fully God and, while distinct, contains the wholeness of the Godhead.

APOLLINARIANISM

Contemporary with Macedonianism was another heresy called Apollinarianism for its founder Apollinarius of Laodicea (died 390) who taught in Antioch. According to his doctrine, man is constituted of three distinct parts: body (soma), animal soul (psyche), and mind or reason (pneuma, nous). Christ, he contended, had no human mind and reason which could lead to sin and corruption. Its place was taken by the Logos. Thus Christ was the divine mind incarnate, a flesh-bearing God. He was a mean between God and man, neither wholly God nor wholly man but a mixture like that of black and white, which produces grey.

The attributes of both God and man according to Apollinarius are not destroyed or lost, just as mixing water and wine does not destroy their own peculiar qualities. The energy of the Godhead may operate either separate from, or in combination with, the flesh. Christ felt hunger only when the Godhead did not operate on the flesh. To explain how it was possible for Christ's deified flesh to undergo the human experiences of birth, growth, hunger, crucifixion and death, Apollinarius resorted to the New Testament doctrine of *kenosis*. "[Christ Jesus], who being in the form of God, thought it not robbery to be equal with God but emptied himself, and took on him the form of a servant" (Philippians 2:67). Thus the Incarnation was an emptying out of God; Christ imposed limits upon himself.

Apollinarius refused to say that Christ was God dwelling in a man, because this would have meant there are two persons in Christ—God and a man. The doctrine of kenosis explained how the Godhead came into contact with human flesh; it was not a conversion of the flesh into divinity or a confusion of the two, but a voluntary limitation. The Godhead can never be contained within the body or reduced to corporeality. Even while on earth, Christ continued to be everywhere; his divinity was unimpaired but permitted him to yield to human modes of existence. The union is so complete that even though we can distinguish between divine and human attributes it is proper to associate them with one another. There is a sharing, an interchange of attributes. The body that the Logos assumed became part of the Lord, and the body's properties also became the Lord's, but neither is the divinity transformed into the flesh nor the flesh into the divinity. It is comparable to fire being applied to iron; the iron becomes red hot like fire but does not change its essence. The interchangeability of the divine and human attributes of Christ became the orthodox view.

It is true that Apollinarius's system did preserve monotheism; it explained the unity of Christ's person and it seemed to make salvation possible. If Christ had been merely a man in whom God dwelt, he could not have saved man from sin and death. Instead, Christ retained his full divine power and was not bound to a human mind chained to passion and emotion. The Divine Logos directs Christ in sinlessness; the conquest of sin in Christ could not have been effected had the Logos not acted in place of the human mind.

Thus Apollinarianism seems logical, but it too had serious defects. The humanity of Christ, as the orthodox party was quick to show, is completely compromised; Christ is less than human if he lacks human reason; consequently, Christ could not have redeemed man. St. Gregory of Nazianzos stated the orthodox position succinctly: "What Christ did not assume he could not redeem."

Apollinarius, moreover, claimed that Christ had always been "the son of man"; he descended from heaven in the flesh and was not really derived from Mary. The flesh, therefore, existed before the Incarnation; the man Christ existed before all creation and before all ages. Yet Apollinarius insisted that the flesh of Christ is not consubstantial with God but is true human flesh. Having foreseen Adam's sin, God provided for the incarnation and future sacrifice of his Son for man's redemption.

Apollinarius introduced a monophysite view of Christ by holding that Christ was "one incarnate nature of God the Logos," thereby rejecting the orthodox dyophysite position that Christ had two perfect natures, one divine and one human. He felt that the dyophysite view destroyed the unity of Christ's person, splitting him into two persons. For Apollinarius "The Word became flesh" (John 1:14) meant only that God had assumed flesh, not that he had become true man.

Both Macedonius and Apollinarius, together with their heresies, were condemned by the Second Ecumenical Council, convoked in Constantinople in 381 by Emperor Theodosius I (379–395). The Nicene-Constantinopolitan Creed was then published and received the full weight of the emperor's authority.

The Second Ecumenical Council of Constantinople also took an extremely important step concerning church administration. The third canon states: "The bishop of Constantinople shall rank next to the bishop of Rome, because Constantinople is New Rome." It is important to note here that the ecclesiastical preeminence of both old Rome and new Rome (Constantinople) hinges not on their being apostolic foundations but on the fact that Rome was the capital of the empire in the past and that now Constantinople is the capital. It was the emperor's prerogative to alter the boundaries of ecclesiastical jurisdiction that allowed him to place the bishop of the imperial residence ahead of both Alexandria and Antioch in the hierarchical lists of precedence. The latter might chafe, but the emperor's wishes had to be honored. The sees of Rome, Constantinople, Alexandria and Antioch were also raised to patriarchates at this council.

NESTORIANISM

While Arius contended that Christ was the first creature of God, deified but nonetheless inferior and subordinate to the Creator, Apollinarius taught that Christ was the Divine Logos who had voluntarily assumed an imperfect human nature. The Nicene-Constantinopolitan Creed, formulated by the First and Second Ecumenical Councils, vindicated the orthodox position that Christ was eternally begotten of the Father and not made, that he was true God and consubstantial with the Father. To counter Apollinarianism it specified that Christ was incarnate from the Holy Spirit and the Virgin Mary and became man. Thus the dyophysite position won out over Apollinarius's monophysite teaching. However, the exact relationship of the two natures in the one person of Christ, divine and human, had not yet been adequately worked out and defined.

For some fifty years following the Second Ecumenical Council there was relative peace in the church. During that time, the theological school of Antioch, in an attempt to clarify dyophysitism, concluded that the Christ who was born of Mary and who died on the cross was the man Christ and not the Divine Logos. As a result, a new period of turbulence was to embroil the church. The ensuing dispute, while doctrinal in essence, was also centered around the rivalry between the patriarchate of Alexandria and the upstart Constantinople, which had replaced Alexandria as second in rank next to Rome. At this time, the great theologian Cyril, Bishop of Alexandria (412–444), ruled his see as if he were a pharaoh.

In 428 Nestorius was elevated to the see of Constantinople; he was trained at Antioch and was a very subtle and acute theologian. He was also a man of violent temperament who made many enemies, among them the powerful Pulcheria, sister of Emperor

Theodosius II (408–450) and the real power behind the throne. Nestorius began to teach that the Virgin Mary could not be called *Theotokos,* "Mother of God," but should be referred to as *Christotokos,* "Mother of Christ," the man. Unfortunately for him, his views offended public piety and gave Cyril of Alexandria the excuse he needed to interfere in the affairs of Constantinople. Cyril first appealed to Celestinus I, Bishop of Rome (422–432), who joined forces with him. Then the Bishop of Alexandria accused Nestorius of cleaving Christ asunder and proclaimed his own doctrine that the two natures in Christ were fused into an indissoluble unity. At the Third Ecumenical Council in 431, Nestorius was accused of having taught that there were two sons, the Son of God and the Son of Mary.

Nestorius was probably misunderstood. He contended that every being has an *ousia,* or essence, which gives him life and being and every essence has a *physis,* or nature, which consists of attributes that make it distinctive. Essence and nature are correlative terms implying each other. To be known in its fullest sense the essence also has a *prosopon,* or undivided external appearance.

Both the man Christ and the Divine Logos have their own ousia, physis and prosopon. This is not like the soul and body; the body needs the soul that it may live and the soul needs the body that it may perceive. Humanity and divinity are whole natures independent and complete in themselves. They can neither change nor add to their being without altering it. How then can the union of the divine and human in Christ be adequately defined? Nestorius understood the Incarnation to mean that the human nature of Christ formed a distinct ousia alongside God the Word. His opponents took this to mean that there was no real unity between the two and accused him of creating a Quaternity in place of the Trinity. Repudiating this, Nestorius insisted that no one but He who was in the bosom of the Father came to earth and dwelt among men. The two natures, human and divine, existed without confusion: the divine nature, or Logos, begotten of God the Father, and the human nature, born of the Virgin Mary. But what kind of union is this when there are two essences, two natures and two persons? From the very moment that Mary conceived through the Holy Spirit, the man Jesus was united with the Divine Logos. The two prosopa merge and become identical. Nestorius flatly denied that there were two distinct persons. Man is known by his human prosopon or bodily form, but God is known by his name, "Creator," and is confessed by man as God. When we put the two together, the divine and human prosopa, one person results, not two.

Perhaps Nestorius's major fault was that he was too abstruse. The truth remains, however, that his teachings did offend the masses because of what seemed to them an unwarranted and unpardonable attack against Mary. As we have seen, Nestorius adamantly refused to call Mary Theotokos, "the Mother of God"; it is true that God passed through the womb of Mary but He certainly did not take his being from her, he logically argued. Mary gave birth to the man Christ and therefore must be called Christotokos, "the Mother of Christ." It was not God but the son, Jesus, who was born; it is improper to speak of Mary as the "Mother of God"; after all, God was! Mary did not conceive God in her womb and give him his being. It is not right that one should say of God that he was suckled and was born of a virgin. We cannot say that God was two or three months old. Man is born and grows old, but not God! These are qualities of human nature; the ousia of God cannot be changed into the ousia of man. God is unchanging. The birth of Christ from a woman was a human birth; his generation from God the Father, however, is without beginning and therefore eternal. If this appears wholly reasonable the real difficulty was that Nestorius refused to admit that such was the intimacy of the human and divine natures that one could predicate of the human nature what is divine and vice versa; this latter was the orthodox position. It seemed that Nestorius was repudiating the doctrine of the "transfer of attributes."

Cyril of Alexandria now moved in to condemn Nestorius for not accepting the "hypostatic" union which he himself advocated. This was due to a confusion of terms that at this early period were still ambiguous in the minds of theologians. The Greek term *hypostasis* was sometimes defined as ousia, essence or substance of the divinity, and sometimes as prosopon, the term for the individual persons of the Holy Trinity. The Cappadocian Fathers taught that there are three persons, or prosopa, in the one hypostasis of the divinity. Although Nestorius preached a prosopic union of the divine and human natures and Cyril taught hypostatic union, probably they both were talking about the same things.

To resolve the new religious crisis that had befallen the church, Theodosius II (408–450) convoked the Third Ecumenical Council at Ephesus in 431. It was a complete shambles. Nestorius found

himself outnumbered by Cyril's party, which was joined by the
Bishop of Ephesus, Memnon, and by many of the bishops of Asia
Minor. Nestorius was summarily condemned and deposed by about
two hundred bishops in all. His own party, supported by John,
Bishop of Antioch (428–441/2), and consisting of only forty-three
bishops, made itself an anti-council and excommunicated Cyril and
Memnon. Complete anarchy reigned in the streets of Ephesus.
Theodosius II was on the side of his bishop Nestorius, but Cyril
cunningly strengthened his position at court by a massive distribu-
tion of bribes to high officials and prominent ladies; he even borrowed 1500 pounds of gold to achieve his goal. In the end Nestorius
was compelled to resign while Cyril returned to Alexandria with
great pomp; the Church of Constantinople had been humbled.

Cyril of Alexandria accepted the view of the two natures in
Christ, but there followed a curious forgery of documents with
telling consequences. The followers of Apollinarius of Laodicea,
whose teachings had already been condemned, now began to cir-
culate their doctrines under the name of the great hero of Nicaea,
St. Athanasius. Their special formula, as we have seen, was "One
incarnate nature of God the Logos"; this had originally been rejected
as seeming to deny the reality of the two natures. Cyril fell into
the clever trap of the Apollinarians and espoused the alleged
Athanasian formula. In order to make it acceptable to the orthodox,
Cyril had to resort to some tortuous reasoning. He explained the
formula as meaning that the two natures, divine and human, were
fused into one incarnate nature. Cyril insisted that Mary be called
Theotokos, since the human and divine natures were unified in one
hypostasis; this is what he meant by the hypostatic union.

Cyril of Alexandria died in 444 and was succeeded by his nephew
Dioscorus (444–451). At the imperial court in Constantinople, Dioscorus had his own partisan, the aged archimandrite Eutyches, the
abbot of a monastery outside the capital. Eutyches used the formula
adopted by Cyril and Dioscorus: "Before the union there were two
natures; after the union there was one nature." He also contended
that the body of Christ is the body of God. "But I do not say," he
argued, "that the body of God is the body of Christ the man." The
body of Christ, moreover, according to Eutyches, was not consubstantial with our physical bodies. Eutyches's teaching seemed heretical and totally unacceptable to the orthodox party. As before, Constantinople and Antioch made common cause; Alexandria, however,
was winning the support of the monks of Syria and of Juvenal, the

Bishop of Jerusalem (422–458), who wanted to liberate his see from the authority of the metropolitan bishop of Caesarea in Palestine.

In 448 Eutyches was summoned by the patriarch of Constantinople, Flavian (446–449), before a local council and was called upon to repudiate his false doctrines. He refused and consequently was pronounced a heretic for his admission that the two natures of Christ had become one after the Incarnation. Eutyches's godson was the powerful court chamberlain, the eunuch Chrysaphios. The latter prevailed upon Theodosius II to convoke another council at Ephesus, but under the presidency of Dioscorus of Alexandria. In the meantime Flavian had won the support of the Bishop of Rome, Leo I the Great (440–461). In 449 Leo sent to Flavian his famous *Tome* in which he claimed that the Pope was entitled to resolve doctrinal quarrels by himself. He condemned the Alexandrian doctrine and stated that even after the Incarnation two natures ought to be distinguished in Christ.

In that same year the Council of Ephesus, called the Robbers Council, was attended by about one hundred forty bishops. It was an easy victory for Dioscorus and his forces. The papal legates were not even allowed to read Leo's *Tome;* Eutyches was reinstated and Flavian was beaten and deposed and died shortly thereafter as the result of his mistreatment. It was a sad day for those who believed in the divine inspiration and guidance of the Holy Spirit. Pope Leo I protested and demanded the convocation of another council in Italy, but Theodosius II refused. In 450, however, the emperor was killed in a fall from his horse, and the imperial court policy changed radically.

The only surviving member of the Theodosian dynasty in the Greek East was Theodosius II's sister, Pulcheria, then fifty-one years old and eager for power. She elevated Marcian (450–457), a retired army officer, to the throne as her husband *pro forma* since she had taken a vow of chastity. A devout dyophysite, Pulcheria now reversed her brother's religious policy.

The Fourth Ecumenical Council was convoked in 451 at Chalcedon, located opposite Constantinople, where its proceedings could be strictly supervised by government officials and where imperial notaries could draw up the reports of the sessions. Nearly six hundred bishops were present and the council no longer had need to fear the attacks of fanatic monks. Dioscorus and a few of his partisans were deposed. The council, however, could not accept Leo's *Tome* as a sufficient definition, as the papal legates had required. A compromise formula was accepted, based both on the *Tome* and on Cyril's letters to Nestorius. To avoid the charge of Nestorianism the condemnation of Nestorius was repeated and a clause was inserted in which the Virgin was expressly called Theotokos.

Christ is said to be perfect in Godhead and perfect in manhood, truly God and truly man, of a reasonable soul and body. He is begotten for all ages of the Father according to the Godhead and born of the Theotokos in latter times according to manhood. His two natures exist in his one person unconfusedly, unchangeably, indivisibly and inseparably. The property of each nature is preserved, concurring in one person and not divided into two persons.

It was at Chalcedon that the title of patriarch was officially granted to the incumbent of the see of Jerusalem. Canon twenty-eight of the Council of Chalcedon gave "equal privileges to the most holy throne of New Rome, rightly judging that the city which is honored with the Sovereignty and the Senate and enjoys equal privileges with the old Imperial Rome should in ecclesiastical matters also be magnified as she is, and rank next after her." Not only did this canon place the patriarch of Constantinople on a footing of complete equality with the pope of Rome, it also granted him patriarchal rights in the provinces of Thrace, Asia and the Pontus. Leo I rejected this canon while accepting all the others. The importance of Constantinople, however, could no longer be seriously challenged.

The humiliation of the patriarch of Alexandria incensed not only the monophysite Copts, who were descended from the ancient Egyptians, but also large numbers of the Greek-speaking populace in Alexandria. The exiled Dioscorus was now replaced by the orthodox Proterius (451–457), but it took military force to install him on his throne. When the Patriarch of Jerusalem, Juvenal, was removed for the monophysite Theodosius the army again had to intervene and restore the orthodox patriarch to his throne.

In 457, the same year as the coronation of Emperor Leo I, a bloody monophysite revolution broke out in Alexandria. On Good Friday a raging mob assassinated the orthodox patriarch Proterius and installed in his place the monophysite Timothy the Cat (457–460; 475–477). In the very same year the monophysite party took forceful possession of the Church of Edessa, and the Nestorian theologians who had settled there were forced to flee to Nisibis on the Persian frontier, where they founded the celebrated Nestorian School of Theology.

In Antioch in 469 the monophysite Peter the Fuller managed to seize the patriarchal throne from the Chalcedonian Martyrios (459–470), but only temporarily. Peter the Fuller popularized the monophysite creed by introducing into the liturgy as part of the *Trisagion*, the "Thrice-Holy Hymn," the phrase "who hast been crucified for us." The divine liturgy now became a battleground of the two theologies. Although the emperor continued the Chalcedonian policy, the monophysites continued to make progress during his reign.

In 474 the Isaurian Zeno (474–475; 476–491) came to the throne. He realized that the divisive nature of the religious controversy posed a grave problem to the unity of the empire. Egypt and Syria and parts of Palestine and Asia Minor had grown in monophysite strength, while Italy, the Balkans, Constantinople, and most of Asia Minor were Chalcedonian. Henceforth, until the Arab conquests of the seventh century, the Byzantine emperors devoted all their energy to solving this singular problem in the vain attempt to find a compromise solution.

The orthodox patriarch of Constantinople, Acacius (472–489), and Peter Mongus (477; 482–489), the monophysite patriarch of Alexandria, now came together and made a joint effort to find a suitable compromise formula that might bring an end to the perilous dissension within the church. Emperor Zeno optimistically adopted their proposal and in 482 issued the famous "Act of Union" (*Henotikon*), which was addressed specifically to the churches subject to Alexandria. This document simply avoided mentioning the issue of the two natures in Christ. It declared that Christ was "of the same nature with the Father in the Godhead and also of the same nature with us in the manhood," but the pronouncement made at Chalcedon concerning the exact definition of the two natures was bypassed. The *Henotikon* endorsed the first three ecumenical councils and condemned both Nestorius and Eutyches, but as for Chalcedon, the stumbling block, it merely stated that "Anyone who has taught otherwise, whether at Chalcedon or elsewhere, let him be anathema!" The creed of Chalcedon was not expressly rejected; neither were those who condemned Chalcedon. As often happens, this attempt at compromise satisfied only the moderates. The extremists of both parties rejected it outright.

There was one especially ominous consequence of the *Henotikon,* however. At Rome, Pope Felix III (483–492), dissatisfied with the Act of Union, called a council and excommunicated Acacius, the patriarch of Constantinople; in retaliation Acacius ceased to commemorate the pope in the diptychs of the church. This was the first serious breach between Constantinople and Rome and is known as the Acacian Schism; it lasted from 484 to 518. At this time both Antioch and Alexandria were occupied by pure monophysites.

Zeno's successor was Anastasius I (491–518), who proved to be an ardent monophysite. The kind of monophysitism he professed was not, however, the extreme doctrine of Eutyches, but a moderate version preached by Severus, Patriarch of Antioch (512–518), the most outstanding religious figure of his time. Severus was neither an Egyptian, nor a Syrian, but a Greek from Pisidia; and he wrote his theological tracts in Greek. His doctrine was essentially the same as that of Cyril; for him, too, Christ was not conceivable as a Savior if He had not suffered as a man. But he also confused the concepts of *physis* and *hypostasis* and accused the orthodox of dividing the person of Christ, which appeared very persuasive to the common masses. Anastasius's steady support of the monophysites alienated the orthodox populace of Constantinople, and several bloody revolts broke out.

In 518 Justin I (518–527) succeeded Anastasius as emperor. Justin was a dyophysite, and one of the very first acts of his administration was to terminate the Acacian Schism. Union with Rome was obtained on the condition that all monophysite bishops be expelled from their sees. Moreover, the names of the emperors Zeno and Anastasius as well as those of the Constantinopolitan patriarch Acacius and his successors were erased from the diptychs of the church. The fortunes of the patriarch of Constantinople depended always on the religious persuasion of the emperor.

Justin I was not only illiterate but he soon became senile, and the administration of state affairs fell to his brilliant nephew Justinian I (527–565). In 527 Justinian succeeded his uncle as emperor. More than any of his predecessors, Justinian took seriously his role as defender of the church. His major concern was to find some way to reconcile the dyophysite and monophysite parties. He thought that his adoption of the Theopaschite (God-Suffers) formula "One of the Holy Trinity suffered in the flesh" might be the answer, but he was to be disappointed. With some difficulty he managed to obtain the pope's approval, but the formula did not touch the main issue and the monophysites rejected it.

Theodore Ascidas, Bishop of Caesarea in Cappadocia, now convinced Justinian that all he needed to do to reconcile the monophysites with the orthodox was to issue, on his own, an imperial edict condemning certain writings that were particularly offensive to the monophysites. The *Edict of the Three Chapters* was issued in 546. The person and works of Theodore of Mopsuestia (died 428), considered to be the father of Nestorianism, along with certain writings of Theodoret of Cyrrhus (died 460) against Cyril of Alexandria, and the letter of Ibas, bishop of Edessa (died 457), censuring Cyril, were publicly condemned.

To have his way Justinian resorted to pressure tactics, and the events that unfolded cover a very sad page indeed in the history of the church. The emperor began by compelling the four eastern patriarchs to sign his edict, but the western clergy, protected by distance, opposed it. In 547 Pope Vigilius (537–555) was summoned to Constantinople to add his support to the imperial cause. Vigilius, unfortunately, was not much of a theologian and apparently did not understand the merits of the controversy. Not only did the pope begin by opposing the *Edict of the Three Chapters,* he also excommunicated Menas, patriarch of Constantinople (536–552), exacerbating the relations between the two most important sees in the empire.

Persuaded finally to read portions of the writings of Theodore of Mopsuestia, Vigilius changed his mind and concluded that they were dangerous. He refused, however, to sign the edict, preferring instead to issue his own independent judgment in which he condemned the *Three Chapters* while defending the decisions of Chalcedon. This created an outcry among the western clergy, who proceeded to excommunicate the pope in a council in North Africa. Vigilius now became alarmed and insisted on the convocation of an ecumenical council as the only means of averting a schism. He assured Justinian that he would exert his full powers to have the edict confirmed. While in the capital the pope managed to alienate the Greek clergy, and once more he excommunicated Patriarch Menas, along with Theodore Ascidas. His actions so incited his hosts that on one occasion Vigilius had to seek asylum in the Church of Saints Peter and Paul.

When finally the Fifth Ecumenical Council—a Council the emperor had not really wanted—sat in Constantinople in 553, Vigilius refused to attend. Afraid his prestige would be injured in the West should he officially condemn the writings of Theodoret of Cyrrhus and of Ibas of Edessa, which had been defended at Chalcedon, he decided to issue another judgement. One can only imagine the consternation of the Greek clergy over the pope's incredible behavior. Confronted by this impasse, the council was forced by the circumstances to condemn Vigilius for his unbecoming conduct. Finding himself now alone, the pope changed his position once more and yielded to Justinian's wishes.

The Fifth Ecumenical Council was attended by only one hundred sixty-six bishops, almost all of whom came from the East. Not only did it fail in its purpose of uniting the monophysites and the orthodox, it caused a schism in the western church because both Milan and Aquileia rejected its decisions. It was not until the papacy of Gregory the Great (590–604) that the Latin Church officially recognized the conclave of 553 as the Fifth Ecumenical Council. Actually, the latter differed significantly from the previous four in that it dealt not with a new heresy that had divided the church, but with a question that had been artificially created by the emperor himself. The Council, in fact, did no more than confirm an imperial edict. The results were nil. Not only did the monophysites remain aloof but, thanks to the energetic Jacob Baradaeus (490–577), monophysite Bishop of Edessa, they acquired a strong organization. Baradaeus spent his life wandering through the imperial provinces of the East disguised as a beggar and ordaining bishops and clergy. The monophysite church of Syria became known as the Jacobite Church from his name.

The problem of monophysitism was to remain the major obstacle to church unity and political stability in the Byzantine Empire until the convocation of the Sixth Ecumenical Council at Constantinople in 680–681. Monophysitism simply took on new forms and the emperors continued to look for new formulae of compromise and conciliation. The next important chapter in the religious controversy began during the reign of Heraclius (610–641). In 629, when the Emperor was in Hieropolis (Baalbek), Athanasius, leader of the Jacobites, came to see him. Heraclius promised to appoint him patriarch of the vacant see of Antioch if he would accept the Council of Chalcedon. Athanasius replied that he was willing to accept the doctrine of the two natures united in Christ, and then he shrewdly asked the emperor what one ought to believe concerning the energies (operation) or wills in Christ. Are they single or double? Thus the stage was set for the final definition of Christ's person.

At this time the patriarchates of Alexandria, Antioch and Armenia had monophysite incumbents. To win these back, a new formula of conciliation had to be found. Not knowing what to reply to Athanasius, the Emperor wrote to Sergios, the Patriarch of Constantinople (610–638); in the meantime he also sought the opinion of Cyrus, Bishop of Phasis in Lazica. In 630, Cyrus was elevated to the patriarchate of Alexandria. Sergios, who was a Syrian by birth and whose parents were Jacobites, wrote back that one must confess one natural will and one energy or operation in Christ. Both Cyrus and Athanasius concurred with the patriarch; the monophysites were content that where one energy or operation is found, only one nature is acknowledged. Cyrus was now sent to Alexandria as patriarch of that important see with the aim of achieving a union with the monophysites. Cyrus was supported by another eminent theologian, Theodore of Pharan, and in 633 they both proclaimed their agreement over the one energy in Christ in a doctrine called monoenergism.

The Jacobites claimed that the victory was theirs: "Not we with Chalcedon, but Chalcedon has communicated with us, confessing in the one energy the one nature of Christ." What was now needed was a theological formula that would express an idea of unity in Jesus Christ capable of satisfying both monophysites and dyophysites. The point of contact hit upon was the single energy. "Jesus Christ has two natures" (this was Chalcedonian), but "these two natures have only one energy" (this was an attempt to win over the monophysites).

The most acute thinker on the side of monoenergism was Theodore, Bishop of Pharan, a see located in the Sinai peninsula. His formula was "the one *theandric* (God-man) energy." The bearer of the one energy, the operant, is the Logos or the one Christ. A single, invisible energy represents the operation of the Logos. "From beginning to end, the whole Incarnation and everything in it, both small and great, is in fact one supreme and divine energy." This was very close to the Christology of Cyril of Alexandria. If Theodore of Pharan was the author and intellectual power behind monoenergism Patriarch Sergios was the real organizer and promoter of the doctrine. He and Heraclius shared the view that the integrity of the church and that of the empire were interdependent.

When Sophronios, Patriarch of Jerusalem (634–638), raised a cry against the Alexandrian Union of 633, Sergios maneuvered to try to save it. In 634 he wrote to Pope Honorius I (625–638) urging that the formula of "two energies" be dropped. The formula invited the impious notion that in Christ there were two contrary wills, contended the patriarch. The will was to be attributed rather to the Logos, since he was the subject of both natures. Pope Honorius replied by disapproving of "two energies" and of "one energy" on the grounds that the former implied Nestorianism and the latter, Eutychianism (extreme monophysitism). Honorius maintained that Scripture teaches equally that God has suffered in Christ and that the humanity has come down from heaven. "Therefore, we also acknowledge one will of our Lord Jesus Christ." This is why Honorius was anathematized along with Sergios by the Sixth Ecumenical Council. Thanks to the pope, monoenergism was now transformed into monotheletism, belief in one will. It was Honorius's authoritative assertion of one will in Christ that led to the *Ekthesis* (Exposition) of 638 drawn up by Sergios and posted in the narthex of Hagia Sophia.

The truth is that both Sergios and Pope Honorius were theologically unsophisticated. They were Chalcedonians, but they assumed that Christ could not have had a human will because it would have opposed the will of the Divine Logos. The change in emphasis from monoenergism to monotheletism marked a major turning point in Christological development. The crucial point in the orthodox stand as it was developed against monotheletism was an insistence upon the will as representative of nature. Orthodoxy regarded the capacity to will as an essential and characteristic feature of human nature as well as of divine nature. In other words, human nature is incomplete without the capacity to will.

It was St. Maximus the Confessor (580–662) who championed and elucidated the orthodox doctrine of dyotheletism (two wills). His teachings became a basic reservoir from which the Sixth Ecumenical Council drew its definitions. Key words in the early phase of monotheletism were "voluntary" and its adverb "voluntarily." According to Philippians 2:8, Christ suffered voluntarily: ". . . and being found in fashion as a man, he humbled himself, and became obedient unto death, even the death of the cross."

The patriarchs of Constantinople, Pyrrhus (638–641; 654) and

Paul II (641–653), concluded that this volition had to be ascribed to Christ's whole person. The will could not be ascribed to nature because all natural things happen according to necessity, not according to choice. Only the Logos possessed the freedom requisite for volition. St. Maximus replied that the completeness of his humanity required not only that Christ really suffer, but that he suffer voluntarily. Voluntariness demanded the recognition of self-determination, said Maximus, and this demanded the separate status of the human will from the divine will; therefore, Christ's human nature had its own will.

Pyrrhus objected to dyotheletism on the grounds that more than one will implied more than one willer. But, he argued, Christ was only one willer—that is, one person, one hypostasis. St. Maximus went to the heart of the difficulty and explained that will belonged to nature and not to hypostasis. He illustrated his point by referring to the Holy Trinity: even though they are three persons, they have but one will because they are of one divine nature. Since there were two natures in Christ there must have been two wills also. Furthermore, the will, like the natures, had nothing in common save the hypostasis of the Logos. The monotheletes, as we have seen, assumed that Christ could not have had two wills because they would have opposed each other. The dyotheletes simply declared that the two wills did not need to oppose each other, for they could concur. Pyrrhus argued that concurrent wills were really one will.

St. Maximus resolved this problem by distinguishing two kinds of wills. On the one hand, there is the "will of the one who wills," which renders one a "willful" person. On the other hand, there is the "will that has been willed," which renders a thing "willed." The "will of the one who wills" belongs to a nature, and it is the kind of will of which Christ has two, one for each of his natures. Moreover the agreement of Christ's human with his divine will was not merely a oneness, but the product of the hypostatic union. In other words, the hypostasis made use of each nature's capacity to will.

This clear distinction between the capacity to will and the result of willing tended to disarm monotheletism. But a further explication of dyotheletism needed to be made. Obviously, Christ's divine capacity to will was in some sense superior to his human capacity to will, because the former belonged to the divine nature, to the Logos himself, who assumed the human nature. The problem was to state in exactly what sense the divine will was superior.

St. Anastasius of Sinai, a younger contemporary of St. Maximus, held the view that the divine will surpassed the human in authority, and to this superior authority the human will was obedient. St. Maximus, however, maintained that the human will was in a causal relationship, and hence, the object of the divine will. In this connection St. Maximus distinguished two aspects of the ordinary man's capacity to will. First, there is a "gnomic will," which weighs different possibilities and then decides among them. Second, there is a "self-determined motion," which executes decisions once they are made. Christ's human nature was unique in that it was without sin. This meant that Christ had no human "gnomic will" according to St. Maximus. Christ had a divine "gnomic will," which distinguished immediately and unerringly between God's will and its opposite. As for the human "self-determined motion," the Logos made it his own. The Logos worked "the human things divinely because by willing mightily, but not under compulsion, he was subjecting himself to the trial of human sufferings." In short, Christ's human nature was self-determined and yet motivated by the Logos; it was possessed of free will and yet able to do only the will of God. This paradox is almost eliminated when we realize that Christ's human nature, being perfect, was completely free from the constraint of sin; the only person behind his human will was the Logos. Insofar as the paradox is not eliminated we are confronted with the mystery of God become man.

To put an end to dissension, Emperor Constans II (641–668), Heraclius's son, returned to the tactics of Zeno's Act of Union. In 648 he published the *Typos* (Type), which simply and naively forbade "all Orthodox subjects being in immaculate Christian faith and belonging to the Catholic and Apostolic Church, to contend and to quarrel with one another over one will or one energy or two energies or two wills." When both Pope Martin I (649–655) and the great Byzantine theologian St. Maximus violently opposed the *Typos*, the Emperor had them seized and convicted on grounds of treason to the state. The Pope was exiled to the Cherson in the Crimea where he died in 655; St. Maximus's tongue was mutilated and his right hand was amputated.

To resolve the issue of monotheletism, Emperor Constantine IV (668–685) convoked the Sixth Ecumenical Council at Constantinople in 680–681. The creed of this Council proclaims that Christ had two natural wills and that his human will follows the divine and all-powerful will and is subject to it without resistance or opposition.

Strangely enough, the Council refers to the notion of Christ's human self-determination, but only in the address to Constantine IV delivered at the last session after the Definition of Faith had been signed. It declares: "For nothing constitutes the completeness of the human nature, except the natural will, through which the power of self-determination in us is also characterized; let it hold thus for the natural energy too!"

Actually, monotheletism forced the church to take a fresh look at the person of Christ. The church, because of the concern over Christ's will, was forced to consider his inward psychology as well as his outward activity. Christ's being was given added depth, and a new criterion for characterizing his human nature was identified: it possessed a human will with accompanying voluntariness. This sequence of events marks the Christological maturity of the undivided church.

ICONOCLASM

Iconoclasm, the conscientious attempt on the part of certain Byzantine emperors to uproot the popular cult of the sacred portrait, called an icon, was the last great theological controversy to convulse the Byzantine church until the official break between the Latin and Greek churches in the schism of 1054 and the subsequent attempts to compel the subjects of the empire to submit to the supremacy of the pope in Rome.

Since earliest times there had always been iconoclastic proponents in the church; this Judaistic heritage, which denounced the making of images of any kind, was later reinforced by the powerful influences exerted by Islam in the eastern border provinces of Byzantium. The iconoclast emperors came from the eastern parts of the empire. Moreover, in the matter of church art, the controversy between monophysitism and dyophysitism was to take on a new direction.

The question that was now raised was this: What is the function of art, especially representational art, in the life of the church and the man of faith? The question has been answered differently in different periods of church history. The primitive church, a small island in a sea of idolatry was, of necessity, opposed to art. Most converts to Christianity came from pagan backgrounds and the existence of statues and representational art of any kind would have tempted the less sophisticated to revert to their old ways. The first examples of any kind of Christian art are to be found in the catacombs dating from about A.D. 200. It is significant that the representations found in the Roman catacombs are either purely ornamental or symbolic depicting examples from the Old Testament such as Noah and the Ark or Jonah and the Whale, which are prototypes of the Christian belief in the resurrection and life in the hereafter. The artists of the catacombs were reluctant to portray Christ, who is often represented as Orpheus beckoning mankind to salvation.

With the Constantinian Peace, church buildings were adorned with exquisite mosaic patterns and animal figures. At the same time there is evidence that the impulse to possess portraits of sacred personages became intensified. Constantia, Constantine the Great's sister, desiring a portrait of Christ, wrote to Eusebius who refused her request saying that he had taken away from a woman portraits of St. Paul and the Savior. Such portraits, therefore, existed even though the church disapproved of them. The church's fear of idolatry and opposition to images, however, did not stop in the fourth century when Christians borrowed the whole apparatus of pagan representational art, but remained a constant undercurrent, manifesting itself at different times and in diverse places. There is, nonetheless, a great abyss between the existence of sacred portraiture in the fourth century and the very special role it assumed in the sixth and seventh centuries.

When Christian painting began to be openly encouraged in the latter half of the fourth century, especially by the Cappadocian Fathers, their argument was based on the usefulness of pictures as educational tools, and the fact that the contemplation of saintly persons was an incentive to noble deeds. This was, until the invention of photography, a most natural, and indeed a universal, attitude.

When we consider the rapid expansion of Christianity, which until the fourth century was a minority religion presupposing actual dedication, but which from this time on became first a privileged religion and soon thereafter the mandatory religion; when we consider that conversion became a practical necessity to hold any office, it is not surprising that pagan customs penetrated Christian practices.

One of these was the need for a palpable object of veneration. The cult of relics and the adoration (*proskynesis*) of the cross both became intensified in the fourth century. Emperor Julian the Apostate (361–363), who renounced the Christian faith and espoused paganism, ridiculed the Christians for worshipping corpses and the wood of the cross. The special adoration of images followed; St. Augustine was the first to mention *picturarum adoratores,* and eventually the icon overshadowed even the cult of relics in the East.

Prostration or proskynesis before images is first attested to in the sixth century. Up to that time references to the worship of images are scanty, but in the second half of the sixth and in the seventh centuries it was intensified to the point of becoming the central religious phenomenon. At the same time in the Latin West, Pope Gregory I the Great (590–604), in response to the iconoclastic attitude of Serenus, Bishop of Marseilles, supported the didactic value of the image while insisting that it should not be worshipped. Why the icon became the object of a special cult in the Greek East at this time is hard to tell; but it is unmistakable that at the death of Justinian in 565 there was a complete change in the religious mood, which most likely was connected with the crisis of the empire. We begin to hear of various devotional practices performed in front of icons: lighting of candles, burning of incense, kissing, kneeling, and images carried in procession with all the rites that were reserved earlier for imperial portraits. Such practices could be justified as marks of respect, but there can be no doubt that in the eyes of the faithful the image was identified with its prototype, whose habitation it was. This is apparent by a great number of fascinating miracle stories belonging to this period: images are made to speak, make promises, bleed when stabbed, defend themselves when attacked, cure the sick, and so on. This magical aspect was very acceptable to the common folk, who had inherited similar beliefs from paganism; it was also acceptable to the educated classes, thanks to the neo-Platonic doctrine of the sympathy existing between image and prototype. It must be remembered that the line between magic and true religion is an extremely thin one. Another magical feature was the use of images in an *apotropaic* capacity: images were placed over doors to ward off the evil eye; they were installed over gates and walls to defend cities from attack, and were carried into battle to protect the armies and bring them victory.

Equally characteristic of this period was the appearance of

acheiropoietai (images produced mechanically or by means other than human). The most famous of these were the images of Edessa and Camuliana. The image of Edessa, an ancestor of the Veronica of Turin, was an impression of Christ's face on a napkin, which in turn produced an impression on a brick. All these acheiropoietai appeared almost simultaneously in the second half of the sixth century and the beginning of the seventh. Apart from their miraculous qualities, the icons also served another purpose—that of providing a genuine portrait of the sacred personage. By virtue of their exactitude, they certainly influenced iconography and imposed a given type of face. This purpose they shared with images purportedly painted in the lifetime of Christ and the Virgin, such as the one of Christ at the Praetorium of Pilate or the famous icon of the Virgin supposedly painted by St. Luke.

Throughout this period, which saw the ever-increasing popular devotion to the icon, an undercurrent of iconoclasm was discernible, especially in the eastern provinces of the empire. Then in the eighty-second canon of the Quinisextum Council of Troullo, which sat in 692, the church proscribed the symbolic representation of Christ as a lamb and required that he be represented as a man in order to emphasize "his life in the flesh, his passion, his saving death, and the ransom for the world that was won thereby." Following this pronouncement the image of Christ appeared for the first time on Byzantine coinage.

With the deposition of Emperor Justinian II in 695, the empire was convulsed by a new "Time of Troubles." For some twenty-two years anarchy beset the empire; six emperors came to the throne and were toppled. The Slavs had overrun the Balkans, and the Arabs, at the zenith of their military power, threatened the very existence of the already tottering empire. In 717 the *strategos* or military governor of the Anatolikon *theme* (province) seized the reins of government and, as Emperor Leo III, defeated the Arabs at the gates of Constantinople in one of the most decisive battles in history. The emperor, commander of the eastern troops, whose family came from Syria, was an iconoclast. In 726 Leo III initiated his campaign against the icons by publishing an edict and ordering the removal of Christ's image from above the Bronze Gate of the Great Palace. Unable to win the adherence of pope and patriarch, the emperor published a new edict in 730; the prohibition of icons was now a law and persecutions of iconophiles were undertaken.

Iconoclasm reached a high point under Leo III's son Constantine V (741–775), who attacked the icons more systematically and unleashed a violent persecution against the monks who opposed his program. The emperor's fanatical agent, Michael Lachanodracon, strategos of the Thracesion theme, on one occasion gathered all the monks and nuns in an open plain at Ephesus and threatened: "Those who wish to obey the Emperor and myself will put on white garments and take wives immediately. Those who will not do so will be blinded and exiled to Cyprus." There were many martyrs that day, but many defected too. In Constantinople, St. Stephen the Younger, the abbot of a monastery in the vicinity of the capital, was dragged through the streets of the city and torn to pieces by the mob. Constantine V paraded monks in the hippodrome, each of whom was forced to hold a woman by the hand while the populace spat on him. The emperor's death in 775 put an end to the violent period of iconoclasm.

Constantine V was followed by his son Leo IV (775–780), an iconoclast much less dedicated than his grandfather and father. He was married, however, to an Athenian, Irene, who was a devotee of the icons. At the death of her husband in 780, Irene became regent to her son Constantine VI (780–797). It took her some seven years to prepare the ground for the convocation of the Seventh Ecumenical Council in 787 that restored icon veneration. During the reigns of Irene (797–802), who blinded her own son and had him deposed, and of Nikephoros I (802–811) and of Michael I Rhangabe (811–813), the empire suffered disastrous defeats. The iconophile emperors, unfortunately, compared unfavorably with the great victories and triumphs of iconoclasts Leo III and Constantine V. In 813, Leo V (813–822), strategos of the Anatolikon theme, of mixed Syrian and Armenian descent, came to the throne. He decided to return to the iconoclastic policies of the victorious emperors, and explained his decision as follows:

Why are the Christians suffering these ills and being subjugated by aliens? I think that this is because the icons are venerated, and for no other reason. So I intend to destroy them. You see that the emperors who accepted and worshipped icons either died in exile or fell in battle. It is only those who did not worship them who died a natural death as emperors, and each one of them was buried with honor in the imperial mausoleum at the Holy Apostles. So I too want to imitate them and destroy the icons, so that both I and my son may live for a long time and that my family may reign down to the fourth and fifth generation.

In 815 a council was held in Hagia Sophia that repudiated the Seventh Ecumenical Council of 787 and confirmed the Iconoclastic Council of 754 convoked by Constantine V as the Seventh Ecumenical Council. In 820 Leo V was assassinated at the foot of the altar in the palace chapel. The subsequent emperors, Michael II the Sta..merer (820–829) and his son Theophilus (829–842), continued the policy of iconoclasm.

Like Leo IV before him, Theophilus also married an iconophile. On his deathbed in 842 he made his wife promise that she would not alter his religious policy, but the promise was made in vain. The throne passed to Michael III, who was only six years old, and Theodora assumed the regency. During the next year, she laid careful plans for the final liquidation of iconoclasm. To protect the memory of Theophilus, Theodora claimed that he had repented on his deathbed. On March 11, 843, the icons were officially restored in a church ceremony that involved a procession of icons and the reading of a text that subjected the leading heretics of the past and present to anathema. This event is commemorated in the Greek Orthodox Church as the Feast of Orthodoxy which always falls on the first Sunday in Lent.

Let us now return to a brief exposition of the iconophile and the iconoclast positions so that we may have a better understanding of the unique meaning of the icon in the Byzantine world. On what grounds were images opposed, and what arguments were used for their defense? The arguments to be presented here were not all produced simultaneously; many had been worked out before iconoclasm developed. The systematic elaboration of a complete theory of images was not achieved until the eighth century, and was further elaborated in the ninth century. Moreover, it also stands to reason that there were different shades of opinion in both parties. Some of the milder iconoclasts objected only to the adoration, not to the existence of icons, which, they conceded, had a certain commemorative value. The main body of the iconoclasts, however, objected both to the adoration and to the manufacture of icons. The most extreme elements, it would appear, considered the abolition of icons as only the first step toward a sweeping religious reform. For the sake of simplicity, each party will be regarded as presenting a common front. The controversy itself may be considered under four headings: appeal to tradition, the image and the beholder, the image and its prototype, and Christology, the central issue.

Appeal to Tradition

The iconoclasts took their stand on the second commandment: "Thou shalt not make unto thee any graven image, or any likeness of anything that is in heaven above or that is in the earth beneath, or that is in the water under the earth" (Exodus 20:4). From the New Testament their chief text was: "God is a spirit: and they that worship him must worship him in spirit and in truth" (John 4:24). They also claimed the authority of John 20:29: "... blessed [are they] that have not seen, and yet have believed," and Romans 1:23 and 2:56: "And [they] changed the glory of the uncorruptible God into an image like to corruptible man ... and worshipped and served the creature more than the Creator." The culmination of the iconoclast argument was that the icons had no authority, either Biblical or patristic.

The iconophile party, of course, had its own texts. Had not the Almighty ordered Moses to place images of the Cherubim in the Tabernacle? Was not man himself made in the image of God? In answer to the second commandment they contended that the prohibition of images was caused by the prevalence of idolatry. Man was then in his infancy, now he was mature. Grace had replaced the Law. There was, of course, no lack of patristic texts of the fourth century and later to justify the use of images.

The most interesting part of the iconophile argument was based on "progressive revelation." True, images were not explicitly mentioned in Holy Scripture, but how about such concepts as the homoousion, the "two natures and one hypostasis of Christ," and the Theotokos? All these are implicit in the Bible.

The Relationship of the Image to the Beholder

The charge of idolatry was, of course, a cardinal one. The iconoclasts insisted that images were made by hand of base matter. The reply was that it is not the wood or the paints that are honored, but the sacred person represented. The didactic element was mentioned, but this argument was more a feature of the earlier rather than the later stages of the controversy. More crucial was the anagogical value of the image, the idea that it leads man from the visible to the invisible, from the material world to the spiritual cosmos. This was not a new point; in fact it went back to pagan apologies of statues, but it was more specifically rooted in the sixth-century system of Pseudo-Dionysios the Areopagite, which exerted an immense influence on theological circles. According to the Pseudo-Dionysian texts, the physical and spiritual worlds formed two superimposed hierarchies, and the soul ascended step by step from the confusion of matter to the unity of spirit: "We are led up, as far as possible, through visible images to contemplation of the divine." In the same century, Hypatius of Ephesus put it this way:

> We leave material adornment in the churches ... because we conceive that each order of the faithful is guided and led up to the Divine in its own way and that some are led even by these (i.e., the material decorations) toward the intelligible beauty and from the abundant light in the sanctuaries to the intelligible and immaterial light.

St. John of Damascus (ca. 674–749), the outstanding apologist of icons, wrote in the eighth century:

> For as we are composed of soul and body, and our soul does not stand alone, but is, as it were, shrouded by a veil, it is impossible for us to arrive at intellectual conceptions without corporeal things. Just as we listen with our bodily ears to physical words and understand spiritual things, so through corporeal vision we come to the spiritual. ... And baptism is likewise double, of water and the spirit. So is communion and prayer and psalmody; everything has a double signification, a corporeal and a spiritual.

The Relationship Between the Image and Its Model

Constantine V is represented as saying that the true image must be of the same substance (consubstantial) as the person represented. This led him to state that the only permissible image of Christ was the Eucharist, the elements of bread and wine, after consecration being of the same ousia as Christ. Here we have a fundamental difference between the two parties. The iconophiles argued that images were of two kinds: natural and artificial. The first is precisely the same as its archetype, both in essence and in similitude. Thus, Christ in his divinity is consubstantial with the Father, and in his humanity, consubstantial with the mother. The second kind, however, reproduces the similarity, but not the essence; in other words, it is different as to ousia, but identical as to person. An artificial image can only express personal characteristics.

The cult of the image follows from its nature. In spite of the difference of ousia, the homage rendered to the image and to its prototype is one, since the image does not have a person of its own. There is, however, a sharp difference between homage or veneration (*proskynesis*) and worship (*latreia*) because the latter is appropriate only to the Holy Trinity.

The link between image and prototype is very close, and if the prototype is holy, the image partakes of his holiness. This may be considered the converse of the anagogical argument: in descending from God to saint, and from saint to the saint's image, there is a certain continuity since each successive step is an image of the one above. St. John of Damascus explains: "The saints in their lifetime were filled with the Holy Ghost and, when they are no more, his grace abides with their spirits, and with their bodies in their tombs, and also with their likenesses and holy images, not by nature, but by grace and divine power." Just as in the Acts of the Apostles the shadow of Peter falling on the sick lying in the streets could work miracles, so the icon, which is the shadow of the person represented, can perform miracles.

Christology

Most crucial to faith was whether or not it was permissible to represent Christ. The iconoclast position was that Christ consists of two natures in one person, and that these admit neither separation nor confusion. Painting, therefore, would either have to represent the divine, to circumscribe what is uncircumscribable, or, if it limits itself to representing the bare man, it must divide the inseparable, the human from the divine nature of Christ. The latter would be the heresy of Nestorianism, the former, the sin of monophysitism.

The orthodox answer to this argument was that if Christ cannot be represented, the completeness of his humanity is denied; he cannot be said to have lived and suffered like other men, and the Incarnation was a useless act. To use the formula of St. Theodore the Studite: "Christ is not Christ if he cannot be represented."

The controversy over the meaning and use of the icon, although echoed in the West, was primarily a Byzantine phenomenon. As we have seen, for the primitive church, representational art threatened the purity of the worship of the one God. The demands of a Christian faith in a pagan society outweighed the claims of culture. This was Semitism and stark asceticism breaking through the aesthetic reality of Hellenism. Perhaps it is closer to the truth to say that iconoclasm was a movement in favor of a "Judaized" Christianity. Semitic Islam followed Judaism in rejecting Greco-Roman art of the human form. In the contest between two opposing cultural forces in the Byzantine Church, Greek representational art won out. Christ was a historic reality and no symbol of him as a lamb could suffice. What was to become the greatest achievement of religious art with its emphasis on the spiritualization of the flesh and matter was now permitted to evolve in the unparalleled art of the mosaic, fresco and portable icon. Theologically, the Byzantine church triumphantly proclaimed the true humanity of Christ, the sanctification and redemption of matter as the Divine Logos himself had assumed human flesh, and the rehabilitation of the icon as a vehicle for the transmission of grace.

After the long crisis of iconoclasm, which raised so many profound theological questions, there was a general belief that perfection had been attained in the Christian faith. Patriarch Photios (858–867; 877–886), the most learned scholar of the ninth century, called a council in 867, which condemned all the heresies of the past; the council was intended to inaugurate a new era. The word "new" occurs throughout the writings of the period. Further ecumenical councils seemed unnecessary. At another council in 880 it was stated, with regard to the definition of faith, that:

> any subtraction or addition, as long as no heresy is stirred up by the Devil, only casts reproach on what is irreproachable and inflicts an inexcusable insult on the Fathers. . . . To cut away or to add would mean that the confession of faith concerning the holy and consubstantial Trinity, transmitted to us from the very beginning, was incomplete.

Orthodoxy, wrote Photios, could not tolerate the slightest blemish. As even a small defect is noticeable in a beautiful body, so in an exact science and especially in theology, the tiniest mistake or modification is at once apparent and leads to great inconvenience.

POLITICAL CONSEQUENCES OF THE CHRISTIAN HERESIES

Arianism, rejected by the orthodox church, was to survive nonetheless, as a political factor of some significance for several centuries. Constantine I, the promoter of the orthodox homoousion formula, ironically was baptized on his deathbed by Eusebius, the Arian bishop of Nicomedia. This same bishop was entrusted with the religious education of the emperor's sons. With Constantine's death in 337 the empire was divided among his three heirs, Constantine II (337–340), Constans (337–350) and Constantius (337–361). By the year 350, Constantius's two brothers were dead as the result of internecine struggles, thus leaving him as sole monarch. The tyrant Constantius was an ardent Arian and he doggedly persecuted followers of the orthodox church.

In 341, at a council of Arian bishops in Antioch, a certain Ulfilas (ca. 311–383), of mixed Cappadocian and Gothic descent, was appointed missionary bishop to his pagan Germanic countrymen. Having invented an alphabet for the Gothic language, based primarily on Greek and partly on runic letters, he translated the Holy Scriptures into his native tongue, a monumental achievement. Ulfilas, it should be noted, happened to be propagating the faith of the Byzantine emperor who was an Arian at the time. Consequently, the Germanic Ostrogoths, Visigoths, Lombards, Burgundians and Sueves, who were subsequently converted to Christianity, adopted Arianism. The Arian Ostrogoths occupied Italy, the Visigoths took Spain and the Vandals settled in North Africa.

By the end of the sixth century, however, Arianism was abandoned by the Germanic peoples for the orthodox faith. Clovis, king of the Franks (481–511), was the first Germanic chief to be baptized into the established church, and thereafter all those northern Germans who were to be absorbed into the Frankish kingdom followed suit.

The semi-Romanized Arian Vandals and Ostrogoths were unfortunately crushed and uprooted by the armies of Justinian in the sixth century, and the Visigoths in Spain adopted orthodox Christianity at the Council of Toledo in 589 under their king Reccared.

The Nestorians, condemned by the Third Ecumenical Council, migrated to Edessa. Persecuted by militant monophysites they were compelled to flee to Nisibis on the Persian frontier where they founded the celebrated Nestorian School of Theology. By the seventh century Nestorian missionaries had carried their sectarian beliefs to parts of India and China. Nestorian communities still survive in south India and northwestern Iran, but the Mongols destroyed those in western China.

Despite the claims made by many modern historians, monophysitism was not an example of a burgeoning nationalism that opposed Greek culture, language and the emperor reigning in Constantinople. There is no literary evidence to support the allegation that when the Persians and Arabs occupied Egypt, Syria and Palestine in the seventh century, the alienated monophysites welcomed them with open arms as liberators.

Many Greek and Greek-speaking Christians were ardent monophysites. The intellectual leaders of the movement were Greeks. Several Byzantine emperors supported the monophysite cause, and the emperors, in general, deserve sympathy for devoting their energies, albeit in vain, to seeking some basis for theological compromise between the contending factions.

The Armenian church, however, by way of exception, originated as a national church. King Tiridates III and his subjects were converted to Christianity in 314. Subsequently, however, Persia occupied the greater part of Armenia. Consequently, not only were Armenian Christians persecuted by the Zoroastrian clergy, they were also unable to send representatives to the crucial Third and Fourth Ecumenical Councils. As a result, they were ignorant of both the Nestorian and monophysite crises. About 506, however, persecuted monophysites fled from Persia to Armenia where they were embraced by their fellow-sufferers. Again, it so happened that at this critical juncture in Christian history, a monophysite emperor, Anastasius I (491–518), sat on the throne at Constantinople. The Armenians gladly accepted the doctrinal views of the monophysite advocates of the imperial faith, and later refused to abandon them when orthodox emperors reigned. However, the Armenians always supported Byzantium against the common enemy, the Persians and later the Arabs. Today, monophysite Christians survive in the Egyptian Coptic, Abyssinian, Syrian Jacobite and Armenian churches. The extremely important political consequences of iconoclasm shall be discussed in the last chapter of this book dealing with Byzantine and Latin relations.

MANICHAEISM, MASSALIANISM, PAULICIANISM AND BOGOMILISM

The Christian heresies of Arianism, Macedonianism, Apollinarianism, Nestorianism, monophysitism, monoenergism, monotheletism, and finally iconoclasm dealt with problems of the Holy Trinity, specifically with how to maintain monotheism while formulating the doctrine of the three persons in the one Godhead. Christology was crucial in these controversies. Besides these, however, there were other religious movements within the empire—equally dangerous to the stability of the state—that were anti-Christian. These were Manichaeism, Massalianism, Paulicianism and Bogomilism.

A common denominator of these sects was Marcionism. Marcion, a sectarian reformer of the middle of the second century, claimed that there are two gods. The just god of the Old Testament, the creator of the world, and the good God revealed by Christ. The creator of the "tree of knowledge of good and evil" introduced evil into the world and therefore could not be considered a good god. For this reason, Marcion rejected the whole of the Old Testament as well as the Incarnation of Christ. He also favored the writings of St. Paul, which he purged of their Jewishness, and despised those of St. Peter.

Manichaeism

The most abhorred of the anti-Christian sects was Manichaeism. There was no greater opprobrium in Byzantium than to be called a Manichee. So detested were they that Emperor Justinian inflicted the death penalty on them. Manichees who obstinately refused to abjure their doctrines were gathered on ships that were then set on fire so that they might be buried in the waves.

The term Manichaeism derives from its founder, Mani, who was born about 216 in the Median capital of Hamadan. Mani travelled to Ghandara in northwestern India, where he was greatly impressed by Buddhism. He was also familiar with Christianity, but in the heretical forms of Marcionism and gnosticism. Their esoteric, revealed knowledge, showing the way to salvation, included a cosmic drama and fall and a corresponding historic drama and fall; a good God and a demiurge who creates the evil world; the repudiation of the Old Testament; the absorption of light by darkness and its restoration; and the need for the soul and spirit to be separated from the evil body. Essentially, however, Mani's religion was rooted in Iranian religion, specifically in Zoroastrianism. The Christian and Buddhist aspects of Manichaeism were meant to make the faith acceptable to Christians in the West and to Buddhists in the East.

The appeal of Manichaeism was strong indeed. Communities were established in Alexandria, and St. Augustine (354–430) became a member of the cult in North Africa. By merging Zoroastrian, sectarian Christian and Mesopotamian religious elements, Mani hoped to replace these conflicting faiths with his own universal religion. The threat he posed, since he was favored by the Persian king Shapur, forced the Zoroastrian clergy to establish a state church; once this was done, the fate of the Christians and Buddhists in Iran, as well as of the Manichees, was sealed. Convicted by the Zoroastrian clergy, Mani was seized and fettered. After great suffering he died in the reign of Bahram I (274–277).

Faithful to Iranian religion, Mani based his belief on conflict dualism. But whereas in Iranian conflict dualism the two primary principles of Good and Evil, Ahura Mazda and Ahriman, were twins of equal status, Mani rejected with revulsion the contention that good and evil could be brothers. For him the two primary elements were God and *Hyle*, the Greek word for matter. He taught that both are eternal, without creation, but once again, the good element, God (who is called Light and Truth), shall ultimately triumph over evil Matter (also named Lie and Darkness).

The body of the Godhead is comprised of the realm of light, that is, of the entire light of the earth and of the heavens. The tetrad of God, his light, his force and his wisdom, is seated upon his throne and has four sides or faces. The three faces of God are infinite, but the light side on the south is bounded by finite darkness. At some time in the past the Prince of Darkness and his demons caught sight of the beauty, peace and harmony prevailing in the realm of light, and they became obsessed with the longing to possess it themselves. Armed for battle, they invaded the realm of light; to ward off the onslaught, God, who could not himself enter the fray because he was pure, called into being the Mother of Life; and she, in turn, gave birth to primaeval man to give battle to the forces of darkness and evil. Air, wind, light, water and fire were the five light elements comprising primaeval man's armor; voluntarily he descended into the darkness, but he was defeated and his light elements were devoured by the enemy. Divested of his light elements and stunned, primaeval man, the redeemer now in need of redemption, called for help. Extending his right hand, the Living Spirit (Mithra) drew him up out of the pit of darkness and back to his celestial home of light.

The Passion and the Redemption of primaeval man, however, is only part of the story. The light elements which have been devoured by the forces of darkness must also be redeemed. This task was given to Mithra. Mithra proceeded to create the earth out of the bodies of the vanquished demons of darkness: the sky was made from their flayed skins, the mountains from their bones and the earth from their excrement. The sun and the moon were fashioned out of the purified particles of light, and the stars were constituted of partially sullied light particles.

To counter Mithra's creation, Matter fashioned Ašqualun and his female companion Namrael. Ašqualun and Namrael now gave birth to Adam and Eve. The story of the earth's creation and man's origin is important for understanding the revulsion for matter and the flesh felt by the Manichees and all those heresies that were influenced later by their ideas.

If primaeval man had been redeemed on the macrocosmic level, Adam, in whom was found the greatest portion of the remaining imprisoned particles of light, had to be redeemed on the microcosmic level of the individual. Adam, too, was sunk deep in slumber, and, having been born deaf and blind, he had no awareness of the light within him. The Third Messenger, the incarnation of redemptive intellect, was dispatched to redeem Adam's soul. Roused from the sleep of death and freed from the demons of darkness by exorcism, Adam was shown that his body was derived from evil while his spirit originated in the celestial realm of light. Finally, Adam was instructed in the redemptive knowledge called *gnosis*, "the comprehension of what was, what is and what will be."

The evil material body, then, is the prison of the celestial soul.

Not only the human body but the animal and plant world also contained particles of light. This led Mani to preach transmigration; to destroy a plant or to kill an animal meant that the guilty party would return in the form of the vegetation or animal life against which he had sinned. All trees, since they contained large amounts of light particles, were considered by the Manichees as crosses of Christ.

In organizing his church, Mani followed the Buddhist pattern. In Buddhism the monks comprise the core of the communities and the lay members are only supporting elements who provide sustenance and protection for the monks; so in Manichaeism there are two groups whose functions and way of life differ greatly. If in Buddhism there are the monks and the laymen, in Mani's church there are the elect or righteous, and the hearers or auditors. The elect must refrain from all blasphemy of thought and word; meat derived from evil matter was forbidden as a food; water, a material substance, was also to be avoided in large quantities, and fruit juices were to be preferred. The elect must also have a reverence for all life and must never destroy plant and animal life. As procreation retarded the reassembly of the light particles, the elect must abstain from marriage and sexual intercourse. The hearers, however, were not expected to follow these difficult precepts; it was their lot to provide the elect with the necessities of life. The hearers were allowed to marry and even eat meat, but on Sunday they abstained both from meat and sexual intercourse. The elect fasted on both Sunday and Monday and for an entire month, a practice that may have been copied by the Muslims, who fast the whole month of Ramadan.

There was a kind of baptismal ceremony before death, a ritual of the laying on of hands on the novice. There was also a kind of sacramental meal during which the elect ate bread provided by the hearers and then sprinkled their heads with olive oil.

If in Manichaeism we see how all matter and flesh were deemed of evil derivation, the significant contribution of Byzantine Christianity, which resulted from the victory over iconoclasm, was that matter was proclaimed as a vehicle of sanctification; by assuming human flesh and becoming a true man, Christ, the son of God, redeemed all flesh; the resurrection of his body was the great divine truth that the body is not evil but in fact sanctified in Christ. Thus, the relics of saints, the True Cross, the instruments of the Passion, were all vehicles of grace.

Paulicianism

In the second half of the seventh century another anti-Christian sect, Paulicianism, was to emerge in Armenia and the Asiatic provinces of the Byzantine Empire. The Paulicians constituted a serious military threat to the empire. Chrysocheir, the leader of the Paulicians based in Tephrike in Armenia, led his armies through Byzantine territory all the way to Nicaea and Nicomedia, and in 867 captured and plundered the city of Ephesus, where he turned the church of St. John the Evangelist into a stable. Finally, in 871–872, the Byzantine Emperor Basil I razed Tephrike, killed Chrysocheir and destroyed the military power of the Paulicians. The Paulicians perished by the thousands.

It is from Peter of Sicily, the imperial ambassador sent by Emperor Basil I (867–886) to Tephrike to negotiate with Chrysocheir, that we learn of Paulician doctrines in some detail. Peter says that Paulicianism began with Kallinike, a Manichaean woman, who sent her two sons, Paul and John, to convert the inhabitants in the vicinity of Samosata on the Euphrates. It may be from Paul of Samosata that the Paulicians derived their name. Originating in Armenia, this sect may only have appeared to contain Manichaean elements.

Constantine, an Armenian from Mananali on the upper Euphrates, was instrumental in propagating Paulicianism in the second half of the seventh century by cleverly using the New Testament to support its doctrines. To avoid suspicion, the Paulicians also used accepted Christian terminology but gave it their own interpretation, which only the faithful understood. By confessing the "orthodox" faith they meant the "Paulician" faith; by "cross," which they spurned denying the real crucifixion of Jesus, they meant Christ, with his arms outstretched; they interpreted the "Mother of God" to signify the "heavenly Jerusalem," and when the body and blood of Christ were mentioned, they understood this to mean his words; baptism for them meant that Christ was the giver of the living water of life.

Peter of Sicily analyzes Paulician doctrine as follows. Of the two principles, Good and Evil, it is the evil principle that is the creator and ruler of this world. The good principle will create the world to come. Thus the Paulicians rejected the Old Testament because it relates the creation of the world by the evil Yahweh. The prophets who spoke for the creator of this world were deceivers; the God of the Old Testament was a cruel and unjust God, completely different from the God of love and compassion of the New Testament. To claim that Christ took on human flesh was blasphemy, because this would have meant that his body was an evil creation of the material world. Actually, Christ was of heavenly origin and only appeared to have taken on human flesh, a doctrine called docetism. If this be true, then both the maternity and the virginity of Mary had to be rejected. Significantly, in view of later Protestant developments, the Paulicians rejected the Eucharist as being the true body and blood of Christ and interpreted the bread and wine given by Christ to his disciples at the Last Supper symbolically to be his words. Again, they rejected the concept of the visible church with its priesthood and, like certain radical Protestant reformers, considered churches to be merely meetinghouses for prayer. Again the Protestants rejected icons and relics. Paulicianism, as we can see, was less sophisticated than Manichaeism and differed from the latter in certain important respects. The Paulicians, as described by Peter of Sicily, were not enjoined to abstain from meat, wine and sexual intercourse; there did not seem to be an elect who must live a life of rigorous asceticism. Far from being monastic in their ways, the Paulicians were men of action and war. In fact, it seems that the Paulicians derived their doctrines from other sources, such as Marcionism. Mani, as you recall, opposed God to matter, while Paulician dualism was between the good God and the evil creator of this world.

Massalianism

The Paulicians were also impressed by Massalianism. In Syriac the term means "those who pray," and in Greek they were called *euchitai*. The Massalians, who originated in the fourth century around Edessa, were condemned in 431 by the Third Ecumenical Council at Ephesus. Their doctrines are of interest because some of them found their way later into the West among the mendicant movements of the twelfth century as well as among the Protestants.

Not only did the Massalians reject the Christian church and its priesthood, they also interpreted the New Testament in an individualistic way. They partook of the Eucharist, but only to deceive the authorities, since they denied the real presence of Christ in Holy Communion. They emphasized prayer as the only way of exorcising the demon that dwells in man, and their claim was that they alone knew the true meaning of the Lord's Prayer. Prayer, by bestowing the gift of the Holy Spirit, purifies the soul of all passions, thus enabling the faithful to contemplate the Holy Trinity while in this prophetic state. Since the vision of God can be achieved by prayer alone, they rejected the sacraments as powerless and unnecessary. This visionary state resulted in the soul's possession by a sacred delirium characterised by jumping and dancing, symbolizing thereby that the vanquished demon was being trampled under foot. Because of this divinely inspired physical agitation the Massalians were also called *enthousiastai* (inspired, possessed of the god) and *choreutai* (dancers).

The Massalians held no possessions and were wholly dependent on charity for the necessities of life; they were the first "mendicant friars." Since manual labor was an obstacle to fulfilling their duty to prayer and contemplation, they renounced all forms of work. Finally, their most fascinating doctrine was that those who had reached perfection through the rigors of asceticism and self-denial no longer had need to observe these restraints. Once the evil demon was driven out of man there was no longer any possibility of sinning. Beginning with extreme asceticism they ended in extreme immorality and the worst sexual excesses. While the Paulicians were noted for their aversion to monks, the Massalians had a particular predilection for the monastic life. In fact, it was as monks that they were able to penetrate orthodox monasteries and disseminate their heretical teachings.

Bogomilism

In the latter half of the eighth century thousands of Armenian families were transferred from Asia Minor to European Thrace in order to stem the invasions of the menacing Bulgars. In 813 the Bulgar Khan, Krum, transported the entire population of 10,000 inhabitants of Thracian Arianople to the northern shores of the Danube; later Sardica and Philippopolis and Macedonia were annexed. The result was that great numbers of Paulicians were incorporated into Bulgarian territory and Paulician missionaries were spreading their doctrines at the same time that Byzantine Christianity was penetrating Bulgaria. The introduction of Paulicianism into Bulgaria became a serious menace to orthodox Christianity and gave rise to the important and dangerous heresy of Bogomilism.

In the 860's Bulgaria became the battleground of Roman and Greek Christianity; missionaries of both churches were accusing the other of introducing heretical practices into that country. Finally, Khan Boris opted for Byzantine Christianity, but the unedifying contest between Christians of the one church probably contributed indirectly to the advance of Paulicianism in Bulgaria. Then by the middle of the tenth century, the teachings of the Paulicians and the Massalians coalesced, and the resulting heresy of Bogomilism assumed specifically Slavonic characteristics. The first important text that survives describing the doctrines of the Bogomils is the treatise *Sermon Against the Heretics,* written about 969 by the priest Cosmas. Cosmas gives us the name of the founder of this sect and the approximate time he began his work of proselytizing. "And it came to pass that in the land of Bulgaria, in the days of the Orthodox Tsar Peter (927–969), there appeared a priest (*pop*), by the name of Bogomil, but in truth 'not beloved of God' (*Bogynemil*)." Cosmas then goes on to enumerate Bogomil doctrines. "They call the Devil the creator of man and of all God's creatures; and because of their extreme ignorance, some of them call him a fallen angel and others consider him to be the unjust steward." The creator of this world then is the fallen angel Satanael. No longer do we have two equal or nearly equal principles, Good and Evil, confronting each other. Satanael is clearly inferior to God and ultimately dependent on him. The Bogomils, according to Cosmas, rejected the Incarnation of Christ and consequently refused to venerate his mother Mary. Like the Paulicians before them, they also reviled the Mosaic Law and the Old Testament in general because it was the work of the evil creator, the Devil. "Although they carry the Holy Gospel in their hands, they interpret it falsely, and thus seduce men." The Bogomils had also learned the trick of outwardly accepting the New Testament in order to avoid suspicion and then interpreting it in their own way.

Since the visible world is the creation of Satanael, it followed that union with God could be achieved only if all matter and flesh were avoided. Meat, wine and marriage, the triad of evils, were renounced as abominable. Bogomil legend states that the very tree of good and evil in the Garden of Eden, whose fruit was the cause of the downfall of Adam and Eve, was actually the vine planted by Satanael himself. This would explain why wine was so abhorrent.

Like the Paulicians, the Bogomils rejected the sacraments and denied the real presence of Christ in the Eucharist, interpreting the sacrament allegorically. Cosmas says: "They felt an aversion to baptized children," and whenever they encountered a child they would "turn away and spit." Not only did they abhor Christian baptism in water, they held John the Baptist to be the forerunner of anti-Christ.

The Bogomils saw no virtue in the cross, even in a cosmic sense, as did the Manichees, as Cosmas says:

About the Cross of our Lord ... they say: how can we bow to it, for on it the Jews crucified the son of God? The cross is an enemy of God. For this reason they instruct their followers to hate it and not to venerate it, saying: if some one were to kill the son of a king with a piece of wood, is it possible that this piece of wood could be dear to the king? So is the cross to God.

Since church buildings, icons and relics were all of material origin, and hence evil, the Bogomils were repelled by them. Churches, in fact, were viewed as the dwelling places not of God but of the evil creator Satanael. "The heretics," says Cosmas, "do not reverence icons, but call them idols ... the heretics mock [relics of saints] and laugh at us when we reverence them and beg help from them." As for miracles, the Bogomil arguments were the same as those of the Jewish authorities in the New Testament against the miraculous powers of Jesus: "They say that the miracles are not wrought by the will of God, but that the Devil performs them to deceive men." Consequently, the whole cult of saints was rejected by the Bogomils. Not only were the orthodox feast days of Christ and of the Christian martyrs not celebrated by them, the Bogomils both fasted and worked on Sunday, the Lord's day.

Like the Massalians, the Bogomils stressed the significance of the Lord's Prayer. "Shutting themselves up in their houses, they pray four times a day and four times a night. ... When they bow they do not make the sign of the Cross." Another Massalian trait the Bogomils adopted was their aversion to manual labor. Cosmas criticizes them as parasites on society and idlers with no fixed abode.

While rejecting the order of priesthood and the sacraments in general, the Bogomils did confess their sins to one another, suggesting thereby the concept of the general priesthood of the laity. This idea, together with their individualistic and rationalistic interpretation of the Gospel, found its way later into Protestantism.

Finally, Bogomilism was a serious political threat to the Bulgarian state, since it preached outright civil disobedience. "They teach their own people not to obey their masters, they revile the wealthy, hate the tsar, ridicule the elders, condemn the boyars, regard as vile in the sight of God those who serve the tsar and forbid every serf to work for his lord."

By 1050 Bogomilism had spread to the western provinces of Asia Minor. The fullest and most systematic account of the Bogomil doctrines is found in the *Dogmatic Panoply* composed by the theologian Euthymios Zygabenos. Briefly these were as follows. Satanael was the first-born son of God the Father and the elder brother of the Son and Logos. The compound name Satanael means God's adversary. Second to the Father in dignity, Satanael was clad in the "same form and garments" as the Father and sat on a throne at His right hand. Stricken with the sin of pride, however, Satanael decided to rebel against the Father and succeeded in persuading the "ministering powers" to shake off their yoke and follow him. As a punishment for their rebellion, they were cast out of heaven, and Satanael's place and seniority rights passed to his younger brother. Exiled from his celestial abode, Satanael decided to create the visible world in imitation of the heavenly one over which he would reign as the Father reigns in Heaven. It is the creation of the visible world by Satanael that is described in Genesis. The Christians falsely attributed the creation of this world to God the Father.

Next, Satanael created Adam's body out of earth and water, but when he set the body upright, the water flowed out of the big toe of Adam's right foot and assumed the shape of a serpent. Then Satanael breathed into the body, hoping to animate it, but again the breath escaped by the same way, animating instead the serpent, which now became a minister of Satanael. Thoroughly frustrated at his attempt to bring his human creation to life, Satanael turned to his Father and begged him to send down his Spirit on Adam; in return Satanael promised that man should belong to both of them. God agreed, and Adam came to life, a compound of a divine soul from the Father and a body created by Satanael. After creating Eve in the same manner, Satanael proceeded to seduce her; as a consequence of this union, Eve bore Satanael a son, Cain, and a daughter, Kalomena. Abel was born later of Eve and Adam. Satanael's seduction of Eve had a serious consequence for him: he was divested of his creative powers and beauty, and God abandoned to him the government of the earth with the hope that the divine soul in all men would resist evil, but this was not to be.

The ministering powers who fell with Satanael now felt betrayed by their leader; taking the daughters of men as wives, they begot the race of giants who rose up to fight Satanael on behalf of mankind. Incensed by this open rebellion, Satanael sent down the flood to destroy all living flesh with the exception of Noah, who had no daughter and who consequently remained faithful to Satanael.

Finally, in the year 5500 from the creation of the world, taking pity on the divine soul imprisoned in the human body, the Father brought forth from his heart the Logos known by the names of Archangel Michael, because he was "the messenger of the Great Counsel," Jesus, as healer, and Christ, since he was "anointed with the flesh." Christ, however, did not really assume human flesh but only appeared to do so (docetism). He entered the world merely by passing through the right ear of the Virgin, and in his nonmaterial body he performed his mission of teaching. Although he appeared to be crucified and to rise from the dead, Christ's redemption actually consisted only in his teaching aimed at liberating man's divine soul from his material body. Descending into Hell, Christ cast aside his mask and bound the enemy Satanael with heavy chains. It was at this time that Satanael lost the "el" from his name, together with all his divine attributes, thus becoming "Satan." Having succeeded in his mission, Christ returned to the Father into whom He was resolved. In other words, Christ was not the Second Person of the Trinity, the eternal Word who was incarnate as true man in history, but only the spoken word of God manifested in Christ's oral teaching. Thus, Christ entered the world through the right ear of the Virgin just as the spoken word enters the ear of the listener.

In view of these doctrines it becomes understandable why the Bogomils rejected the Old Testament, which, they taught, describes the works of Satanael as the creator. The Mosaic Law, the law given to Moses on Mount Sinai, was the work of Satanael. The only Old Testament figures who were saved were the ancestors of Jesus. In this regard, however, the Byzantine Bogomils differed from their Bulgarian coreligionists: the Bulgarian Bogomils rejected both the Mosaic Law and the Old Testament prophets, while the Byzantine Bogomils accepted the Psalter and the sixteen Books of the Prophets from the Old Testament, and the New Testament in its entirety. This also explains why the Byzantine Bogomils recognized the ancestors of Christ and the sixteen Prophets of the Old Testament as saints. Rejecting the cult of icons, they revered the iconoclasts, whom they considered "alone Orthodox and faithful." With the exception of these, the Bogomils rejected all other Christian saints, whose relics they believed were inhabited by demons. Their view of demonology according to Zygabenos was that "the demons fly from them alone like an arrow from a bow; they inhabit all other men (non-Bogomils) and instruct them in vice, lead them to wickedness and after their death dwell in their corpses, remain in their tombs and await their resurrection in order to be punished together with them."

The chief residence of Satanael in the past had been the Temple of Solomon in Jerusalem, but after its destruction he took up his abode in Hagia Sophia in Constantinople. The special habitat of demons, however, was water, the element from which Satanael created the world. Thus, the Bogomils detested the idea of baptism by water. Nonetheless, the Bogomils called the ceremony of initiation into their own sect the Baptism of Christ, which, however, was consummated through the Spirit. After a period of severe asceticism and spiritual preparation, the baptized candidate was fully initiated by the higher ceremony of Perfection.

Since the body, fashioned by Satanael, was evil, at death the bodies of the Perfect were believed to dissolve into dust, never to rise again; instead, the divine soul put on the immortal garment of Christ and entered the Father's Kingdom.

The Bogomil community imposed a severe discipline on its members by demanding that they recite the Lord's Prayer seven times a day and five times a night and that they fast from meat, cheese and eggs on Monday, Wednesday and Friday of every week until the ninth hour of the day.

Uprooted from Byzantium by Emperor Alexios I Komnenos (1081–1118), Bogomilism returned to its original stronghold in Bulgaria, enriched and fortified by its evolution in the empire.

The increasing intercourse between the East and the West fostered by commerce and the Crusades introduced these Bogomil or neo-Manichaean ideas to western Europe. In 1167 a certain Niketas of Constantinople presided over a meeting of the Cathars or Albigensians at Saint-Felix de Caraman near Toulouse. This infection of Eastern heresy introduced new "protestant" ideas to the Catholic West and caused grave dislocation in southern France and northern Italy.

Chapter 3

Byzantine Christianity and Mysticism

No description of Byzantine Christianity can be complete without some discussion of one of its greatest concepts, its mystical vision of God. The chief goal of Byzantine religious life was to transform Adam into Christ. Thirsting after divine perfection, the Byzantine soul was consumed by a divine love; it saw Christ as the Bridegroom and viewed the Kingdom of Heaven as the Bridal Chamber.

The great danger of the heresies, which threatened to destroy the fulfillment of Christ's promise of union with God, was that their unbounded and undisciplined free thought created unacceptable new doctrines instead of interpreting the accepted dogmas of Divine Revelation. Byzantine orthodoxy remained a religion and did not become a philosophical system because it did not discuss the originating principle (God), but mystically affirmed the dogma of his being. To those who examine the divine through human reason, the things of faith appear to be foolish; the reason for this is that whatever has relation to God is simply beyond reason and philosophic syllogisms. God is, after all, incomprehensible; just as he did not transmit his essence to man in creation, so he did not transmit the knowledge of his essence to man. What we understand of God is not his essence, but something about his essence, the categories of his essence: God is *anarchos*, without beginning, and *aoratos,* invisible. The Greek *alpha privative* in such terms of definition shows that they are negative attributes and as such are called *apophatic* in Greek. God is not *one* of many beings, not because he does not exist. but because he is beyond all beings and fills everything. He is an ocean of infinite being and is described as uncircumscribable. God is the source and ground of all being. Being is the essence of the personality of man. Christianity is concerned with the salvation of being and not only with the comprehension of essence as were the ancient Greeks. That is why St. John of Damascus (ca. 674–749) considered *agonia* as the highest degree of fear and characteristically defines it as the "fear of the Fall." Agonia became the essential passion of man after the fall. In its depth it is the expression of the natural desire for being. Since man was created out of nothing, it is natural for him to desire to remain forever in the state of being; the terrifying fear that death promotes is the fear that we shall lose all being completely. From this fear Christian existentialism saves man and opens to him the road to salvation.

The Byzantines, however, did not reject philosophy. Philosophy for them, as indeed for Aristotle, was largely a matter of logic and dialectic; it was for this reason they called philosophy the handmaiden of faith. They were perfectly willing to use Aristotelian logic to explain Christian metaphysics; thus it was that basic Aristotelian terms took on a new content in Christian metaphysics. The conclusions between the two systems were necessarily different and it was this exactly that constituted the creativity of Byzantine thought. This was the problem with the heretics: They did not attempt to define with exactitude, clarity and consistency the meaning of the basic terms they used to develop their ideas.

St. John of Damascus resorted to arguments of reason to combat superstition and to explain such natural phenomena as thunder and lightning. As a Christian philosopher he rejected the contention of Plato, Aristotle and the Stoics that the whole universe is animated, alive. "No one ought to think," he wrote, "that the heavens and the stars have a soul because, in truth, they are soulless and insensient." As for matter St. John argued: "Do not condemn matter, for it is not a dishonorable thing. Nothing created by God could be so. This heresy was adopted by the Manichees. Dishonorable is whatever, not being the work of God, is our invention, that is, sin."

Ethical and theological reasons led St. John of Damascus also to reject augury and astrology. Astrology, it is argued, does away with laws, justice, praise and blame, everything that the Christian bases on the conviction that there is free will. Astrology attributes everything in man's life to agents outside of himself; for it is the position and movement of the stars that decide man's fate, and this with a necessity that is beyond appeal. The same holds true for sorcery and fortune-telling. In fact, Stoicism and neo-Platonism had accepted all these superstitions. The ethical majesty of man, however, was basic to Christianity. External necessity was thus shattered, and free will and responsibility replaced it with an internal moral necessity.

For the Byzantine theologian there was no antithesis between faith and reason. "Some men say that it is not necessary to study nature," wrote St. John of Damascus. "We do not want to study nature, they say, but theology. We ought to know that these are words of the indolent and lazy. The study of nature, which is the basis of theology, proves theological truth. The student will see the Spirit of God in nature." The reason the Byzantines did not concentrate on natural sciences, however, was that their basic concern was the salvation of man. It is not important whether the sky is a sphere or a hemisphere; what is essential, however, is that all things were made by the Word of God. Philosophical thought, therefore, ought not to be concerned with details but should confine itself to general statements of the truth. The reason was not antipathy for knowledge, but a difference in emphasis. Byzantine theology successfully synthesized the two great forces of the soul, mysticism and rationalism. With its mystical vision it conceived the basic religious truths that were then entrusted to rational formulation.

Byzantine Christianity was also influenced by neo-Platonism, especially in the form it had permeated the writings of the Christian author known as Pseudo-Dionysios the Areopagite. These writings, which belong to the end of the fifth century, were an attempt to combine neo-Platonic theories and Christian dogma into a unified system of Christian mysticism. The treatise *On Divine Names* deals with the names and attributes of the "suprasensual and hidden divinity" who is true being, as opposed to evil, which is non-being. The names attributed to God, such as Good, Being, Mind, and so on, belong to *cataphatic* (affirmative) theology. The treatise *On Mystical Theology*, however, presents an opposite view. None of the names we attribute to God are really suitable; this is apophatic (negative) theology. All we can say is what God is not, since He is beyond comprehension. Pseudo-Dionysios deals throughout with the subject that henceforth was to constitute the trunk of mystical philosophy and theology—the mystical union of the soul with God. The destiny of man is to become God-like and to be united to him. Pseudo-Dionysios, then, was the bridge that allowed neo-Platonism to cross over to Christian theology, and that gave the main direction to Christian mysticism. Thus Greek philosophy, in its last stage of evolution as neo-Platonism, found a way to survive in Christian dress. But there was an evident danger in Pseudo-Dionysios's attempt to Christianize neo-Platonism. Christianity and neo-Platonism, in fact, were two almost contemporary movements—two analogous answers to almost the same spiritual problems. Both were theocentric and described the dual movement of beings: their repulsion from the first principle and their return to it. It was this similarity that enabled neo-Platonism to penetrate Christian thought in the first place. But there is essentially a great difference between neo-Platonism and Christianity. While Greek philosophy inquires after the essence of being, Christianity seeks the salvation of all being. Again, neo-Platonism was a philosophical theory, founded on a logical premise, which seeks to divide the genus into its species and then to make possible the return of the species to the genus. In place of this logical step-by-step procedure of neo-Platonism, Christianity posits history, which is the sequence of events, each of which is the result of free will and not of a natural, eternal necessity. Christianity must not be viewed as a philosophic system that gives a logical and systematic explanation of the universe. God is all-powerful and omniscient; for the man of faith that is enough. Because of Pseudo-Dionysios's incorporation of neo-Platonic theories, Christianity was in danger of being transformed into a philosophy. In his system the historic appearance of Christ almost lost its central importance for the redemption of man.

It was left to St. Maximus the Confessor to defend the historicity of Christianity as essential to its truth and majesty. As a scholiast of Pseudo-Dionysios, St. Maximus accepted from this Christianized neo-Platonism only that which referred to man's alienation from God and to his being made over in God's likeness (his *theosis* or deification), but in such a way as not to sacrifice the historicity of Christianity while extolling its mystical essence. Thus the Christ of the Gospel is an inviolate historical reality. The penetration of neo-Platonic propositions into Byzantine theology allowed for the development of a Christian mysticism just as Aristotelian logic aided in the reasonable formulation of dogma. In this way, Christianity avoided the two evils of the intellectualism and fatalism of neo-Platonism. Man's free will was preserved, and Christianity remained a springboard for action.

Before proceeding to discuss the chief characteristics of Byzantine mysticism as it evolved in the great monastic institutions of the empire, a few introductory words ought to be said about the development of Byzantine monasticism in general.

There were in Byzantium two great streams of asceticism which coexisted: one, contemplative; the other, an open war on the flesh. The monastic discipline that evolved to deal with the latter view is represented in the several treatises on virtues and opposing evils. They remind us of the view of matter as evil and of the asceticism of the cynics in their struggle to attain virtue. The great representative in Byzantium of this particular kind of asceticism was St. John of the Ladder (525–605). He wrote a popular treatise, *The Ladder,* referring to the heavenly ladder which the patriarch Jacob saw in his dream. The thirty chapters or rungs into which it is divided symbolize the thirty years of Christ's hidden life before his public ministry. So popular was this work that it was translated into Syriac, Latin, Spanish, French and Slavonic.

John began with the idea that the monastery is a preparatory school for the life to come. The monk spends all his life there as a student in the hard struggle to gain perfection, a struggle directed against both himself and others. *The Ladder* is to serve as his guide, pointing out to him the method to achieve victory. In this difficult task the monk cannot hope on his own to gain perfection; this would be the worst form of egotism. He must attach himself to a worthy master, for the true shepherd will lead not only the studious and diligent but even the recalcitrant and coarse souls to God.

The starting point for the evangelical life is resignation from all worldly concerns; the goal is *apatheia* (impassibility), which can be reached only in successive stages as one passes from one rung to a higher one. The monk must make himself "a dwelling place for the incorporeal powers."

The overt act of resignation from the external and mundane cares of this life must be followed by a total inner break with these things. We can abandon the world only when we become inseparably attached to God through contemplation. Only thus can we reach the final rung of apatheia, which is "death of soul and death of mind before the death of the body." The ascetic will now be ready to put on another ego or self and enter into a new life, accepting God who surpasses all human measure. As the physical world dies in him, he is reborn to the contemplative life.

In this perfect isolation, the monk will have as his faithful companion his daily rehearsal for death. But what is death? Death is separation from God. The rehearsal for death is a daily mortification; in every moment the spirit must surrender itself in an endless sigh. To rehearse for death is to struggle against death and to struggle for immortality.

Once the monk has overcome the weakness and the evils of both flesh and soul, once he is alienated from the world and raises himself in contemplation above creation through love of virtue and of God, then he will reach the rung of holy *hesychia,* the peace of body and soul whose end is impassibility in which the soul is finally liberated from the confusion and agitation of the passions.

It now remains for the ascetic to be united to God. Intimate and familiar prayer, the dialogue between man and God, will achieve this. The characteristic of the pure soul is its continuous, unbroken love for God. The soul that is joined to God in purity will have no need to be taught by the mind. The inner, eternal mind will be its mystagogue, its guide and light. Man does not reach God by way of intellectual activity and dialectic, but only through the erotic attachment of the soul to him. John of the Ladder is a lover (*erastes*) of God. We are told that during his forty years as an anchorite his soul was aflame with the fire of divine Eros. Man must love God, and he does this through unceasing prayer. While St. John of the Ladder emphasized man's love for God, it remained for St. Symeon the New Theologian (944–1022) to speak adequately of God's love for man, thereby achieving the wholeness of love.

For St. John of the Ladder, impassibility must be the final condition of man's passions, but the same holds true even for the mind. While for the Stoics apatheia is the final end in the struggle for perfection enabling man to accept his fate ungrudgingly, for St. John of the Ladder it is not the final end, but only the means that enable him to make the final jump in which he surpasses himself and consummates his ultimate destiny, theosis. Of course, this does not mean that man becomes God in essence; he becomes God-like through God's own precious gift of divine grace.

Alongside this practical and empirical mysticism of St. John of the Ladder, so strongly influenced by oriental views, Byzantium developed a higher form of mysticism that was more genuinely Greek and whose philosophical propositions were brought into complete harmony with Christian faith. Thanks to St. Maximus the Confessor and St. Symeon the New Theologian, the emphasis of mysticism was turned to the inner religious life and to its direct and immediate spiritual relation to God.

St. Maximus accepted two kinds of truth, since two different organs were used to attain them: reason (*logos*) and mind (*nous*). By reason he meant common human knowledge resulting from the use of syllogism. For such knowledge to be possible there has to be a correspondence between the sensible and the intelligible world. Is there truly a correspondence? Plato tried to resolve the problem with the theory of ideas. St. Maximus used allegory and symbolism instead. Each of these two worlds, he said, is an allegory and symbol of the other. Thus the intelligible world finds its concrete form in a mystical manner, in the species of the sensible world that are symbolic. And the sensible world, through knowledge (gnosis), enters into the intelligible world, where it is organized by logical arguments. In this way we can comprehend the non-phenomena through the phenomena, and, more importantly, from the spiritual contemplation of the non-phenomena we can comprehend the phenomena. This system of symbolism and allegory thus presupposes a completely rational theory of knowledge.

The second kind of truth, however, is the vision of the mind that unites man to God. This is not truth in the usual sense of the term. It is rather that which is meant by "life in God." The virtues of prayer, prudence and love are required to attain this truth, for without these the soul cannot achieve perfect communion with God. Love pacifies the soul, prudence overcomes desire or concupiscence, and prayer cleanses the mind from all thoughts and presents it naked before God.

Thoughts are perceptions of things, either sensible or intelligible. The grace of prayer releases man from such perceptions and binds him to God. The mind, now turned to God, is deified through divine illumination. No amount of ascetic practices, deprived of love, can lead man to God; love alone enables us to become God, thanks to Christ, who became man out of love for him. When, then, does prayer release man from perceptions and thoughts that weigh him down? When he feels that being is superior to knowing. Knowing is a characteristic attribute of man. Being is a characteristic attribute of God. Only God's grace can enable man to achieve true being. As man erases from his soul every vestige of thought, perception and comprehension, being will deluge him. This cataclysm of being which displaces knowing is not so much a method for the attainment of truth as it is a rule of morality and philosophy, which together lead to the perfect life. For St. Maximus, contemplative reasoning becomes an inner search, a philosophical synthesis that embraces the universe and pursues not only the struggle against the flesh but also the illumination of the mind which transforms all things. This does not mean, argues St. Maximus, that because being is superior to knowing, knowing is useless and ought to be ignored. Knowing is the necessary first step, and we must be trained in its school. Knowing prepares us for the goal of attaining vision and, through vision, the ultimate end of theosis. Knowing reveals the mysteries found at the root of things, and by surpassing the condition of knowing we are able to move into the sphere of being.

To understand well this Christian *anthropologia* in its depth, where lies hidden the vision and the theosis that is man's destiny, we must resort to the Old Testament. St. Maximus was profoundly impressed by God's decision in Genesis 1:26: "And God said: 'Let us make man in our image and in our likeness.'" In these words the great theologian sought the essence of man and especially of Christian faith. By image is meant the mind, free will and the supernatural gifts of immortality and impassibility with which man is endowed. Likeness (*homoiosis*) refers to the moral order, the practice of virtue. The term "likeness" refers to the capacity or potential of man to become God-like. Only he who is good and wise can attain this condition. God's decision obligates us to understand human nature, the complete nature given man by his Creator, and to act in accordance with that nature, or reason (image), and in accordance with the moral law, or virtue (likeness).

Human nature, seen in this light, posits the exigent duty on every Christian to turn back, to find his original condition, or, better, to realize within himself the nature God gave him. This return to man's original condition is the objective of St. Maximus's asceticism. It constitutes the call to self-knowledge. The means for the success of this objective is the purely Greek means of decreasing daily the irrational part of the soul. St. Maximus's optimism stems from his confidence in regenerated human nature. He calls us to become just and holy, to unite with God in the light of the spirit. For St. Maximus, asceticism is not a martyrdom of the unclean flesh but rather the purification of the spirit and of the soul so that we may be united with God, who is pure spirit and truth.

The complete fulfillment of human nature demands the second supernatural gift, apatheia, an impassibility which will lead to the real sinless man. St. Maximus returns to the original blessedness of Eden; he is nostalgic for the lost paradise. After the "Fall," Adam became the type of fallen nature. Because Adam misdirected his capabilities from their natural attraction to God, he subjected his spirit to his senses and sought his happiness thereafter in sentient being. Man lost that inner harmony which the unity between himself (the subject) and God (the object) provided. Disorder replaced harmony; the senses replaced God, and with the senses came all the dangers and deceits stemming from them. Instead of rising, man fell. Christ, however, achieved the reconciliation of man. He became man outside of sin in order to make man God outside himself. Man's likeness to the divine nature must correspond to God's likeness to human nature. Man cannot discover God within himself. Within himself he shall discover only his own nature in its original wholeness and the spiritual thrust that ultimately leads to theosis. Man's deification takes place in an ineffable and mystical manner. Although reason and knowledge are useful instruments, St. Maximus recognizes that the rational road is inadequate to lead man to God. It is *ephesis,* the burning desire to be united to God, and the reward of theosis that together constitute the basis of St. Maximus's mysticism.

In the person of St. Symeon the New Theologian we have the crowning achievement of the synthesis of the spiritual way of St. Maximus and of the asceticism of St. John of the Ladder. A truly great mystic, St. Symeon was also one of Byzantium's greatest poets. Boundless love and ineffable joy spring forth from his soul when he communicates mystically with God. Let us briefly discuss the way leading to theosis as charted by this remarkable mystic and poet.

First, says St. Symeon, in agreement with St. John of the Ladder, a saintly man must be chosen as one's guide, spiritual father and teacher. Having found him with the help of God's grace, one must completely surrender himself to him.

Next, one must comprehend that the most sacred gift granted by God to man is freedom of choice. Freedom of choice is limited by the nature of our passions. Of the two kinds of passions that we meet in man, natural and spiritual passions, the former are immutable, serving natural needs such as hunger, thirst, sleep and so on; thus they do not belong to the realm of freedom of choice. Originally, the passions of the soul, primarily concupiscence and the emotions, did belong to the sphere of freedom of choice, but after the "Fall" man lost both his freedom of choice and his freedom from sin. Having now become a slave to sin, must we then despair for man? No! There is still a ray of hope and salvation because in the slave of sin there still remained a small but precious trace of free will: the desire to be saved. It is this desire for salvation that opens to man the way to discover the sickness of his mind and senses. It is because we do not realize that we are sick that we are insensitive to the great need for therapy. Whoever finds himself in this condition is not yet a true Christian. "If he were, he would partake of the life and the light because Christ is life and light. Such a one is dead; he has not yet been illuminated by the rays of the spiritual sun of righteousness." Only the God-man (*theanthropos*) can give true health and liberate man from utter corruption. But to achieve this condition we must "offer Christ our will together with the effort and labor of our intelligence united to our rational self, not by way of good deeds but by way of faith, so that Christ may see and free us through his divine grace." It is not that good works are superfluous but rather that faith, as the root, illuminates the way leading to good works, thus sanctifying and liberating the soul; since the soul governs the body, once it is sanctified, then the body too is sanctified. At this level man becomes free and self-governing. Understanding now how sacred indeed is the gift of free will he will say to God:

I thank Thee for having honored me with free will.... As a scorner and ingrate I deemed that the value of free will is like the unloosing of an irrational animal from its bonds and that is why once I was loosened I strayed far from the reign of Thy power and threw myself over a cliff of many evils.

St. Symeon realized all too well how difficult the temptation of sin makes this task: "The temptation of the Devil is that which makes man to sin both willingly and unwillingly, in knowledge and in ignorance." Or again:

So does the hawk which flies with wings to find food and is deceived by the hunter who sets up his nets to ensnare it. Below he spreads his net and above he places the bait; the hawk, seeing the bait, descends to eat it and is caught in the net and then the hunter seizes it and sews up its eyes and holds it in his hand in his power against its will. The Devil is like that. He knows that the mind of man is always in movement, and that is why he goes near man and dangles sensuous pleasures as bait before his thoughts, and beneath the pleasures he places sin as a net which is like a delicate and light hand because the Devil without sin cannot catch the human soul. . . . And when man is caught, then the devil sews up his eyes, that is, he beclouds his mind. . . . When the intellect of man inclines rationally to sin, then the intelligible tyrant and dynast of souls who stands behind, ever vigilant, in the blinking of an eye, convinces the intelligence to consummate the sin with the act. . . . Man contracts from committing sin, but when instigated by the Devil he performs it.

This is the reason the mind must be healed first. Christ must first dwell there; then the reason and the acts of man will be restored to health. The deeper man senses his weakness the stronger will be his sense of contrition and humiliation. When divine grace finds him contrite and humbled, it will overshadow and visit him. Before man begins to sing hymns and pray to God he must be reconciled to Him. How then must man pray? If he lifts up his hands, eyes and mind to heaven and thinks divine thoughts and sheds tears and weeps, then be assured that he is on the way to self-deception. "Such as these see light with the eyes of their body and smell sweet scents and hear voices with their ears . . . and gradually they are possessed by demons." Again he who "prefers to read always instead of learning to pray is deceived and alienates himself from salvation and is completely insensitive even though he may have Holy Scriptures at his finger tips." If he concentrates on himself and examines his thoughts and attends to the words of his prayer and if he is at war with himself and can find no peace or the time "to live virtues and to receive the crown of righteousness," then he makes war on his enemies in the night. The moonlit night is only better than a moonless one.

Fortunately there is another kind of prayer: "obedience to the spiritual father, which makes man unconcerned for all things and consecrates him only to God." Prayer is association and dialogue with God. The spiritual condition of man who reaches this height is dramatically drawn for us by St. Symeon in the poem *Who Is the Monk?*

The monk is he who is uninvolved with the world
And unceasingly speaks to God alone.
Seeing, he is seen, loving, he is loved
And ineffably becomes an illuminated light.
Glorified he appears to be impoverished
And becoming familiar he is a stranger.
O strange and ineffable marvel!
Possessing infinite wealth I am a pauper
And thinking I have nothing I possess much
And I say "I thirst" while having an abundance of waters!

St. Symeon the New Theologian expresses the condition of the man who is truly close to God and simultaneously is aware of the immeasurable distance that separates him from God. Ever aware of the presence of God and of his *engagement* with Him, all of man's life is sanctified and all life is a prayer. United to Christ, his total self becomes Christ: "I move my hand and Christ is my hand." United to Christ, St. Symeon acquires free access to Him. He speaks to God as a friend speaks to a friend, and peace and joy fill his soul. Peace, joy, exhilaration, total freedom, absolute creativity—these are the characteristics of the man who is reborn when God dwells in us. Such a man, of course, can have no egotism in him. Even the monk will give his soul for his fellow man as did Christ. St. Symeon invites all men to be united to Christ. The purpose of Christ's incarnation was exactly this: "For man to see Christ and to be united to him. Whoever considers this impossible denies both the Old and New Testaments."

Since man is able to achieve union with Christ, we may enjoy the greatest optimism. Man, in other words, is not condemned to live forever bound by the iron chain of an immutable nature. Man's nature is "mutable and changeable as is habit" since the Christian "who is united to the divine nature of Christ is altered by its power and is changed both in nature and in habit to the most divine and becomes god by grace like unto Him who caused the change, that is, Christ the sun of righteousness." This then is the great message the Byzantine mystic brought to mankind: man's nature is alterable; he can break its bonds when he becomes worthy to receive within himself the light of God. To accomplish this great work God has not left man unaided. "Within all of human nature he placed a loving power so that the rational nature of man might be helped by the natural power of love." In other words, man attains to the love of the Gospel, which is voluntary; to have any value the soul must accept it freely and man must combine within himself both reason and its natural loving power. How, then, does man alter his nature, becoming thereby an "earthly angel"? Love is born first of the fear of the Lord; by this St. Symeon meant the fear born of the knowledge of one's sins. It is this fear of sin that leads to the conviction of the Lord's love of mankind. But once love is born in the soul, fear is uprooted and love stands alone, queen of the soul, "being a divine and holy spirit." This is the paradox of love:

> In love there is no fear whatever,
> Nor again does love without fear in the
>   soul bear fruit.
> The tree blossoms and bears fruit
>   through labor;
> Again its fruit uproots the whole tree.
> The fruit remains alone; how can there be
>   fruit without the tree?

St. Symeon contends that "faith in Christ alone cannot save us if we do not receive the grace of the Holy Spirit knowingly." And grace comes only to the soul that is enflamed with love for the Lord.

> Seeking ... Him whom I desired,
> Whom I loved, with whose beauty I was pierced,
> I was enflamed, I was consumed, I was all afire.

To such a soul comes the holy fire, which "becomes intelligible unintelligibly in union with the ineffable." Then "the mind made pure in the light of God becomes God." That is why "it is good to be baptized, but one must receive intelligible perception of the intelligible light, that is, of the mystical life."

In this fashion only is the total and complete alteration of the mind achieved, as it progresses from natural love to voluntary love and thence soars upward on pinions made strong for the great flight. When man reaches this perfection, God embraces him mystically and caresses him, and then the soul "comes to revelations of the Lord and speculations and hears ineffable words." After this union "follows divine knowledge, the wisdom of the Word, and the abyss of the hidden purposes and mysteries of Christ."

Just what does St. Symeon mean by divine knowledge? Whatever the saints and the Scriptures say concerning God are not mere conceptions but a true vision of "those things which truly are." "They must have seen, not only heard; because the only way for someone to know God is through the vision of the light, the light of knowledge, which is sent out from that light."

We cannot know God indirectly through rational syllogisms, but only through direct vision, the same vision with which the saints knew him and to which we shall be raised when we are purified. Thus the direct vision of God becomes the highest purpose for every man and not only for a chosen few and only in rare situations as in Platonic ecstasy.

The vision is the crown with which every athlete will be rewarded at the end of the race. It is the common good that invites every man to regeneration. The mystical philosophy of St. Symeon is a categorical statement of spiritual freedom and human independence, which is subjected only to the divine light. With this view St. Symeon established the historicity of Christianity for which St. Maximus struggled so hard. The vision is direct sight and not an intellectual journey in which the mind sees what exists. The mystic sees but does not interpret; it is only afterward that he describes the vision. His conviction that God exists, therefore, is unshakeable.

"To ask what God is is not only audacious, it is foolish and stupid." God is beyond essence (*hyperousios*). Man, as man, cannot know God, but the moment he surpasses his humanity he is united to God and sees him. This is the meaning that the vision of the holy fire has for us. Although St. Symeon the New Theologian was not the first to speak of the vision of the holy fire, he was the first to give it such breadth and depth. He insists: "If no man sees God, he will never know Him nor will he learn His holy will." From the moment man achieves theosis, "whatever he says or does or writes he does not say or do or write these things but the Holy Spirit does so." It must be emphasized, however, that:

... the power of the Holy Spirit, which he who loves God puts on, does not appear perceptible in the form of fire; these things happened only in apostolic times for the benefit of the faithful, but it is seen spiritually in the form of spiritual light and it comes with peace and joy as the prologue of the eternal and first light, as radiance and brilliance of eternal blessedness.

With this light, then, "the eyes of the heart are cleansed, that is, the mind and the intelligence, and they see ... God." Then the soul views its smallest mistakes "and comes to the greatest humility and, reflecting the majesty of that glory, is filled with joy and gladness and wonders at this unhoped for miracle which it has seen, and immediately sheds many tears. And in that way man is totally changed and knows God and is known first of God." The grace of the Holy Spirit makes man "both friend and son of God and God as much as it is possible for men." Yet, despite our union with God, the God whom we see is like the sun in water. The sun itself we shall see only after our death. And if we are deemed worthy in our lifetimes to see Christ "we shall not die nor shall death overcome us." God, who is omnipresent, never leaves our side; it is because we have separated ourselves from God that we do not see him. The Kingdom of God is always at hand. God is to man's soul what man's soul is to his body. The genius of Byzantium was that it knew how to put new life and meaning into old forms.

HESYCHASM

In the fourteenth century, Byzantine monasticism made its last great contribution to orthodox religious life. This remarkable movement was known as *hesychasm,* coming from the Greek word for quietude, the silence that results from complete seclusion from the world. At the beginning of this century, the monk Gregory of Sinai (died 1346) came to Mount Athos and introduced what was claimed to be the highest form of monastic life. The hesychasts of Mount Athos believed that a particular position of the body during the hour of prayer contributed greatly to achieving ecstatic love, which, in an immediate rather than a gradual experience, brought them to true union with God. The hesychast sat with his body bent and his chin resting on his breast so that his eyes were fixed on the area of the navel while repeating over and over the Jesus Prayer: "O Lord, Jesus Christ, Son of God, have mercy on me the sinner." At the same time he held his breath in a disciplined fashion.

Actually, the hesychasts were concentrating their attention on the position of the heart. Union with God, they said, is attained when the spirit succeeds in attracting the mind to the depth of the heart. Only the activity of the heart leads to pure truth, because it is a simple and pure activity without any form, a gift of divine grace. Thus hesychasm was an anti-intellectual movement of mystical love leading to union with God and emphasizing the role of the heart as the key. The bounds of love opened up by the Lord's commandment of love are expanded more and more until they embrace the whole life of man. As a result of this mystical discipline, the monks of Mount Athos contended that they were able to see a powerful light around them which inundated their whole being with ineffable joy. They added that this light was the same as the uncreated light which comes from God, and which was seen by the Lord's disciples, Peter, John and James, on Mount Tabor at the glorious moment of the Transfiguration of Christ (St. Mark 9:2–3).

At this time Barlaam, a Greek monk from Calabria, came to Constantinople to study Aristotle in the original. Aristotle, of paramount importance in the Latin West, had been chiefly studied in Arabic translations. The influence of Aristotle reached its zenith with St. Thomas Aquinas, who fused Aristotelianism with Christian theology in his *Summa Theologica*, which still remains the accepted philosophical approach of Roman Catholicism. Barlaam, proud of his own learning, created a great stir in Byzantium by maintaining that the wisdom of the Latins (whom the Byzantines still considered to be barbarians) was superior to that of the Byzantines. Barlaam's challenge led to public debates in 1330 in the palace before Emperor Andronikos III Palaiologos (1328–1341). The learned priest, Nikephoros Gregoras, was chosen to rebuff Barlaam. Gregoras undertook to unmask Barlaam as a shallowly educated man; famous for his own mathematical and astronomical expertise (he had advised the emperor to update the calendar), Gregoras attempted to show how the learning of the West was confined to the physics and logic of Aristotle.

Barlaam was disgraced in the debate and afterward sought refuge in Thessalonica. Since Mount Athos was not too far from this city he decided to visit this center of Byzantine monasticism. While on Mount Athos he learned of hesychasm from an ignorant monk and forthwith he began to ridicule the movement. He derided the hesychasts as Massalians and navel watchers (*omphaloskopoi*) and made bitter accusations against them. Since they claimed to see the divine and uncreated light of God with their physical eyes, argued Barlaam, the hesychasts were perverting the truth, since every visible thing to man's eyes is necessarily created. If the light of Mount Tabor was visible to the Lord's disciples, then it follows that it could not have been the uncreated light of God. The real vision of the divine, contended Barlaam, is learning and knowledge, promoting thereby the position of extreme rationalism. Whoever has knowledge and wisdom knows the truth, and whoever knows the truth knows God and remains near him. Once one has mastered Pythagoras, Plato and Aristotle, one will have attained to full comprehension of the truth. Secular knowledge, then, is a catharsis of the soul without which it is impossible to reach God and be united to him. Barlaam was no mystic, and the hesychasts were wholly mystical in their approach to the Truth who is God. Barlaam consequently based his arguments on the model of Greek logic, and he followed the methodology of Aristotelian Thomism. It was no accident that later Barlaam became a cardinal of the Roman church. The question dividing the two camps can be summarized as follows: Is true theology inquiry or vision? What scandalized Barlaam and his followers was the contention of the hesychasts that they saw the uncreated light; they viewed this as the materialization of God.

The great champion of hesychasm was St. Gregory Palamas (1296–1360). He was a noble brought up in the court of Andronikos II Palaiologos (1282–1328). As a young man Palamas abandoned the court, was tonsured a monk in Thessalonica and lived in a hermitage near Berrhoea. Barlaam's violent attack against the hesychasts, however, compelled Palamas to come out of his retreat. To support the method of hesychastic prayer and to repel the ridicule and abuse of Barlaam, Palamas based himself on the Christian teaching that the human body, the holy temple of the Holy Spirit who is God, is not the cause of evil. The doctrine that man's body is the source of evil is both neo-Platonic and Manichaean in origin; the Christian position is that the body is an absolutely necessary counterpart of man's hypostasis. The Barlaamites located the mind outside the body and contended that the mind during prayer must be external to the body. Palamas argued that the mind is inside the heart, its treasure chest. If neo-Platonic ecstasy takes man outside of himself, in hesychasm the mind is purified through the heart. Palamas attempted to formulate a theory which springs from the deeper roots of Christianity. He wanted the mind to be baptized in the heart and ruled by the heart; rediscovering its own essence, the mind springs from the heart, returning to God.

Barlaam, however, contended that there is no vision that surpasses the intellectual capabilities, and he ridiculed the claim of the hesychasts that mystical vision alone provided the brightest proof that God exists and is above all beings. "Our holy faith," wrote Palamas, "is a vision of our hearts in a special way because it surpasses all the intelligible capabilities of our soul." Only when the uncreated light inundates the heart does the true man enter into his true work, ascending the eternal mountains, viewing the invisible, entering completely into the land of the miracle. For Palamas it is the illuminated heart, not the intellect, that leads man to God and saves him.

To Barlaam's arguments that the light of Mount Tabor was material, created and sensible, Palamas made a distinction between essence and energy. There is, said Palamas, an infinitude of divine energies, and one of these is the uncreated light of Mount Tabor. These divine energies spring from the essence of God as from an endless fountain. The divine essence is described as the divine darkness (*gnofos*), whence flow the divine energies that constitute the manifestations of God. Man, aided by divine grace, is united not to the essence but to the energy of God. But the divinity is not divisible as are physical bodies: all those who receive within them one divine energy have received the plenitude of divinity, all of the Godhead, since the energy cannot be separated from its source, which is God. God's providence, omniscience and creativity are all manifestations of the divine energies. The problem is the relationship between essence and energy, a problem similar to monotheletism but seen from another vantage point.

The Barlaamites saw the relationship between cause and effect only in a logical framework: God—creation—creatures. The Palamites, with the aid of divine grace, saw God with their very eyes. The Barlaamites attained theosis or deification only through the mind; the Palamites, by way of divine grace. The Palamite did not inquire after a logical proof of God's existence; he sought but to see God and to live in him. The hesychast, however, did not deny that God is infinite and uncircumscribable because God, whom the mystic sees, is a single divine energy and not the divine essence itself. The moment the Transfiguration of Christ took place, God allowed the door of divinity to open a little to those to whom he gave his grace, and the God who dwells therein was revealed to his initiates. The divine uncreated light, then, is not something that now exists and then disappears, nor is it circumscribable. Those who saw Jesus on Mount Tabor passed from the flesh to the spirit. How this occurs only God and those who have experienced it know.

NIKOLAOS KABASILAS

The last great mystic of Byzantium was Nikolaos Kabasilas (died 1471). He carried St. Symeon's thoughts and teachings to their fruition. With Kabasilas, the mystical vision made an important advance. He wrote:

> The law of the spirit, which is love of God, is a law of friendship and gratitude. To follow this law one need not expend effort or expense or shed perspiration. . . . Nor is it necessary to leave your work or to go to out-of-the-way places, to live a strange life and to wear strange garments. You need not do all these things. You can stay at home and without losing your riches you can spend your time in the continual study of God and man, in the study of the relationship of man to the divine. . . . And, moreover, preparations for our prayer are not necessary, nor are special places or voices, when we supplicate God. Because there is no place where God is absent, it is not possible for God not to be with us, since God is closer to them who call upon him than their own hearts. He will come to us even if we are evil, because God is good.

What is truly fascinating about Kabasilas is that for him all contention with the flesh is removed, and gone too are all the external conditions and forms of life considered so necessary in the past to the monks. Piety is exclusively the work of our inner disposition and of our will. That is why the external abandonment of the world as practiced by the anchorites is not a prerequisite of mysticism.

Man can transform his daily social life with the study of exalted spiritual matters and by voluntarily subjecting his will to God's.

Kabasilas, then, was not a mystic of ecstatic conditions. His purpose was to describe the reality of divine grace within the common Christian worshipper. And this he did with an exceptionally powerful theological insight. The *Life in Christ,* his great theological study, for him is the "life of Christ" that enters every Christian with a mystery of familiarity. It is natural, said Kabasilas, for every thing to be more attached to itself than to anything else. Yet our union with Christ is still more powerful. Blessed men feel themselves attached more to the Savior than to themselves. Christ is at the same time paradoxically a stranger to us and our dwelling place. It is exactly in this that the New Testament differs from the Old Testament, that is, in the presence within us of Christ, who sets the soul of man in order and transforms it. It is the Christian's sacred obligation to discover within himself the pure essence of virtue, the value of human nature and God's love for mankind.

> Neither temples nor anything else are as holy as man with whose nature God himself communicates. He who will come seated on the clouds is a man as certainly as he is God. Each one of us can shine brighter than the sun, rise to the clouds, fly to God, approach him so that God will look at him with sweetness.

Here, again, we find ourselves at the Socratic starting point, but with new depth: Discover the value of your nature and build your life upon it. If, after this discovery, man considers the poverty in which he exists while possessing such a rich nature—because he has allowed sloth and sleep to entangle him—great sorrow and many tears will accompany him all his life. From the day, however, that man makes his life as it should be, then joy and happiness will be his forever. It is not in the hermit that the spiritual man will be found, but rather in the excellent human nature through which God communicates with every man. Kabasilas invites every Christian to make this discovery. Religious thought is emancipated from every bond to external conditions. From the asceticism of the body we ascend to the spiritual heights of man. This is one of the great concepts of Byzantine theology.

Kabasilas is indeed remarkable, because he does not follow the views of earlier mystics, such as St. John of the Ladder, who rejected science and secular learning as deceitful; nor does he denigrate reason. With exceptional zeal he himself cultivated astronomy and other sciences. His appreciation of science is such that he calls the saints imperfect beings "because they did not accept in this world a human good while they were able to do so. And every being who cannot raise to actuality that which is in him potentially is imperfect." Thus, Kabasilas makes a giant step in the direction of complete reconciliation between religious mysticism and the wisdom of this world.

The contention that Byzantine theology was stagnant is one of the great misconceptions of historians!

Chapter 4

Byzantine Christianity and the West

As Europe was barbarized during the early centuries of our era and the capital of the Roman Empire was transferred from old Rome on the Tiber to New Rome on the Bosphorus, the western half of the Roman Empire declined and the Greek half emerged in the full bloom of its vigor. When the West in its turn revived from its dark ages, this regeneration, together with the appearance of the Turks on the eastern frontiers, signalled the decline and fall of the greatest Christian empire in history. The balance of history was now reversed: the rise of the Latin West was partly purchased at the price of the fall of the Greek East.

Events in the Christian East and West proved, once again, that there could be no political victory or defeat without corresponding religious consequences, and no religious victory without political repercussions. Political needs could and did corrupt and shatter religious cohesion. Religious conviction could and did negate the necessity of political compromise. The religious alienation and political rivalry between Byzantium and Europe resulted finally in the murder of the Byzantine state by the Fourth Crusade in 1204. It was another two and a half centuries before it succumbed completely to the Ottoman Turks, but the mortal blow had been struck by Italians, Normans and Franks.

The remarkable political and religious achievements of Byzantium were ever the source of two irreconcilable reactions on the part of the European West: attraction and repulsion, fascination and revulsion. It seems that a society can admire the intellectual, spiritual and political achievements of another society while despising the people responsible for them. Latin arrogance and disdain were countered by Byzantine suspicion and growing hatred. The Latin infiltration of the Greek East finally demoralized the Byzantine state. The demands of ecclesiastical and theological submission to the papacy as a sine qua non for military assistance against the Turks was understood by the Byzantines as a demand that they sell their souls to preserve their bodies. The threads of political life and religious faith in Byzantium were interwoven into one seamless robe, and the final attempts to separate the two resulted in the ultimate destruction of the fabric. That is why the opposing phenomena, reconciliation and ever-increasing alienation, could be at work at the same time. This dichotomy finally severed the politico-religious cohesiveness, integrity and unity of the Byzantine soul, thus destroying its will to resist.

Four factors in combination led to the collapse of Byzantine civilization: religion, political ideology, culture and economics. Although Greek East and Latin West shared a common Greco-Roman and Judeo-Christian heritage, historical events projected them into different and often opposing directions. Consequently, alienation and estrangement made implacable enemies of brothers begotten of common parents. The story of how this happened is one of the most fascinating and instructive lessons in history.

THE POLITICS OF RELIGION AND
THE RELIGION OF POLITICS

We have already discussed the religious heresies that for brief periods of time alienated the Latin West from the Greek East. The Byzantine emperors were exercised primarily by the need to reconcile rival religious factions in order to preserve the unity of the state. This is what lay behind Zeno's *Henotikon* (482), which led to the Acacian Schism (484–518), the first serious breach between Rome and Constantinople; the unedifying account of Justinian's *Edict of the Three Chapters* (546) and Pope Vigilius's ludicrous reactions; Heraclius's *Ekthesis* (638) which led to the anathematization of Pope Honorius I by the Sixth Ecumenical Council; the *Typikon* of Constans II (648); and the arrest and conviction of Pope Martin for treason and his subsequent exile to the Cherson.

During these first six centuries, despite the growing animosity between Constantinople and Rome, the pope was a citizen of the empire. The sixth and seventh centuries, however, proved fateful for the intensification of the alienation of Greek East and Latin West.

On the one hand, Justinian's policy of *renovatio*, leading to the reconquest of Italy from the semi-Romanized Ostrogoths, was a tragic error; in 568 the barbarous Lombards moved into Italy from the north and occupied large areas, filling the vacuum left by the destruction of the Ostrogothic forces. Ravenna, the imperial capital of Italy, was now cut off from Rome, and the pope became responsible for the military defense and political administration of that key city. The pope, by virtue of political accident, had become a secular ruler, a fact of tremendous historical consequence. In a letter to Empress Constantina, wife of Maurice, Pope Gregory I the Great (590–604) wrote:

> It is now seven and twenty years that we have been living in this city beset by the swords of the Lombards. How much we have to pay them daily from the Church's treasury, in order to live among them at all, it is impossible to compute. I will merely say that, as at Ravenna the emperor has a paymaster for the First Army of Italy, who defrays the daily expenses as need arises, so at Rome for such purposes I am paymaster.

The same pope clashed head on with the patriarch of Constantinople, John the Faster (582–595), over the latter's use of the title Ecumenical Patriarch. If the emperor was monarch of the Byzantine oikoumene, meaning the inhabited Christian empire, then the patriarch of the empire's capital city was the "ecumenical" ecclesiastical leader of that empire. Following the devastation of Italy as a result of Justinian's reconquest, the population of Rome fell to about ten thousand. The glory and the power of empire resided in Constantinople. Papal prestige and primacy in the Greek East was involved. Gregory the Great became obsessed by the titular claims of the patriarch of Constantinople:

> I am compelled to cry aloud and say, *O tempora! O mores!* ... Priests who ought to lie weeping on the ground and in ashes seek for themselves names of vanity and glory in new titles.... Doctors of the humble, chiefs of pride, under the form of a lamb we hide the teeth of a wolf.

Within a century of Pope Gregory I's death the bishops of Rome consented to be honored as "ecumenical" popes, the very title that was characterized by Pope Gregory I as foolish, proud, pestiferous, profane, a diabolical usurpation and a mark of the forerunner of anti-Christ!

CAUSES OF ESTRANGEMENT

At about the same time that the invasion of Italy by the Lombards was under way, the Slavs of the lower Danube, some one hundred thousand strong, in concert with the Asiatic Avars, poured over the frontier into Thrace and Illyricum; the permanent Slavization of the Balkan peninsula had begun.

The profound significance of the Slavic occupation of the Balkans was that the most important Latin-speaking elements of the Byzantine empire were eliminated. The only Latin centers that remained were Carthage, Ravenna, Rome and Naples, but these were too distant to influence the linguistic predominance of Greek, which became the official language of the Byzantine state under Heraclius (610–641). The Slavic penetration into Greece affected significantly the ethnography of Sicily and south Italy. Large numbers of Greeks from the Peloponnesus emigrated to these safer territories. Ironically, as a result, the effective jurisdiction of the papacy was reduced to lands where the Greek element was considerable. Of the thirteen popes between 678 and 752, eleven were Greek speaking!

The Slavic occupation of the Balkans was one of the chief causes of the estrangement between Latin West and Greek East. The Via Egnatia, the old Roman road that led directly from Constantinople to Dyrrachium (Durazzo) on the Adriatic coast, was now blocked; the land bridge between Byzantium and the West was ominously closed. Despite Muslim control of the Mediterranean, it was still safer to travel by sea than over land.

The Byzantine empire, as we have seen, was considered to be the continuation of the Roman empire, universal and eternal in nature. But with the Germanic barbarian invasions in the West and the eventual collapse of the western Roman Empire, the subsequent occupation of the Balkans by the Slavs in the sixth and seventh centuries, and the Muslim control of the Mediterranean Sea by virtue of their seizure of Syria, Palestine, Egypt, North Africa and Spain, the sea and land routes between Christian East and West were effectively blocked. This enforced separation led to differences in liturgical practices, religious usages and traditions, church organization and, finally, doctrine.

The ever-growing estrangement between Greek East and Latin West is clearly seen in the reorientation of the Byzantine government eastward rather than westward. The narrowed Byzantine field of vision is shown in Byzantine chronicles written in the eighth century by the monk Theophanes and the patriarch of Constantinople, Nikephoros. The work of Theophanes (died 818) is built on a chronological skeleton. The narrative is divided into years, and, at the beginning of each year, Theophanes marks the regnal year of the Byzantine emperor and of the Persian king, who is later replaced by the Arab caliph, and by the year of the reigning five patriarchs, first of the bishop of Rome and then followed by the patriarchs of Constantinople, Alexandria, Antioch and Jerusalem.

It is significant that the names of the popes drop from the lists completely after 574–575 and reappear again only in the second quarter of the eighth century. The papal register was dropped not because of any clash between Rome and Constantinople, but simply because the popes were no longer of any interest to Byzantium. Greek East and Latin West had gone their separate ways. The reappearance of papal names in the eighth century was due to papal opposition to iconoclasm. But in listing the popes of this period, Theophanes was surprisingly inaccurate. He confused Popes Gregory II (715–731) and Gregory III (731–741), listing them as one person. Moreover, Theophanes was mistaken about the years of Pope Zacharias's pontificate (741–752) recording his reign as lasting twenty-one years instead of eleven. In contrast Theophanes was remarkably accurate about the Arab caliphs, because the Muslims were Byzantium's chief enemies.

Again it is quite remarkable that in the chronicle written by Nikephoros, patriarch of Constantinople (806–815), the author makes only three brief references to the West in his entire treatment of the seventh century. These two chronicles are concerned primarily with Byzantine wars against the Arabs, and, secondly, with the Slavs in the Balkans. In fact, for these two chroniclers, the terms "the West" and "Europe" regularly mean the Balkan peninsula. By the middle of the ninth century Emperor Michael III (842–867) was calling Latin a "barbarous Scythian language"! The one Christian empire was now divided along cultural as well as political lines.

RELIGIOUS DIFFERENCES

The cultural and political division between the two halves of the Christian world resulted in religious differences that were to become crucial by the eleventh century. A reading of the canons of the Quinisextum Council in Troullo (691–692) convoked by Emperor Justinian II significantly reveals this cleavage in religious customs that had already emerged. One of the chief areas of friction was the issue of married clergy. In the Byzantine empire, and in former Byzantine possessions—Syria, Palestine and Egypt—there had always been married clergymen as well as celibates. Until the early fourth century bishops might be married, but from that century on the church canons state that bishops must henceforth be celibate. In the West, however, the Spanish Council of Elvira (ca. 300) insisted that the clergy, bishops, priests and deacons renounce cohabitation with their wives and the desire to beget children (Canon thirty-three). It must be understood that in Byzantium a married man was allowed to become a cleric, up to the order of the episcopate, but no cleric was ever allowed to marry. Canon six of the Quinisextum Council proscribes marriage after ordination beginning with the rank of subdeacon. Canon thirteen goes on to condemn the Latin practice of forcing celibacy or separation from wives on deacons and priests. Canon forty-eight stipulates that even a married priest may be ordained a bishop if his wife first agrees to enter a convent.

Differences in liturgical practices and fasting requirements were also emphasized by the Quinisextum Council. Canon fifty-two prescribes the liturgy of the Pre-Sanctified Gifts to be celebrated during the Great Lent, with the exception of Saturdays and Sundays and March 25, the Feast of the Annunciation. Canon fifty-five condemns the Latin practice of fasting on Saturdays; the only exception is Saturday of Holy Week. Finally, Canon ninety proscribes kneeling from sundown Saturday to sundown Sunday in honor of the Lord's Resurrection.

Pope Sergius I (687–701) refused to accept these decrees discrediting Latin practices; consequently, the emperor dispatched an emissary to arrest him, but times had changed! Not only was the emissary obstructed from carrying out the emperor's order, he barely escaped with his life. Hostility and intolerance of one another's traditions were to be the bane of Christian East and West.

The mounting friction between the popes and emperors of the Byzantine Empire led to far-reaching consequences for the evolution of the papacy into a great temporal power. The necessary preoccupation with the Arabs in the East and the Slavs in the Balkans led iconoclast emperors Leo III (717–741) and Constantine V (741–775) to neglect Italy. To support his military program in the East, Leo III increased the taxes on the church estates in Italy. Furthermore, he was particularly odious as an iconoclast. In 731 Pope Gregory III, in retaliation, condemned the iconoclasts in a synod. Unable to chastise the pope by force, the emperor is said to have confiscated the patrimonies of St. Peter in Sicily and Calabria and to have transferred jurisdiction over the dioceses of Calabria, Sicily, Crete and Illyricum to the patriarchate of Constantinople. It should be observed that these areas were predominantly Greek speaking. In the meantime, Byzantine imperial power in Italy had been severely curtailed by the Lombards, who had severed communications between Rome and the Byzantine military and administrative center, the exarchate of Ravenna. To repeat, it was the need to defend Rome and the surrounding territories that transformed the pope into a temporal prince.

In 751 Ravenna was captured by the Lombard king Aistulf, and the Byzantine exarchate was at an end. Aistulf now threatened Rome, and since the Byzantine authorities were powerless to help, Pope Stephen II (752–757) travelled across the Alps in 754 and met Pepin the Short in the royal palace of Ponthion on the Marne. An agreement of far-reaching consequences was struck between

Roman pope and Frankish king. The pope, it seems, addressed Pepin as *Patricius Romanorum* (Patrician of the Romans), illegally granting him the official Byzantine title designated for the imperial exarch of Ravenna. The pope next anointed Pepin and his sons. The Franks, on their side, agreed to make war on the Lombards, and a document was issued defining the extent of the territories and the rights that were to be granted to the papacy after the defeat of the Lombards. In two campaigns Pepin defeated the Lombards and secured to the papacy the dominion over Rome and over the Byzantine provinces of central Italy as well. This is known as the *Donation of Pepin the Short.* The Pope of Rome was truly a temporal ruler in his own right. The Byzantine government protested, but in vain. The Papal States were to survive until 1870.

Since the actions of both Frankish king and Roman pope were illegal vis-à-vis the legitimate Christian empire of Byzantium, a forgery was conveniently drawn up by an unknown cleric to support the pope's extraconstitutional claims. According to this document, known as the *Donation of Constantine,* Constantine the Great, suffering from leprosy, was miraculously cured through the intercession of the Bishop of Rome, Sylvester I (314–335), and, in gratitude, the emperor was baptized at the hands of his benefactor. Actually, Constantine was baptized on his deathbed by Eusebius, the Arian Bishop of Nicomedia. The *Donation of Constantine* decrees that all ecclesiastics are subject to the bishop of Rome to whom the emperor transfers "the city of Rome and all the provinces, districts and cities of Italy and of the regions of the West." This amazing document then claims that the pope is the supreme arbiter of the universal church as well as temporal overlord of the entire western half of the empire. For some seven hundred years in the West the glaring falsity of the *Donation of Constantine* was accepted as truth until it was shown to be a blatant forgery by Cardinal Nicholas of Cues in 1433 and by the papal secretary Lorenzo Valla in 1440.

With the intervention of the Franks in Italian affairs, the days of the Lombard kingdom were numbered. Charlemagne succeeded his father Pepin the Short, and in 774 he destroyed the Lombard forces under their king Desiderius. That same year he was festively received in Rome by Pope Hadrian I (772–795), who crowned him King of the Lombards. North Italy now became a part of the Frankish empire. Charlemagne assumed the role of protector of the papacy and confirmed, and perhaps extended, Pepin the Short's

Donation. Papal allegiance had turned from Byzantium to the Franks. In 781, Pope Hadrian I stopped dating his acts by the Byzantine emperor's regnal year. In Italy, Byzantine possessions were confined to Venice, Naples, Calabria and Sicily.

As a result of his military victories against the Saxons, Bavarians and Avars, Charlemagne had become master of the West. Apart from the Arabs in Spain, there was no one to resist him in the field, and by waging war against the pagan Saxons and Avars, and Muslim Arabs, Charlemagne showed himself to be the protector of Western Christendom.

It is in the sphere of political ideology that the pervading influence of the Byzantine empire over Charlemagne can be most strongly observed. Coveting the title of emperor, which legitimately belonged to the ruler of Byzantium, he could no longer be satisfied with the lesser titles "rex" and "Patrician of the Romans." Charlemagne might scoff at the impotence of Constantinople to interfere seriously in the affairs of Italy, but he recognized the legal title of the Byzantine monarchs to the Roman empire. Political unrest in Constantinople gave Charlemagne the opportunity to advance his own cause.

In 780 the Byzantine Emperor, Leo IV, died, leaving his wife Irene in control of the government on behalf of their little son Constantine VI. For over fifty years Byzantium had been in a state of turmoil over the policy of iconoclasm initiated by Emperor Leo III. Irene was an iconophile determined to restore the sacred image in orthodox Christian worship. She was also an extremely ambitious woman intent on keeping the reins of government in her own hands. Anxious to consolidate her position by establishing friendly relations with Rome and the West, she concluded a pact with Charlemagne's daughter Rotrud. A Byzantine official, the eunuch and notary Elissaeus, was dispatched to educate Rotrud in the Greek language and the intricate ceremonial of the Byzantine court. This marriage arrangement was evidently a political move intended to deflect any Frankish attacks against Byzantine possessions in Italy.

Irene, however, was not satisfied with the regency; she wanted to rule in name as well as in deed. In 787 she convoked the Seventh Ecumenical Council to reestablish the icon in Byzantine worship. Pope Hadrian I recognized the ecumenical character of the council to which he had sent his own legates.

Constantine VI was now seventeen years old. Successful in her ecclesiastical policy, Irene was determined to eliminate all possible rivals for the supreme power. Fearing the combined power of Charlemagne and her own son should the marriage with Rotrud be carried out, Irene broke off the engagement and obliged Constantine VI to marry Maria of Amnia, a girl of modest family and without political advantage.

Charlemagne was furious and became more determined than ever to undermine the spiritual supremacy of Byzantium. To achieve this end he made an overt attack against the religious orthodoxy of the Byzantine emperors. The scholars at his court were commissioned to draw up the *Libri Carolini,* the Caroline Books, in an attempt to show that the Byzantine church had succumbed to heresy—not by rejecting icons, but by accepting them too wholeheartedly. The ground was thus laid for the Council of Frankfurt that took place in 794. Charlemagne's purpose was to condemn the decrees of the Seventh Ecumenical Council of Nicaea in 787. Being very Byzantine indeed, the Frankish king convoked on his own prerogative an orthodox council to annul the decrees of an ecumenical council under the presidency of Irene and Constantine VI. His plan was to demonstrate that the rulers of Byzantium were heretics. The Council of Frankfurt, which was attended by two papal legates, then condemned the decrees of the Seventh Ecumenical Council, which had been ratified by two legates of the same pope. Despite the fact that Pope Hadrian I had given his sanction to the Seventh Ecumenical Council, the *Libri Carolini* argued that the papal legates had fallen into theological error. Indeed, the Latin translation of the Greek texts of the Seventh Ecumenical Council was faulty. Charlemagne's court scholars took advantage of this fact to prove that heresy was involved. The Council of Nicaea had made a subtle distinction, as we have seen, between veneration and worship. Charlemagne's theologians considered this distinction to be too subtle to be practicable and accused the Byzantines of worshipping icons. For them, icons had only a didactic purpose, serving as books for the illiterate and as decorations. They did not accept the interpretation that the honor given to icons is conveyed to the prototype represented. They even insisted that candles and incense should not be offered to them.

Despite these pronouncements against the theology of the icon, the Seventh Ecumenical Council had already resolved the issue in favor of the iconophile view, and the Council of Frankfurt failed to arouse any enthusiasm in support of its attack. It was another theological issue, espoused by Charlemagne's theologians, that was to prove disastrous to the cause of Christian unity: the Council of Frankfurt officially adopted the *filioque* clause into the Nicene-Constantinopolitan Creed. From this moment the filioque controversy was to become a major divisive issue between the Byzantine and the Latin churches.

The Creed, as originally composed by the church fathers who sat in the First and Second Ecumenical Councils, states that the Holy Spirit proceeds from the Father. In the sixth century, however, in Spain, theological controversy between Spanish Catholics and Arian Visigoths was intense; to defend the orthodox position that Christ was consubstantial with the Father against the Arian position that he was a deified creature, not of the same essence as the Father, and, therefore, inferior and subordinate, the Catholics inserted the filioque formula into the Creed so that it now read: "... the Holy Spirit, the Lord and lifegiver, Who proceeds from the Father *and from the Son* [filioque]. ..." When the Arian Visigoths were finally converted to orthodox Christianity under their king Reccared in 589, the filioque clause was retained in the Nicene-Constantinopolitan Creed.

CHARLEMAGNE'S LEGACY

From Spain the filioque passed to the Carolingian court at Aix-la-Chapelle, where it found an eager advocate in Charlemagne. His intention was to use it to discredit the Byzantine emperors. Consequently, the Council of Frankfurt officially adopted the filioque formula, but without papal sanction. Soon thereafter, in 808, the patriarch of Jerusalem complained to Pope Leo III (795–816) that Frankish Benedictine monks on the Mount of Olives were causing scandal because they were reciting the unwarranted filioque addition in the Creed. The pope wrote to Charlemagne, diplomatically suggesting that although there was nothing theologically objectionable to the filioque, it would perhaps be a mistake to depart from the universally accepted version. He himself was careful to omit the word from the Creed, which he had inscribed in silver plaques around the interior of St. Peter's.

The *Libri Carolini* also insisted that the priests and "kings" of the East, tempted by arrogance, pride and vainglory, had sacrificed the salvation of their souls and destroyed the unity of the church. They attacked the Byzantine emperors for making idols of themselves and for claiming "to govern with God" and "to be divine"; in ridicule they spoke of the emperors' "divine ears." The *Libri* also refused to accept their title of *Isapostoloi* (Equal to the Apostles), rebuking them for chasing after transient things. Charlemagne and his supporters forgot that Constantine the Great himself, the founder of the Christian imperial cult and the great model of the secular ruler, was designated as the Thirteenth Apostle. The real aim of the *Libri Carolini*, however, was political: to accuse the Byzantines of theological corruption. The Byzantine court, however, passed over the charges of the barbarian Franks in contemptuous silence. Charlemagne was assuming Byzantine imperial prerogatives; as guardian of the faith he was imitating strong Byzantine emperors, and as such he attempted on his own to decide matters of dogma.

Desiring further to emulate the Byzantine emperors who resided in a capital city, Constantinople, then "New Rome," Charlemagne decided to found a fixed residence of his own at Aix-la-Chapelle. Since in Constantinople the center of imperial administration was the magnificent complex of buildings called the *sacrum palatium* (the sacred palace), Charlemagne undertook the erection of a *sacrum palatium* of his own. Charlemagne's architects were now commissioned to erect a palace-chapel at Aix-la-Chapelle in imitation of the famous Chrysotriklinos, the golden audience chamber used for Byzantine imperial ceremonies. Travelling to Ravenna, the seat of the former Byzantine exarchate, they were able to copy and modify the Byzantine church of San Vitale. Charlemagne's building program seems to indicate that by 798 he was seriously entertaining the thought of assuming the role of emperor. His court poets even referred to Aix-la-Chapelle as "New Rome"!

The tragic turn of events in Constantinople now gave Charlemagne the opportunity he sought. Constantine VI ineptly attempted to assume sole rule of his empire. Irene schemed to discredit her son; she encouraged Constantine to put his wife, Maria of Amnia—the wife Irene compelled her son to marry in the first place—in a convent and to take as wife his mistress and Irene's lady-in-waiting, Theodote. The Byzantine church was scandalized, since he had illegally divorced Maria. In 797, Irene perpetrated one of the most shocking crimes in Byzantine history. In the very room, the Purple Chamber, where Constantine VI was born and had first seen the light of day, Irene deprived him of his sight and officially deposed him from the throne.

Irene had usurped imperial power, thereby creating what was to be interpreted in the West as an irregular and unconstitutional situation: the throne could not be occupied by a woman alone. Irene, moreover, now assumed the masculine title of Faithful Emperor (*pistos basileus*)!

In 798, papal affairs proved to be as irregular as imperial matters in Constantinople. Pope Leo III, accused of being a rake and a tyrant, was partially blinded and imprisoned by his enemies, among whom were members of the family of the former Pope Hadrian I. Both the Roman papacy and the Byzantine imperial dignity appeared to be in jeopardy. Seizing upon this fortuitous coincidence, Charlemagne's court scholars maintained that the salvation of both church and state rested on Charlemagne's shoulders as the "governor of Christendom."

Leo III escaped and fled to Charlemagne, seeking protection and support. After returning to Rome with the papal fugitive, Charlemagne presided over a synod in Rome at which Leo III was reinstated as pope. In gratitude the pope accepted the Carolingian court view that the imperial throne of Constantinople was really vacant since, in defiance of ancient tradition, a woman ruled. Pope Leo III now conceived the idea of nominating Charlemagne as emperor. In other words, Charlemagne was not succeeding to the western Roman Empire—whose last recognized emperor was Julius Nepos (474–475), not Romulus Augustulus (475–476), who was a puppet ruler only—but indeed he was to be viewed as the successor to Constantine VI!

During the mass of Christmas day in 800, as Charlemagne rose from prayer in the Church of St. Peter in Rome, Pope Leo III crowned him emperor. The Roman congregation acclaimed "To Charles the Augustus, crowned of God, the great and pacific emperor, long life and victory."

Charlemagne's problem now was to gain recognition of his imperial title and status from Byzantium. In spite of the sophistic arguments used to justify Charlemagne's coronation and assumption of the imperial title, he himself must have felt the illegality of his position. His court scholars now hit upon an ingenious plan: envoys accompanied by papal representatives were sent to Constantinople with a proposal of marriage to Irene, "thus uniting the East to the West." Irene may have been seriously considering the offer when suddenly a coup d'état took place, deposing her in favor of Nikephoros I (802–811). Byzantium had an emperor, and the course of events was altered radically.

Immediately after his elevation, the Byzantine emperor Nikephoros negotiated a draft of a treaty with Charlemagne that gave Byzantium Venice, maritime Dalmatia, Naples, Calabria and Sicily. The acceptance of this treaty on the part of Charlemagne depended upon Byzantine recognition of his imperial title. Nikephoros, however, refused, and the treaty was scrapped.

The Bulgar problem was extremely acute at this time. The Bulgar khan, Krum, inflicted a disastrous defeat on the Byzantine imperial forces and killed Nikephoros; Krum even made a goblet of the slain emperor's skull. With his hands tied in the Balkans, the new emperor, Michael I Rhangabe (811–813), decided to appease Charlemagne by recognizing his title in return for which the proposed treaty negotiated under Nikephoros was accepted. Charlemagne was now greeted as "Emperor," but not "Emperor of the Romans," a title reserved only for the Byzantine emperor at Constantinople. The latter more and more began to use the Greek title of basileus.

SCHISM

Charlemagne's legacy to the papacy and Latin Christianity was the cause not only of mischief but of subsequent division within the one Christian community of Byzantine East and Latin West. Thanks to the prestige of Charlemagne's name, the filioque was gradually adopted in Germany, in Lorraine, and in some parts of France during the course of the ninth century. In the latter half of that century it became a crucial and, indeed, a divisive issue between Byzantium and the West. Charlemagne won his point, but at the cost of theological unity.

The immediate cause for the eruption of the filioque controversy between the two major sees of Christianity—Rome and Constantinople—was the prize of the Slavic peoples, whose conversion was now to be fiercely contested by both centers. The fact that such a contest was possible shows clearly the serious cleavage between the two. The battle was enjoined in two geographically separated areas —Moravia and Bulgaria. Latin Christianity won out in Moravia, where German missionaries eventually succeeded in ousting the Byzantine mission founded in 863 by Saints Cyril and Methodios. The Bulgar khan, Boris, playing both sides for as much as he could get (he wanted a patriarch subject to his authority), negotiated with the German king, Lewis II; but, defeated in battle by the Byzantines, he was baptized with the Emperor Michael III (842–867) acting as his godfather by proxy. When Photios, the learned Patriarch of Constantinople, refused to comply with Boris's request for an autonomous church, the Bulgar khan turned to Pope Nicholas I in 866. The pope was anxious to take advantage of this new opportunity and immediately dispatched two bishops to Boris's court. In a letter, Pope Nicholas I denigrated the usages of the Byzantine church; and Boris, pleased with the results of his clever tactics, drove all the Greek priests from Bulgaria. Photios, of course, was furious over this unexpected turn of events and sent out invitations for a council to take place in Constantinople. The council met in the fall of 867; Pope Nicholas I and the Latin clergy in Bulgaria, who had been spreading "heretical" doctrines (specifically, the filioque formula), were condemned. The Churches of Rome and Constantinople mutually excommunicated each other.

Patriarch Photios composed treatises condemning the filioque addition as heresy. The Byzantine view was that the unwarranted filioque clause upset the delicate balance of the Holy Trinity. Christ himself, it was argued, expressed the proper relationship of the Three Persons. "But when the Comforter is come, whom I will send unto you from the Father, even the Spirit of Truth, which proceedeth from the Father, he shall testify of me" (John 15:26). Thus the Holy Spirit proceeds eternally from the Father and is sent temporally, that is, in time, into the world by the Son. God the Father *begets* his Son eternally, but the Holy Spirit *proceeds* eternally from the Father. God the Father is neither begotten nor proceeds from any of the other persons. The Greek view of the Holy Trinity was that of an isosceles triangle, with God the Father at the summit. The Western position not only seemed to be un-scriptural, but by creating two principles from which the Holy Spirit was said to proceed—Father and Son—the triangle of the

Trinity was improperly inverted. Not only the orthodoxy of this new doctrine, but the whole structure of church government and the proper source of dogma was at stake! In Byzantine theology the only inspired doctrinal authority was the ecumenical council, where the Holy Spirit preserved the Fathers from error and guided them surely to the truth.

The Fathers had, moreover, expressly forbidden any addition or subtraction from the Creed. The Western Church's insertion of the filioque clause was an overt act of defiance against the authority and inspiration of the church fathers sitting in ecumenical councils. A succeeding ecumenical conclave might amplify the decisions reached by a previous council, but it was unthinkable that it should alter those decisions. Moreover, to tamper unilaterally with the Creed was an act of heresy. No pope alone had the right to pronounce judgment in favor of the filioque without consulting with the four other major patriarchates. The classical Latin response was that the filioque was only an amplification of doctrine, not an alteration or addition.

The filioque controversy was to remain a major obstacle to the theological union of Roman and Greek churches. The schism between Rome and Constantinople, created by the filioque and the Christianization of Bulgaria, was not lasting. When Photios ascended the patriarchal throne a second time in 877, he was recognized by Rome.

It should be observed that it was the fortuitous combination of political turmoil and theological differences that ignited the flames of schism between Latin West and Greek East. Religious disputes alone do not explode into international crises; it is the insertion of a political wedge that finally separates the two halves of an original whole.

Despite differences in religious usages and even doctrine, Greeks and Latins succeeded in living in harmonious coexistence in at least two regions—southern Italy and the Holy Land. At the time of the mutual excommunications of Pope Nicholas I and Photios, the patriarch of Constantinople, a Breton monk named Bernard the Wise travelled to Jerusalem. He worshipped in the Church of the Resurrection at the Easter services conducted by the Greek patriarch Theodosius (863–879), who was responsible to the Muslim officials for the Latin and Greek communities in Jerusalem. Bernard described the unique ritual he witnessed:

I must not, however, omit to state that on Holy Saturday, which is the eve of Easter, the office is begun in the morning in the church, and after it is ended the Kyrie Eleison is chanted until an angel comes and lights the lamps that hang over the aforesaid sepulchre; of which light the patriarch gives their shares to the bishops and to the rest of the people, that each may illuminate his own house.

The Latins in the Holy Land at this time do not appear to have been alienated from the Greek church.

The same holds true for south Italy. With the dissolution of the Carolingian empire into a mass of little principalities, the Byzantine government created two new *themes* as outposts in south Italy: these were Longobardia (Apulia) and Calabria. Here Greeks and Latins coexisted and shared their cultures. The cities south of Naples were in Byzantine territory, and Byzantine troops defended such Latin monasteries as the famous foundation of St. Benedict, Monte Cassino. The Latin clergy sang the praises of the Byzantine emperor, Leo VI the Wise (886–912), in gratitude for this solicitude: "Hail, O great Leo, of loftiest power, ornament of the Romans, and child of God. . . ."

Calabria was entirely Greek in population, and the cities of Longobardia were mainly Greek, whereas the countryside was inhabited by Lombards and Latins. Spiritual jurisdiction over the Christians of these regions was divided; the patriarch of Constantinople named the bishop of the theme of Calabria, while the pope named the bishop for the heel of Italy (where the population was mixed between Greeks and Latins). At the same time, the suzerainty of the Byzantine emperor was acknowledged there.

The tenth century and the first half of the eleventh century was an era of papal corruption. Citing a report brought back to Otto I of Germany concerning Pope John XII (955–964), Liutprand of Cremona writes in his *Chronicle of Otto's Reign:*

Pope John is the enemy of all things. What we say is a tale well known to all. As witness to its truth take the widow of Rainer, his own vassal, a woman with whom John has been so blindly in love that he has made her governor of many cities and given to her the golden crosses and cups that are the sacred possessions of St. Peter himself. Witness also the case of Stephania, his father's mistress, who recently conceived a child by him and died of an effusion of blood. If all else were silent, the palace of the Lateran, that once sheltered saints and is now a harlot's brothel, will never forget his union with his father's wench, the sister of the other concubine Stephania. Witness again the absence of all women here save Romans: they fear to come and pray at the thresholds of the holy apostles, for they have heard how John a little time ago took women pilgrims by force to his bed, wives, widows and virgins alike. . . .

At this time of the "papal pornocracy" and general malaise in Western monastic life, which reflected the need of reform in the Latin church, the holiness of life in the Greek monasteries was greatly admired. The life of St. Neilos of Rossano (d. 1004) is particularly instructive in this regard. A Lombard prince of Capua, guilty of murder, sought absolution from the Byzantine saint's hands. When Neilos visited the monastery of Monte Cassino, the Latin monks came out to greet him with candles and censers; he responded by chanting Greek hymns in honor of St. Benedict. It is evident that at this time, in practice, the Greek and Latin rites were not at all opposed and, in fact, were held in deep mutual respect. It is significant that St. Neilos was invited not only to discuss the differences in customs and usages between the two rites, but to give the Byzantine view of the filioque clause.

A new era of friction between Byzantium and the West was sparked by the coronation as Holy Roman Emperor of Otto I, the Saxon king of Germany, at St. Peter's on February 2, 962, by Pope John XII. Thus Charlemagne's empire was refounded. Otto I now schemed to seize Byzantine Italy by winning over the Lombard princes in the south. In a show of force he attacked the Byzantine city of Bari, but he was unsuccessful. At the same time he dispatched his envoy, Liutprand, Bishop of Cremona, to the imperial court at Constantinople with a proposal of marriage between Otto I's son and heir, Otto II, and the daughter of the deceased Byzantine emperor, Romanos II. The emperor who now sat on the throne of Byzantium was the extremely competent Nikephoros II Phokas (963–969), who was furious over the attack on Bari. He purposely offered terms Otto I could not possibly accept and demanded that Otto renounce the title of "Emperor" for that of rex, restore Ravenna to Byzantium and break with the Lombard princes of south Italy.

Nikephoros also humiliated Liutprand, and the proud bishop retaliated by composing his *De legatione Constantinopolitana* (*the Embassy to Constantinople*), in which he venomously attacked the emperor and everything Byzantine.

The bishop's first audience was not with the emperor but with his brother Leo, and the topic of conversation centered immediately around the issue of the imperial title assumed by Otto I, a title that no Byzantine emperor since Michael I was willing to recognize in any Western ruler. Describing this incident to his master, Liutprand wrote:

> We tired ourselves with a fierce argument over your imperial title. He called you not emperor, which is basileus in his tongue, but insultingly, rex, which is king in ours. I told him that the thing meant was the same though the word was different, and he then said that I had come not to make peace but to stir up strife. Finally, he got up in a rage, and really wishing to insult us received your letter not in his own hand but through an interpreter.

The issue of the assumption of the imperial title by Otto I was a source of constant friction. Nikephoros insisted on referring to Otto as rex. "Do you want a greater scandal," he asked Liutprand, "than that he should call himself emperor and claim for himself provinces belonging to our empire? Both these things are intolerable; and if both are insupportable, that especially is not to be borne, nay, not to be heard of, that he calls himself emperor."

The dispute on political ideology boiled over when "an ill-omened embassy came from the apostolic and universal Pope John" to Constantinople on behalf of Otto I and then officially referred to Nikephoros as "the emperor of the Greeks" and to Otto I as "august emperor of the Romans." The Byzantine officials reacted severely. "The audacity of it," they cried, "to call the universal emperor of the Romans, the one and only Nikephoros, the great, the august 'emperor of the Greeks,' and to style a poor barbaric creature 'emperor of the Romans'!" The papal envoys, whose master was referred to as a stupid and silly blockhead, were forthwith cast into prison for such impudence.

Liutprand gloated in depicting the basileus as "a monstrosity of a man, a dwarf, fat-headed and with tiny mole's eyes; disfigured by a short, broad, thick beard, half going grey; disgraced by a neck scarcely an inch long; piglike by reason of the big close bristles on his head; in color an Ethiopian." Liutprand ridicules the imperial "robe made of fine linen, but old, foul smelling, and discolored by age." Then he made the kind of comment that became the stereotyped view of Westerners concerning Byzantine emperors and Greeks in general: Nikephoros is "bold of tongue, a fox by nature, in perjury and falsehood a Ulysses."

The emperor, however, was very direct in informing Liutprand of the exact cause of his animosity toward him. Otto I had illegally laid claim to Rome and was guilty of slaying by the sword, hanging, blinding and exiling Byzantine citizens in Italy and of burning their cities. Nikephoros considered the bishop of Cremona as nothing more than a spy! Liutprand countered that Otto I had done only what the Byzantine emperors had been unable to do—free Rome from the tyrant's yoke and from the rule of harlots. The bishop also argued that Byzantine lands in Italy, where "race and language" are Latin, actually belong to the kingdom of Italy. Nikephoros goaded Liutprand charging: "You are not Romans, but Lombards." Liutprand was beside himself, and, defying court etiquette, he interrupted his host. His rebuttal is most instructive in showing how the Germanic nations felt about "Romans":

> History tells us that Romulus, from whom the Romans get their name, was a fratricide born in adultery. He made a place of refuge for himself and received into it insolvent debtors, runaway slaves, murderers and men who deserved death for their crimes. This was the sort of crowd he enrolled as citizens and to whom he gave the name Romans. From this nobility are descended those men whom you style "rulers of the world." But we Lombards, Saxons, Franks, Lotharingians, Bavarians, Swabians and Burgundians so despise these fellows that when we are angry with an enemy we can find nothing more insulting to say than "you Roman!" For us in the word Roman is comprehended every form of lowness, timidity, avarice, luxury, falsehood and vice. . . .

Liutprand also stressed two charges, which later were to be repeated time and time again in criticism of the Byzantines: all heresies emanated from Byzantium, and the Germanic peoples are a warrior folk who prefer the sword to diplomacy. In the words of the bishop of Cremona:

All the heresies have emanated from you and among you have flourished; by our western peoples they have been either strangled or killed. . . . As for the Saxon people, since they received the holy baptism and the knowledge of God, they have not been stained by any heresy that rendered a synod necessary for its correction; of heresies we have had none. You declare that our Saxon faith is young, and I agree. Faith in Christ is always young and not old among people whose faith is seconded by works. Here [Byzantium], faith is old, not young; works do not accompany it, and by reason of its age it is held in light esteem like a worn-out garment. I know for certain of one synod held in Saxony where it was enacted and decreed that it was more seemly to fight with the sword than with the pen, and better to face death than to fly before a foe.

Westerners and Greeks were also different in dress, a fact that emphasized political and religious differences. When Liutprand was ordered to remove his hat in the presence of the emperor while riding in the imperial park and to put on instead a bonnet, he protested that in his country "only women wear bonnets while riding; men wear hats." He continued, saying that Byzantine envoys to the West are allowed to wear their "long sleeves, bands, brooches, flowing hair, and tunics down to their heels, both when they ride or walk or sit at table with us; and what to all of us seems quite too shameful, they alone kiss our emperors with covered heads." To emphasize further the differences between Byzantium and the West he cited the dress, food and personality traits of the respective rulers of the two halves of Christendom, who "differ from one another in character as much . . . as rational beings differ from those devoid of reason." Liutprand's views, of course, are heavily weighted in favor of Otto I:

The King of the Greeks has long hair and wears a tunic with long sleeves and a bonnet; he is lying, crafty, merciless, foxy, proud, falsely humble, miserly and greedy; he eats garlic, onions and leeks and he drinks bath water. The King of the Franks, on the other hand, is beautifully shorn, and wears a garment quite different from a woman's dress and a hat; he is truthful, guileless, merciful when right, severe when necessary, always truly humble, never miserly; he does not live on garlic, onions and leeks nor does he spare animals' lives so as to heap up money by selling instead of eating them. . . .

Liutprand came to the defense of Pope John XII for calling Nikephoros "emperor of the Greeks" with this specious reasoning:

> But the pope, . . . in his noble simplicity thought that in writing thus he was honoring the emperor, not insulting him. We know, of course, that Constantine the Roman Emperor came here with the Roman knighthood and called the city he founded by his own name. But as you have changed your language, customs and dress, the most holy pope thought that the name of Romans, like their dress, would displease you.

It is important that we understand the significance of dress. The Byzantine officials reminded Liutprand that in Otto's native land of Saxony the people were dressed in skins. In the highly civilized society of Byzantium, purple cloth was the visible symbol of imperial authority. The highly developed silk industry producing garments of iridescent, peach-colored purple, and gold embroidery was a much-prized Byzantine monopoly until the twelfth century. The attire of the emperor and the nobility and the vestments of the bishops were all made of such precious stuffs. Privately owned factories were strictly regulated and manufactured silk of second quality, while the imperial factories alone were allowed to produce first quality silk. The process of silk manufacture in Byzantium was a highly guarded state secret, and only materials of inferior quality were sold to foreign merchants for export. Thus, foreign officials coming to Constantinople often tried to smuggle the royal purple out of the country. One of these was Liutprand, who was caught red-handed. Five very valuable pieces of purple cloth and all purple vestments found in Liutprand's possession were confiscated. The irate bishop complained that the Byzantines considered:

> . . . all the Italians, Saxons, Franks, Bavarians, Swabians—all the nations—as unworthy to appear abroad in such ornate vestments. How improper and insulting is it that these soft, effeminate creatures, with their long sleeves and hoods and bonnets, idle liars of neither gender, should go about in purple, while lords like yourselves [Otto I], men of courage, skilled in war, full of faith and love, submissive to God, full of virtues, may not!

When Liutprand countered that Nikephoros had given his word that he might purchase as many vestments of any material as he liked, he was censured in no uncertain terms:

> But these stuffs are prohibited ... and when the emperor spoke as you say he did he could not imagine that you would ever dream of such things as these. As we surpass all other nations in wealth and wisdom, so it is right that we should surpass them in dress. Those who are unique in the grace of their virtue should also be unique in the beauty of their raiment.

Finally, Liutprand informs us that Nikephoros had ordered the patriarch of Constantinople, Polyefktos (956–970), "to raise the church of Otranto to the rank of an archbishopric, and not to allow the divine mysteries throughout Apulia and Calabria to be celebrated in Latin, but to have them performed in Greek."

On his return journey to Italy via Greece, the bishop of Cremona complained of the meanness of Greek bishops who, he said, are "rich in gold coins" but "poor in servants and utensils." He ridiculed their simple life and frugal table. Greek bishops "sit by themselves at a bare little table, with a ship's biscuit in front of them, and instead of drinking their bath water they sip it from a tiny glass." The humble ecclesiastics did their own buying and selling and closed and opened doors themselves!

Thus, Byzantine religion, diplomacy, food and drink, manners, ceremonial, etiquette and official splendor, as a matter of policy and personal simplicity, went against the grain of the mores and customs evolved in the Germanized West.

EVENTS LEADING TO THE SCHISM OF 1054

The successor of Nikephoros, John I Tzimiskes (969–976), reversed Byzantine imperial policy, and in response to the request of a new German embassy, the princess Theophano was married to Otto II in 972. In return, Otto I relinquished his claim to south Italy, which was now united into one Byzantine province as the catepanate of Italy.

During the first years of the reign of Tzimiskes's successor, Basil II (976–1025), south Italy was frequently invaded by the Muslims of Sicily. The Byzantine *catepan* (military governor) was unable to protect the inhabitants. As a result they appealed to Otto II (973–983), but, suffering a humiliating defeat at the hands of a Muslim raiding party in Calabria, he was forced to beg to be taken aboard a Byzantine ship for escape to safety. The young Holy Roman Emperor died at the age of twenty-eight in Rome; in 991 Theophano died without having seen her son, Otto III, crowned Holy Roman Emperor. Not only had his mother brought Byzantine culture to the German court, Otto III had been raised as an admirer of Byzantine civilization. Consequently, Byzantine prestige and influence now reached its greatest height in Italy.

Otto III believed unrealistically that he was destined to reconstitute the universal Roman empire. "Ours, ours is the Roman Empire," he was told by Gerbert Aurilliac. "Born of Greek blood thou surpassest the Greeks . . .; thou rulest over the Romans by divine right." Did Otto's Byzantine mother instill in him such grandiose but futile dreams? Poor Otto III could not even rule Rome, from which he was excluded by the Italian aristocracy! In 1002, he too died a young man without ever surrendering his Byzantine titles.

In 1009 there was inaugurated a chain of political events in south Italy that culminated in the Schism of 1054 and in the loss of these territories to the Byzantine empire. In 1016 a certain Lombard by the name of Melo, who several years before had taken Bari and then was driven out by Byzantine troops, went on a pilgrimage to the famous shrine of St. Michael on Monte Gargano. As fate had it, he met there a group of Normans brought south from Normandy by the economics of feudalism, the practice of primogeniture. Melo invited the Normans to serve him as mercenaries in his war against Byzantium. The Normans, who were looking for such an opportunity, received in Rome the tacit approval of Pope Benedict VIII (1012–1024) and of Emperor Henry II, the successor of Otto III, both of whom were anti-Byzantine. Byzantine influence, so strong in the German courts of Otto II and Otto III, had now crumbled.

Melo and his Norman mercenaries were defeated by the Byzantine forces under Basil Boiannes, the new catepan of Italy, who reestablished Byzantine control over the Lombards and extended Byzantine authority to the border of the papal states. But the Normans kept pouring into south Italy, and by 1041 Byzantine control over Apulia was reduced to the coastal towns. Byzantine political unrest and suspicions at this most critical juncture deprived south Italy of its competent commander, George Maniakes. The Normans seized the opportunity handed them when their chief William Iron-Arm, son of Tancred de Hauteville, was made Count of Apulia (1043–1045) by Guaimar V, the Lombard prince of Salerno. The Normans occupied and controlled the interior of the Italian heel, while the Byzantines held on to Calabria and the coast. The half-brother and successor of William Iron-Arm, Robert Guiscard "the Sly," continued the struggle against the Byzantines from 1045; by 1059 he had conquered all of south Italy and had assumed the title Duke of Apulia and Calabria (1057–1085).

Pope Clement II (1046–1047) recognized the authority of the Normans in south Italy as local princes, which made the Byzantine government very unhappy. However, the reform pope, Leo IX (1049–1054), opposed the Normans because they had seized much church property and were guilty of mercilessly pillaging the inhabitants.

In 1051 the Byzantine emperor, Constantine IX (1042–1055), sent Argyros, the son of the Lombard Melo, to Italy with the title "Duke of Italy and Sicily" and with huge sums of money to buy off the Normans. He was to lure them to Anatolia to fight the Turks who had made their first appearance on the eastern frontiers of the empire. The Normans, who had already won rich lands for themselves in south Italy, had no desire to fight for the Byzantine government. Argyros, Pope Leo IX and Henry III (1046–1056) now allied themselves against the Normans, who were called "the Christian Saracens" because of the misery they inflicted. In three battles Argyros was defeated by the Normans, and the pope, leading his army behind the banner of St. Peter, was beaten decisively at Civitate in June of 1053, taken prisoner and kept under house arrest at Benevento.

It must be understood that the causes of the Schism of 1054 were intimately bound up with the political events we have been describing in south Italy. The emergence of the reform papacy at exactly this time provided the necessary catalyst to produce ecclesiastical schism.

The great reform movement, which reached its climax in the eleventh century, originated in two key centers, Lorraine and the Abbey of Cluny. It was directed against two specific evils, Nicolaitism and simony. Nicolaitism designated the marriage of clergymen, considered to be fornication, as well as the practice of concubinage followed by countless churchmen in the West.

Simony derives from Simon Magus, a figure in Acts who sought to purchase the miraculous curative powers of St. Peter. A simoniac is either one who paid money to receive the appointment to an important bishopric or monastery—as was the common practice of the time—or the lord, duke, count or king who bestowed such an office on a cleric in return for payment.

One of the first acts of Leo IX was to condemn simony and married clergy. Claiming the lands of the forged *Donation of Constantine,* he led the papal armies against the Normans in Byzantine south Italy where, as we have seen, he was defeated and taken prisoner.

The patriarch of Constantinople at this critical moment was the extremely ambitious and able politician Michael Keroularios (1043–1058). When the patriarch was informed that Greek customs and usages in Italy were being repressed by the Normans with papal blessing and by reforming synods throughout Italy, he countered by ordering the Latin churches in Constantinople to adopt Greek usages. When they refused, he had them closed down toward the end of 1052. Since the Greek communities of Apulia and Calabria were at stake, Keroularios assumed an even more militant stand. He instructed Leo, the Archbishop of Ochrid, to send a letter to John, the Latin Bishop of Trani, condemning Latin practices. The old charges were repeated: fasting on the Sabbath, the enforced celibacy of the clergy, eating strangled meat, and not singing "alleluia" following Septuagesima, the third Sunday before Lent. Although the filioque was not mentioned, a new charge appeared: the Latin use of *azyma* (the Greek term for unleavened bread) in Holy Communion. This latter practice became important to the patriarch of Constantinople because he was attempting at this time to integrate the monophysite Armenian Church into the orthodox Church of the Byzantine Empire. The Armenians followed two practices that were surprisingly similar to Latin usages: fasting on Saturdays and the azyma for communion. The Byzantine theologians considered these practices to be purely Judaistic, and it was primarily because of the Armenian question that Keroularios insisted that the Latin churches in Constantinople conform to Greek usages.

The azyma, as it turned out, became the popular liturgical issue between Byzantium and the Latin West. This can be easily understood when one realizes that to become deeply involved in the subtleties of the filioque it is necessary to have theological and philosophical training, whereas the average man could and indeed did get excited over a tangible and visible element such as the azyma used by Latin Christians. Keroularios not only refused to give Argyros Holy Communion when he demanded an unleavened wafer, he also considered him a heretic for so doing! For Western Christians the issue was crucial: "If the oblation of unleavened bread is not the true body of Christ, then the Latin Church is deprived of eternal life." No one, of course, is willing to say that he and his ancestors are damned. In the Greek Church the leaven in the communion bread, called *enzyma,* was important as the symbol of the Holy Spirit, the Giver of Life.

The incredible animosity generated between Greeks and Latins over the azyma can be seen in the martyrdom of thirteen Greek monks on the island of Cyprus in 1231. Cyprus at this time was under the rule of the Lusignan dynasty, and the Latin Church was in ecclesiastical control of the Greek island. Pope Gregory IX (1227–1241) directed Eustorge, the Latin Archbishop of Nicosia, to excommunicate "heretic" Greek monks who refused to use unleavened bread in the performance of the Eucharist. The Greek monks refused, arguing that they used enzyma as it was handed down to them from the beginning by those who were eyewitnesses—the Apostles and, after them, the ecumenical councils. They claimed that those who receive azyma for Communion were heretics, fallen from the truth. The Greek monks were then dragged on the ground, beaten and called dogs, and their beards were pulled by their jailers. Three years later they were condemned to death for refusing to repent; their feet were tied to the tails of horses and mules, and after being dragged through the marketplace and the riverbed, where their flesh was torn on the stones, they were burnt at the stake.

In the *Life of St. Luke* (died 1114), Bishop of Asyla (Isola Capo Rizzuto), we read that the saint condemned the Latins for "acting pharisaically" and for "judaistically" celebrating the azyma. Infuriated, the Latins attempted to burn him to death in a hut, but St. Luke celebrated the liturgy with enzyma while the fire was raging. The hut was totally destroyed, but the saint emerged unscathed!

Unfortunately, Leo of Ochrid's aggressive document fell into the hands of the chief papal secretary, the vain and truculent Humbert, Cardinal of Silva Candida. Both Pope Leo IX and Humbert knew little Greek, but they were outraged at the contents. The pope instructed Humbert to draft a reply, in which Keroularios is simply referred to as "bishop" and is taken to task for using the title of "ecumenical"; the patriarchate of Constantinople indeed should revere Rome as her mother. The pope wisely ignored the issues of azyma and clerical marriage but protested the closing of the Latin churches in Constantinople. Keroularios, who probably realized that the empire needed the alliance of the pope in its struggle against the Normans, sent back a conciliatory reply promising to inscribe the pope's name in the diptychs throughout the empire, provided his own name was inscribed at Rome. He insisted, however, on using the title Ecumenical Patriarch for himself and offended the pope by referring to him as Brother, instead of Father as past patriarchs had done in recognition of the pope's seniority.

At this critical moment the pope fell gravely ill; consequently, Cardinal Humbert was given free rein to handle the matter as he saw fit. Humbert decided to lead an embassy to Constantinople and chose Frederick of Lorraine, chancellor of the Roman see, and Peter, Archbishop of Amalfi (which contained a large Greek population) to accompany him. Humbert had prepared two letters, one for the patriarch and one for the emperor. Disregarding patriarchal protocol, the legates merely thrust the papal letter at the patriarch and stomped out! The contents of the papal reply were vitriolic. The pope insisted on being recognized as the supreme head of the church; he castigated Keroularios for using the title "Ecumenical" Patriarch and berated the Greek attack on the unleavened sacramental wafer. Any church separated from Rome, he warned, is nought but a synagogue of Satan! The canonicity of the patriarch's election was placed under suspicion; and, finally, the pope hoped that the papal legates would find Keroularios duly repentant!

On April 15, 1054, Pope Leo IX died, thereby invalidating the legal standing of the papal legates. His successor, Victor II, who was appointed by Henry III, did not arrive in Rome until the following April. In the meantime Cardinal Humbert behaved abominably. The Byzantine monk and theologian Niketas Stethatos reiterated the charges against the Latin practices of using unleavened bread, fasting on Saturdays and banning the married clergy, and then—like the Quinisextum Council—condemned the Latin practice of celebrating an ordinary rather than a liturgy of the Pre-Sanctified Gifts during the weekdays of Great Lent. Humbert, livid with rage, attacked the Greek usage of adding warm water to the Communion wine. For the Byzantine Church this both commemorated the water that issued from the wound made in the Lord's side and symbolized the warmth and ardor of faith.

The Byzantine emperor, Constantine IX (1042–1055), afraid that the needed alliance with the papacy against the Normans was being jeopardized by such unfruitful theological polemic, compelled Stethatos to retract his attack and apologize publicly. The intransigent cardinal, elated by this victory, then raised the question of filioque. The patriarch remained silent throughout these developments and preferred simply to ignore the papal legates. Frustrated by Keroularios's determined refusal to submit, Humbert committed one of the great follies in history. On Saturday, July 16, 1054, just as the divine liturgy was about to begin, Cardinal Humbert and his colleagues stalked into the Church of Hagia Sophia and dramatically laid on the altar a bull of excommunication against Michael Keroularios and all his followers. The papal legates then marched out of the church, ceremoniously shaking the dust from their feet!

When the bull of excommunication was translated, the charges levelled against the Greek Church were found to be blatantly erroneous. Keroularios was refused his title of patriarch, and all his adherents were condemned as simoniacs. (Simony was actually the dominant vice, as we have seen, of the Latin Church.) Keroularios and his supporters were also taken to task for encouraging castration. (In fact, the island of Favignana off Sicily and Verdun in the West boasted of eunuch "factories.") The Greek ecclesiastics were also falsely accused of insisting on the rebaptism of Latins and of allowing priests to marry. This latter charge was technically incorrect, since a married man may be ordained a deacon and then a priest, but no ordained cleric may marry in the Greek church. Greek clerics were accused of refusing Holy Communion to men who shaved their beards. Actually, while the Byzantines disapproved of shaven clerics, they did not deny the sacrament to clean-shaven men. Perhaps most amazing of all, the Byzantines were accused of omitting a clause in the Nicene-Constantinopolitan Creed, when, in fact, the Latins were guilty of adding the filioque to the Creed. The double curse of "Anathema Maranatha" (I Corinthians 16:22) was hurled at Patriarch Keroularios, and he and his followers were vilified as prozymite heretics because they used enzyma instead of azyma.

The populace of Constantinople rioted when they heard the news, and the emperor, fearing for his throne, ordered the bull of excommunication consigned to the flames. On Sunday, July 24, 1054 the patriarchal synod anathematized the Latin envoys and their sympathizers. The schism, separating the one Christian church into Roman Catholic and Greek Orthodox, had been consummated. The robe of Christ had been rent in two. The damage was never undone; the whole of the Eastern Orthodox world—Alexandria, Antioch, Jerusalem, Russia and southeast Europe—joined Constantinople against Rome. For the future of Christianity these developments have taken on immense significance. Yet these events were hardly noticed in the contemporary records of Byzantium. After all, schisms had taken place before and had always been healed.

Actually, the differences between the two churches need not have erupted into permanent schism. The legates, who had no legal standing, since they could not represent a dead pope, condemned only Keroularios and his adherents, while the patriarchal synod condemned only the papal legates. The Byzantine church did not in any way involve the papacy or the western church in general. A subsequent pope could have repudiated the legates' actions without any loss of prestige, but Humbert's influence among the reformers was too strong at the time.

One of the most moving moments of the Second Vatican Council, which terminated its sessions in December of 1965, was the mutual revocation of the excommunications of 1054 by Pope Paul VI and Patriarch Athenagoras I of Constantinople. Although communion between the Roman and Greek churches has not been restored, at least the unfortunate acts of history, wrought by fallible men, have been renounced by the two churches.

The Schism of 1054, it should be emphasized, involved only a handful of high churchmen and was little noticed by the masses. It was only with the events inaugurated by the First Crusade and culminating in the Fourth Crusade that sufficient hostility was generated among the inhabitants of the Byzantine empire to make reconciliation impossible.

On the basis of the lives of the Greek saints of the eleventh and early twelfth centuries, we constantly come across indications that, despite the schism, Greeks from Byzantium travelled to Rome to worship at the tombs of Saints Peter and Paul. Saint Christodoulos (d. 1101), founder of the Monastery of St. John the Evangelist on Patmos, visited Rome with the double purpose of escaping his parents, who wanted him to marry, and of venerating the tombs of the Holy Apostles. Saint Meletios (ca. 1035–1105) not only sailed from Jerusalem on a pilgrimage to Rome, he also sailed to Spain where he venerated the tomb of St. James the Apostle at Compostella. Having befriended a group of some sixty or more Westerners detained by the governor of Attica in Greece while on their way to the Holy Land, his fame was advertised throughout the West on their return home. Two relatives of St. Cyril of Thrace (d. 1110) voyaged to Rome in the hope of being healed of their sicknesses by venerating the tombs of Saints Peter and Paul. Again, in the very heart of orthodox monasticism, Mount Athos, Leo, the brother of Pandulfus II, Duke of Benevento (981–1014), had founded a monastery for Amalfitan monks, who followed the rule of St. Benedict.

Throughout the period leading to the Schism of 1054 the policy of the Byzantine government had been, as we have seen, to seek an alliance with the papacy against the aggressive newcomers to south Italy, the hated Normans. In 1058 Robert Guiscard penetrated Byzantine Calabria, and in the following year the new pope, Nicholas II (1059–1061), a Cluniac reformer, reversed papal policy. Conveniently overlooking the humiliating defeat of Pope Leo IX at the hands of the Normans at Civitate, he used Norman troops to rout a rival pope, Benedict X. Then at the Council of Melfi in 1059 in south Italy, Pope Nicholas, as suzerain, invested one Norman, Richard I, as Prince of Capua and another, Robert Guiscard, as Duke of Apulia and Calabria. The Normans, in effect, received papal blessing and confirmation for seizing Byzantine possessions! The loss of Bari in 1071 to the Normans is regarded as the final collapse of Byzantine power in south Italy. It was, nonetheless, Byzantine culture and ideals that exercised the greatest effect on the mind of Guiscard, who became obsessed with the desire to be recognized by Constantinople as the legitimate governor of south Italy. By 1072 Roger I, brother of Robert Guiscard, was master of Sicily; his son Roger II became the first Norman king of Sicily (1130–1154). The Norman kings of Sicily adopted Byzantine ceremonial and dress and imitated the Byzantine basileus. The magnificent churches of Mantorana and the Capella Palatina were Byzantine in conception and were probably decorated by Greek artists. History has borne out, however, that a nation's imitators are often its greatest enemies.

In the same year Byzantine Bari fell to the Normans (1071) the Byzantine forces, under the Emperor Romanos IV Diogenes (1068–1071), suffered a disastrous defeat in one of the most decisive battles in history near the Armenian town Manzikert, north of Lake Van on the upper Euphrates. The frontier defenses had been sadly neglected by the imperial government and the reduced Byzantine army, no longer manned by native provincial troops, was dependent upon undisciplined and poorly armed Slav, Turk and Frank mercenaries. In fact, a Norman, Roussel de Bailleul, was the commander of an army division. Not only was the brave emperor taken prisoner by the Seljuk sultan, Alp Arslan, the empire had lost its ability to defend the frontiers. Anatolia, the heartland of the Byzantine empire since the conquest of Islam in the seventh century, was now overrun and occupied by Turks. Byzantium was threatened with collapse. A partial recovery began only in the region of the great Alexios I Komnenos (1081–1118).

Meanwhile, Byzantine relations with the West continued to deteriorate. In 1073 the ambitious reformer and canonist, Gregory VII Hildebrand, ascended the papal throne, and in his *Dictatus Papae* advocated the most extreme interpretation of papal supremacy over both ecclesiastical and secular princes. This document declared that the pope is the divinely appointed sovereign, whom all must obey and to whom all earthly rulers are responsible, not only for their spiritual welfare but for their temporal good government. The following claims for the papacy were set forth: The Roman Pontiff alone can be called Universal (Dictate II). The pope's name, *papa,* is the only one of its kind in the world (Dictate XI). Actually, the patriarch of Alexandria in the fourth century was the first to use the title. In the Greek East, it later degenerated in meaning and became the title for any priest (papas). The pope alone may wear the imperial insignia—mitre, gloves and red shoes (Dictate VIII), and he is the only one who may have his toe and feet kissed by a prince (Dictate IX). Defining the primatial authority of the see of Rome in respect to secular powers, Dictate XII declares that the pope has the right to depose an emperor and Dictate XXVII makes the claim that he may relieve subjects from their oath of allegiance to wicked rulers.

On the basis of his *Dictatus Papae,* Hildebrand proceeded to confer the royal crown on both Demetrios Zvonimir of Croatia in 1075 and Michael of Zeta in Serbia as papal vassals! Byzantium now lost all of the western Balkans. Michael VII Doukas (1071–1078), who succeeded the unfortunate Romanos IV Diogenes as emperor, initiated a correspondence with Hildebrand, and for the first time a Byzantine emperor threw out what henceforth became standard bait—in exchange for military assistance against the Turks, Michael VII hinted at the possibility of the reunion of the two churches. This tempting offer was to establish for almost 400 years the diplomatic pattern between Byzantium and the Latin West. In 1074 Pope Gregory VII hatched an extraordinary scheme. He would lead an army of Western crusaders to liberate the Christians of the East; in gratitude they would humbly acknowledge papal supremacy. The idea was as yet premature, but the seed had been sown, and soon it would bear fruit. Michael VII also arranged a marriage into the imperial family for Helen, daughter of the Norman Robert Guiscard, Duke of Apulia and Calabria; but when the emperor was deposed, his successor, Nikephoros III Botaneiates (1078–1081), put the prospective bride into a convent. Guiscard was furious at this turn of events, since it deprived him of the influence he expected to exercise in the Byzantine court. Pope Gregory VII himself depended on the support of Norman troops in his life-and-death struggle with Henry IV, and in response to pressure from Robert Guiscard he excommunicated the usurper Botaneiates. It seems that as early as 1078 Guiscard, encouraged by the papacy, had designs to take Constantinople, and when Alexios I Komnenos replaced Botaneiates on the imperial throne in 1081, Hildebrand excommunicated him as well. The question is inescapable: If the Schism of 1054 had been viewed at the time as permanent, why the need repeatedly to excommunicate succeeding Byzantine emperors?

COMMERCE

No less ominous for the coming collapse of the Byzantine Empire than the political and religious events of the eleventh century were the shortsighted economic policies of the imperial administration. The emerging maritime cities of Italy (such as Bari, Amalfi, Pisa and especially Venice and Genoa) were to form the third side of the arrowhead of the Norman and papal alliance aimed at the jugular vein of Byzantine life.

Liutprand of Cremona informs us that from the middle of the tenth century Venetian and Amalfitan merchants were not only engaged in items of lawful trade with Byzantium, but were guilty of smuggling contraband—the precious purple fabrics of Byzantine manufacture—into the West. Unfortunately, the Byzantines failed to export the products of Byzantine industry to foreign markets themselves, preferring instead to allow foreign merchants to come to their markets with their imports and to export Byzantine goods. The whole world marketed at Constantinople, and the Byzantines were proud of draining off the gold of Christendom in this manner. But Byzantium was to pay dearly for this grave economic fallacy that encouraged foreign merchants to penetrate the commercial markets of the empire. More ominous still, Italian ships were allowed to replace the imperial navy, a fatal and tragic mistake. Survival depended as much on control of the seaways as on frontier defenses. The enemy comes by sea as well as by land.

Venice was a Byzantine city. It was built on islands in the lagoons and marshes at the head of the Adriatic Sea by settlers from the mainland who sought security from the devastating invasions of Huns, Ostrogoths and Lombards in the fifth and sixth centuries. In the eighth century the doge of Venice was an elective official chosen by an aristocracy of merchants; nonetheless, he was a Byzantine official, and he borrowed the dress and ceremonial of Byzantium for his court. As Venice was a city of the empire, all Byzantine ports were open to Venetian merchants. They imported salt, fish, wheat, wine and lumber in return for finely fabricated Byzantine products and spices from the Far East, which they exported to the West. Venice became a prosperous commercial power, and its success and example was one of the major factors leading to the economic and political revival of the West. Since Venice was too distant an outpost to be under the direct control of Constantinople, it moved in the direction of virtual equality and almost total independence and autonomy.

The Byzantine government, often in need of Venetian help and shipping, unwisely allowed the merchants of Venice many exemptions and privileges, which made it difficult for Byzantine merchants to compete. In 992 Byzantine Emperor Basil II issued an imperial *chrysobul,* allowing the Venetian merchants considerable reductions in import and export duty payable at Abydos, the port of entry. Moreover, the empire was to rely on Venice for part of the fundamental job of ferrying troops around the Mediterranean. Thus, the decline of the imperial fleet was foreshadowed; the empire was to become dependent on a commercial power. Basil II also authorized the Venetians to defend the Dalmatian coast against Muslim pirates. Having succeeded in clearing the Adriatic of pirate nests, Doge Pietro II Orseolo (991–1008) in 1001 assumed the title "Doge of Venice and of Dalmatia." Venice had become a great naval power. A significant Venetian ceremony was conceived to commemorate the expedition of 1001: the doge threw his ring into the sea, thereby symbolizing the union of Venice with that element which made it great. The emperor rewarded the doge by giving the hand of his niece to Orseolo's son in marriage.

In 1082 Emperor Alexios I Komnenos concluded a disastrous treaty with the Venetian republic that exempted Venetian ships from taxes and customs duties. The ports of the empire were opened to them; Venetian merchants were found in the Peloponnesus, the Archipelago, Thrace, Crete, Rhodes and Anatolia; their ships sailed into the Black Sea to the Crimea and to the end of the Sea of Azov, exploiting the trade routes from central Asia. Commercial traffic between East and West was in the hands of the Venetians. Their Italian rivals, who were less privileged, had difficulty competing, and the decay of the Greek merchant marine enabled the Venetians to keep the monopoly they had won. Byzantine merchants were victims of the imperial economic system of restrictions, while the emerging capitalism of the West—based on loans and partnerships—was flexible and adaptable enough to encourage Western expansion. Besides reaping the wealth of Byzantium, the Venetians were granted their own quarter in Constantinople; they were provided with quays for docking and unloading, a bazaar of their own, Latin churches to worship in and a Venetian magistrate to administer their own affairs. Watching the Venetians grow rich and arrogant at their expense, the Byzantine merchants grew more hostile each day. By 1170 some sixty thousand Westerners were in Constantinople, ten thousand of whom were Venetians.

THE CRUSADES AND THE FALL OF CONSTANTINOPLE IN 1204

On Easter day, April 4, 1081, Alexios I Komnenos was crowned emperor of a tottering empire. Following the disastrous defeat of

Manzikert, Anatolia was overrun by Seljuk Turks; only the Byzantine cities in the coastal areas remained free. In the Balkans the Slavs of Serbia and Dalmatia were in revolt; Turkish Patzinaks continually crossed the Danube to raid imperial lands. Robert Guiscard, that inveterate enemy of Byzantium, crossed over the Adriatic, took Avlona and then besieged Dyrrachium.

The energetic and competent Alexios succeeded in routing the Normans from Dyrrachium in 1085 by defeating Bohemond, Robert's son. Bohemond never forgot this humiliation and hated the Byzantine emperor with a fury. In this same year, Pope Gregory VII, who had excommunicated Alexios I, died in exile after Rome had been plundered and devastated by the Norman troops who supported him.

The loss of the heartland of Anatolia, from whence the majority of Byzantine troops were recruited, was critical to the survival of the empire. Alexios I had to rely more and more upon foreign mercenaries. Apparently, he sent an embassy to the Council of Piacenza, which sat in 1095, to appeal to Pope Urban II (1088–1099) for Western knights to fight in his armies against the enemies of the empire. The Turkish advance across Anatolia, moreover, had blocked the roads leading to the Holy Land, thereby causing Western pilgrims untold hardships. Pope Urban was impressed, and the opportunity to launch a great Western offensive against the infidel appealed to his chivalrous nature. Moreover, he believed that this great cooperative endeavor might lead to the healing of the schism between East and West. On November 27, 1095, at Clermont in south central France, in a rousing and impassioned sermon delivered in French, the pope succeeded in convincing the great ecclesiastics and nobles of Europe. The response was electrifying: cries of *Deus le volt,* "God wills it," filled the air. The First Crusade was launched.

Holy War

In no other area, with the exception of religion, can the differences in attitudes and culture between the Byzantine East and the Germanized West be better seen than in the concept of warfare. The barbarization of the West had ushered in a feudal military society which sought to justify its habitual pasttime; the Germanic code of chivalry gave preeminence to the military hero. In this regard, the papacy itself was barbarized; there was nothing more disconcerting to the Christians of the Byzantine empire than the theory of papal warfare and the idea of "holy war." The Byzantines were shocked to see bishops, clad in armor, fighting and leading armies to battle; in disgust they called them "war mad" (*areiomaneis*).

The holy war, that is, war in the interests of the Roman church, was encouraged by the papacy. In his *The City of God,* St. Augustine admitted that war might be waged by the command of God, and in the sixth century Pope Gregory I the Great was paymaster to the troops defending Rome against the Lombards. In the mid-ninth century Pope Leo IV (847–855) declared that anyone dying in battle for the defense of the church would receive a heavenly reward. Pope John VIII (872–882) is given credit for taking the step of ranking the victims of a holy war as martyrs whose sins were remitted. Liutprand informs us that Pope John XII advanced against the army of the Holy Roman Emperor Otto I "equipped with sword, shield, helmet and cuirass." We have already seen that Pope Leo IX led an army against the Normans. Pope Alexander II (1061–1073) sent the banner of St. Peter to the Norman, William the Conqueror, to sanction his conquests against fellow Christians. Pope Gregory VII ascribed holiness to warfare by virtue of the fact that the pope participates in or blesses a war. Assuming imperial prerogatives, the "Universal Pope" wore the red buskins reserved in the past for Byzantine emperors, and—having usurped the responsibility of the emperor as vicegerent of Christ to defend the Christian oikoumene against conspirators, barbarians, heretics and blasphemers—he declared war against the church's enemies. In his conflict with Henry IV, Hildebrand declared that all those who fell in the field of battle fighting the enemy of the church were martyrs.

The papacy gave the knights of the West a status parallel to that of the monks, the *milites Christi* (soldiers of Christ), so-called because they were engaged in spiritual warfare against the demons. The priest replaced the father or lord in the elevation of the son and vassal to knighthood. After an all-night vigil of prayer in the chapel there followed the Benediction of the Sword, to be used in defense of churches, widows and orphans; the sword became a hallowed instrument, and forgiveness was granted for malicide, the justifiable death inflicted upon the wicked, as opposed to homicide. The western knight must be ready to fight and kill not only pagans and infidels but schismatics and heretics as well.

The Byzantines, in contrast, did not consider death in battle glorious; nor did they believe that to be cut down in the field by an infidel was martyrdom. They maintained the original meaning of the word: the martyr died without resistance, armed only with his faith. The canons of the Greek church stated that anyone guilty of killing in war must refrain for three years from taking Holy Communion as a necessary sign of true repentance; moreover, the soldier who had taken the life of another man was barred from holy orders. Describing the fierce bellicosity of a Latin priest bent on destroying as many Byzantine troops as possible by the might of his own hands, Anna Komnena writes:

> For the rules concerning priests are not the same among the Latins as they are with us; for we are given the command by the canonical laws and the teaching of the Gospel, "Touch not, taste not, handle not! For thou art consecrated." Whereas the Latin barbarian will simultaneously handle divine things, and wear his shield on his left arm, and hold his spear in his right hand, and at one and the same time he communicates the body and blood of God, and looks murderously and becomes 'a man of blood,' as it says in the psalm of David. For this barbarian race is no less devoted to sacred things than it is to war.

The leaders of the crusades could never understand the Byzantine preference for diplomacy and the payment of money to warfare and bloodshed. Western knights, who knew next to nothing of military science, accused the Byzantines of cowardice for retreating from the field when losing in order to fight another day under better circumstances. It will be instructive to quote from the sources. As early as 900 the *Taktika,* the military manual of Byzantine emperor Leo VI the Wise (886–912), stressed the difference between disciplined, well-organized Byzantine armies (whose generals were masters of military strategy and tactics and who thereby added theory to empiric knowledge) and the Frankish knights (who fought for individual glory).

> The Frank believes that a retreat under any circumstances must be dishonorable; hence, he will fight whenever you choose to offer him battle. This you must not do until you have secured all possible advantages for yourself, as his cavalry, with their long lances and large shields, charge with a tremendous impetus. You should deal with him by protracting the campaign, and if

possible lead him into the hills, where his cavalry are less efficient than in the plain. After a few weeks without a great battle his troops, who are very susceptible to fatigue and weariness, will grow tired of the war, and ride home in great numbers. . . . You will find him utterly careless as to outposts and reconnaissances so that you can easily cut off outlying parties of his men, and attack his camp at advantage. As his forces have no bonds of discipline, but only those of kindred or oath, they fall into confusion after delivering their charge; you can therefore simulate flight, and then turn them, when you will find them in utter disarray. On the whole, however, it is easier and less costly to wear out a Frankish army by skirmishes and protracted operations rather than to attempt to destroy it at a single blow.

The *Alexiad,* written by Anna Komnena, daughter of Alexios I, gives us a revealing picture of Byzantine military tactics and the art of diplomacy, as opposed to the Crusaders' concept of warfare:

He [Alexios] knew Bohemond to be a man of consummate guile and energy and, although he was quite willing to accept open battle with him . . . yet he never ceased working against him by every other possible means and device. . . . For I [Anna] hold that a general ought not always to try to gain victory for himself by drawing the sword, but that, when opportunity and circumstances permit, he should occasionally have recourse to wiliness and thus ensure complete victory for himself. For, as far as we know, it is the prerogative of generals not only to deal with swords and fighting but also with treaties.

To sow dissension among the ranks of Bohemond's forces, Alexios sent letters to the Norman's most intimate followers with the intention that they should be intercepted, falsely incriminating his chief supporters of planning to betray their leader. The use of cunning and trickery in warfare bewildered the Franks. Anna further describes the importance of the Byzantine tactic of winning wars without fighting by the use of "quick wit" and stratagems.

The First Crusade

When the Emperor Alexios solicited professional soldiers from the West to serve as mercenaries in his armies, he had no idea that a flood of irresponsible peasants—led by brigands and crusading armies out to get loot and lands for themselves—was to be loosed upon his already battered empire.

The anonymous author of the *Gesta Francorum et aliorum Hierosolimitanorum* (The Deeds of the Franks and the other Pilgrims to Jerusalem), a vassal of Bohemond, in his own words indicts the motley host of Peter the Hermit, who reached Constantinople on August 1, 1096, and immediately proceeded to alienate the Byzantine populace:

> But those Christians behaved abominably, sacking and burning the palaces of the city and stealing the lead from the roofs of the churches and selling it to the Greeks, so that the emperor was angry and ordered them to cross the Hellespont. After they had crossed they did not cease from their misdeeds, and they burned and laid waste both houses and churches.

Refusing to heed the advice of the emperor to wait for the regular troops and knights, the pilgrims scattered in all directions, ravaging the country. The Turks took them by surprise and besieged them in the abandoned fortress of Xerigordos, cutting off their water supply. The Westerners were soon to learn what warfare against the Turks was like:

> Our men were therefore so terribly afflicted by thirst that they bled their horses and asses and drank the blood; others let down belts and clothes into a sewer and squeezed out the liquid into their mouths; others passed water into one another's cupped hands and drank.... Of the remainder, those who would not renounce God were killed;... some were put up as targets and shot with arrows, others sold and given away....

The crusaders, divided into four armies, each taking a different avenue to Constantinople, finally began to appear one by one at the walls of the city. Knights from Lorraine, France, Normandy, Flanders and Germany, and Normans from south Italy comprised the hosts. Emperor Alexios was now confronted by a crisis of major proportions. He realized that he had to find a way to protect Byzantium from total ruin at the hands of the crusaders and to use the Western knights to restore Byzantine power in Anatolia and Syria.

Having been instructed in Western feudal customs, the emperor, in return for provisions and assistance against the Turks, insisted that the leaders of the crusade take an oath of fealty to him. This meant that the lands taken by the crusaders from the Turks would belong to the emperor as suzerain over vassals. From the very beginning, the Franks showed their suspicion of and hostility to the Byzantine emperor. Godfrey of Bouillon had to be compelled to pledge fealty, while Raymond of Saint-Gilles consented only to swear not to undertake any designs against the life and honor of the emperor. Once again the alienation of Western and Byzantine cultures was dramatically emphasized when an impudent Frankish knight showed his disdain of imperial court etiquette by defiantly sitting himself down on the emperor's throne. The incident is recorded by Anna Komnena:

Thus they all assembled, . . . and after the oath had been taken by all the Counts, a certain venturesome noble sat down on the Emperor's seat. The Emperor put up with him and said not a word, knowing of old the Latin's haughty nature. But Count Balduinus stepped forward and taking him by the hand raised him up, rebuked him severely, and said, "It was wrong of you to do such a thing here, and that too when you have promised fealty to the Emperor; for it is not customary for the Roman Emperors to allow their subjects to sit beside them on the throne, and those who become his Majesty's sworn bondmen must observe the customs of the country." He made no reply to Balduinus, but darted a fierce glance at the Emperor and muttered some word to himself in his own language, saying, "Look at this rustic that keeps his seat, while such valiant captains are standing round him." The movement of the Latin's lips did not escape the Emperor, who called one of the interpreters of the Latin tongue and asked the purport of his words. When he heard what the remark was, he said nothing to the Latin for some time, but kept the saying in his heart. As they were all taking leave of the Emperor, he called that haughty-minded, audacious Latin, and enquired who he was and of what country and lineage. "I am a Frank of the purest nobility," he replied, "all that I know is that at the crossroads in the country whence I come there stands an old sanctuary, to which everyone who desires to fight in single combat goes ready accoutred for single combat, and there prays to

God for help while he waits in expectation of the man who will dare to fight him. At those crossroads I too have often tarried, waiting and longing for an antagonist; but never has one appeared who dared to fight me." In reply to this the Emperor said, "If you did not find a fight when you sought for it then, now the time has come which will give you your fill of fighting."

Anna fully understood the economic reason that impelled the dispossessed younger sons of the Norman nobility to join the crusade. Bohemond, the leader of the Normans of south Italy, she writes, "was sad in mind, as he had left his country a landless man, ostensibly to worship at the Holy Sepulchre but in reality with the intent of gaining a kingdom for himself or, rather, if it were possible, to follow his father's advice and seize the Roman Empire itself." To persuade Bohemond to pledge fealty to him the emperor had a special chamber in the palace filled with precious garments and gold and silver coins, and then instructed the official who was to show the Norman these riches "to throw open the doors suddenly." Overwhelmed by what he saw, Bohemond exclaimed, "If all these treasures were mine, I should have made myself master of many countries long ere this!" With magnanimity the imperial attendant replied, "The Emperor makes you a present of all these riches today." Bohemond, of course, pledged fealty, but Raymond, Count of Saint-Gilles, warned the emperor that the Norman had "acquired perjury and treachery as a species of ancestral heritage, and it would be a miracle if he kept his oath."

In June of 1098, the crusading armies took Antioch, which was given to Bohemond to govern as a principality. Not only did he not keep his pledge of fealty to Alexios I, he attempted to add lands to his principality at the expense of Byzantium. In 1100 the ambitious Bohemond was taken prisoner on an expedition against the Turks, and in 1103 he was ransomed, free once more to resume his struggle against the Byzantine empire. To escape the net spread out by Alexios I for his capture, Bohemond conceived of the following remarkable plan: he had the rumor spread abroad that he had died, got into a wooden coffin punctured with holes to allow him to breathe, and then to simulate the stench of death he had a dead cock placed in the coffin with him. Once the ship, which was carrying the coffin, reached Corfu and there was no longer any danger of being captured by the emperor's officials, the Norman "Lazarus" emerged from his malodorous sepulchre.

Anna writes that Bohemond's one obsession was "the downfall of the Roman hegemony." In Corfu he contemptuously demanded to see the Byzantine governor. "Speaking haughtily in his barbarian language" the Norman ordered the official to deliver a message to the emperor:

> But I myself, who was reported to thee and thine as dead, am going to my own country as a living man to myself and mine and full of dire intentions against thee. For to shatter the Roman Empire under thy sway, I died when alive, and came to life when dead. For as soon as I reach the continent opposite and see the men of Lombardy, and all the Latins and Germans and the Franks, our subjects and most warlike men, I shall fill thy towns and countries with many murders and much bloodshed until I plant my spear on Byzantium itself.

Tragically, Bohemond persuaded Pope Pascal (1099–1118) to adopt the Norman policy, directed at the destruction of Byzantium, as the official crusading policy. Alexios was vilified as a traitor to the cause of Christianity because he had refused to allow the crusaders to loot and plunder the venerable Christian city of Nicaea (where the First and Seventh Ecumenical Councils had taken place), once the Turks had surrendered it. Bohemond urged the papacy to stamp out the heresy of the Greeks. Indeed, the papacy was to sacrifice the possibility of the reunion of the churches in order to support the selfish interests of Norman adventurers. Recruiting a new army, Bohemond, with papal blessing, launched an attack against Dyrrachium, but once again the proud Norman was defeated by Alexios I and was forced to accept the humiliating terms of the Treaty of Devol, whereby he recognized Alexios as his suzerain. The emperor understood very well the single-minded policy of the Normans; in the words of Anna, "for he had long grasped the fact that the Franks were dreaming of the Roman empire."

What kind of impression did these Western knights make upon the sophisticated court of Byzantium? "Now the Frankish counts," writes the imperial princess, "are naturally shameless and violent, naturally greedy of money, too, and immoderate in everything they wish, and possess a flow of language greater than any other human race.... Their talkativeness and hunting instinct and their finicking speech are known to all who are interested in studying the manners of mankind." The Byzantine statesman was trained by education to discipline his mind and to follow the rules of rhetoric when stating his views. The continued disregard of imperial court etiquette on the part of the Western leaders who visited the emperor, "their speech long-winded," showing "no reverence for the emperor," was indeed appalling to the court officials. At the end of the day, when Alexios retired to his bedroom for rest and nourishment, the importunate knights followed him, allowing the beleaguered emperor no peace. The perceptive description of the chief characteristics of the Franks was ominous to say the least: insolence, violence and greed. Inevitably the Byzantine empire was to fall beneath their blows. The First Crusade was a harbinger of the terrible things to come for the Christians of the Greek East.

The anonymous author of the *Gesta Francorum* stresses the violence of those followers of the Prince of Peace and God of Love. Describing the fall of the Muslim city of Marra to the First Crusade, he writes: "Our men entered the city, and each seized his own share of whatever goods he found in houses or cellars, and when it was dawn they killed everyone, man or woman, whom they met in any place whatsoever. No corner of the city was clear of Saracen corpses."

The account of the crusaders' entry into the holy city of Jerusalem on July 15, 1099, is even more shocking:

> ... so our men entered the city, chasing the Saracens and killing them up to Solomon's Temple [Mosque of Omar] ..., so that all the temple was streaming with their blood.... After this our men rushed round the whole city, seizing gold and silver, horses and mules, and houses full of all sorts of goods, and they all came rejoicing and weeping from excess of gladness to worship at the Sepulchre of our Savior Jesus, and there they fulfilled their vows to him. Next morning they went cautiously up on to the Temple roof and attacked the Saracens, both men and women, cutting off their heads with drawn swords.... They also commanded that all the Saracen corpses should be thrown outside the city because of the fearful stench, for almost the whole city was full of their dead bodies. So the surviving Saracens dragged the dead

ones out in front of the gates, and piled them up in mounds as big as houses. No one has ever seen or heard of such slaughter of pagans, for they were burned on pyres like pyramids.

When Alexios I Komnenos died in 1118, the First Crusade had succeeded in carving out the four crusader states of Edessa, Antioch, Tripoli and Jerusalem. Alexios's son and successor, the extremely competent John II Komnenos (1118–1143), had no intention of renouncing the suzerainty of Byzantium over the Latin states. Constance, the daughter of Bohemond II, Prince of Antioch (1126–1130), had been formally betrothed to the emperor's son, Manuel. When Bohemond II died, Fulk, the King of Jerusalem (1131–1143), married Constance off to Raymond of Poitiers, who was made the new Prince of Antioch (1136–1149). John II Komnenos now decided to punish this act of insolence, and he launched a campaign directed primarily against Raymond. After having taken possession of Cilicia, the emperor appeared before Antioch in 1137, claiming that city and all the adjacent provinces as belonging to him according to the pledge of fealty made by the Latin knights to his father, Alexios I. Raymond of Antioch capitulated before the superior forces and siege engines of the emperor and swore allegiance and fealty to him.

John II, described by William of Tyre as "a man of great courage" and "lofty spirit," in the spring of 1138 summoned Raymond and Joscelyn II, the Count of Edessa, to join him in laying siege to Caesarea. While the emperor fought furiously, exposing himself to danger and taking no time for rest or even food, the Prince of Antioch and the Count of Edessa sat on the sidelines, "playing at games of chance."

Disgusted at the behavior of his Latin vassals, John II lifted the siege and returned to Antioch, where he was received with great ceremony. The Latin patriarch, the clergy and the people greeted him, punctuating the procession with songs of praise, the sound of musical instruments and joyous applause. Joscelyn, however, maliciously spread the rumor "throughout the city that Antioch had been sold to the Greeks ... and that the citizens would be forced to leave the homes of their forefathers and depart from their ancestral possessions." The incensed Latins fell upon members of the imperial household, pulled them off their horses and flogged and despoiled them. Those who resisted were forced to withdraw from Antioch.

William of Tyre cites only the ruse of Joscelyn as responsible for Latin fears, but at bottom lay the religious problem. In the Treaty of Devol, Bohemond acceded to the imperial demand that a Greek patriarch be restored to the see of Antioch. The Latins refused to comply, and John II's appearance at Antioch aroused the suspicions of the Latin clergy that the Latin patriarch would be removed for a Greek appointed from Constantinople. In the meantime, Pope Innocent II (1130–1143), alarmed by the emperor's claims to suzerainty over the Latin states, struck out by issuing a bull forbidding all Latins to serve in his armies.

The Latin occupation of Antioch and Jerusalem proved to be extremely important for the future unhappy church relations between Latins and Greeks. The papacy's formula for resolving schism in the Greek East was to set Latin hierarchs over the Greek Orthodox population; nothing could have been more unacceptable to the Greeks.

In the spring of 1143, John II Komnenos, taken by surprise by a wild boar while hunting, accidentally and fatally wounded himself by piercing his own hand with the point of a poisoned arrow. When the physicians suggested amputation of his hand in order to save his life he replied: "It would be unseemly that the Roman empire should be ruled by one hand." His youngest son Manuel, who, according to William of Tyre, "stood high in the estimation and favor of the entire army, particularly with the Latins," was chosen to succeed him.

The brilliant reign of Manuel I Komnenos (1143–1180) was one of the most feverish in all Byzantine history. Extremely cultured, a well-read and skilled writer, eloquent in speech and learned in debating the subtleties of theology, this fascinating occupant of the imperial throne unfortunately conceived grandiose but unrealistic political programs. He spent most of his time negotiating or fighting with the French, Germans, Hungarians, Serbs, Normans, Venetians, Turks and the papacy. He dreamed of reconquering Italy and of being crowned emperor at Rome in alliance with the papacy, as master of Christian East and West. To achieve his far-fetched diplomatic purposes he poured a veritable river of gold into the West when it was needed more to defend the empire in the East against the Turks. But Byzantium was a Mediterranean power, and the complex events unfolding there could not be ignored by an emperor who dreamed of reuniting the old Roman empire under his sway.

Even Manuel's father, the great John II Komnenos, had flirted with the papacy, holding out the bait of the reunion of the churches under the pope of Rome in return for the latter's support in re-establishing the unity of the one Christian empire. The secular sword would be wielded by the Byzantine emperor, John II wrote Pope Innocent II in 1141, while the pope would wield the spiritual sword. It was Manuel's design to consummate his father's plans. And, in fact, he did succeed in establishing Byzantine suzerainty over the Latin Crusader states, which, as they deteriorated, turned to the emperor for protection.

Raymond of Antioch thought the death of John II Komnenos an opportune occasion to invade Byzantine territory, but Manuel struck back quickly by dispatching both fleet and army in retaliation. The Prince of Antioch was compelled to renew his pledge of homage to the Byzantine emperor and to accept a Greek patriarch sent from Constantinople. In this same year, on Christmas day, 1144, the Latin County of Edessa fell to Zengi, the emir of Mosul. The hatred of the Muslims for the Latins was demonstrated when they put to the sword all Franks and sold their women into slavery while sparing the eastern Christians.

Second Crusade

In the West, St. Bernard of Clairvaux preached eloquently for a new crusade, and both Louis VII of France and Conrad III of Germany accepted the leadership of the Second Crusade. The results of this new enterprise were to be totally disastrous. Not only were the western armies decimated by famine, pestilence, and Turkish victories, the relations between Greeks and Latins were further strained and western determination to destroy Byzantium was intensified. On their side, the Byzantines welcomed another inundation of their lands by countless western armies as they would an uncontrollable plague of locusts. It is with this growing hostility between Byzantium and the West that we are concerned.

The German armies were the first to cross the Balkans to Constantinople, and their disorderly conduct and criminal acts against the inhabitants predisposed the latter against the French, who followed later and were made to pay for the misdeeds of Conrad's men. Odo of Deuil, monk of St. Denis and Louis VII's chaplain, confirms the deepest fears of the Byzantines:

The Greeks, however, closed their cities and fortresses and offered their wares by letting them down from the walls on ropes. But food furnished in such measure did not suffice our throng. Therefore the pilgrims, unwilling to endure want in the midst of plenty, procured supplies for themselves by plunder and pillage.

Some thought, however, that this state of affairs was the fault of the Germans who had preceded us since they had been plundering everything. We found also that they had burned certain settlements outside cities.

Niketas Choniates informs us that Conrad III had previously requested of Manuel permission to cross over Byzantine territory and to have roadside markets set up for the provisioning of his troops and horses. Manuel agreed, but asked that the crusaders first swear oaths that their passage would be "God-loving" and free of attacks against the Byzantine populace.

The Germans, however, completely undisciplined, plundered everywhere as they moved on to Constantinople. Odo of Deuil relates the insolent and uncivilized disregard of Conrad and his troops even for imperial property:

Before the city stood a spacious and impressive ring of walls enclosing various kinds of game and including canals and ponds. Also, inside were certain hollows and caves which, in lieu of forests, furnished lairs for animals. In that lovely place certain palaces which the emperors had built as their springtime resort are conspicuous for their splendor. Into this "place of delights," to give it the proper name, the German emperor burst and, destroying practically everything, under the very eyes of the Greeks seized their delights for his own uses. . . .

The Byzantines were also scandalized by the fact that women from the West participated in the crusades and took part in actual combat. Niketas Choniates records the impression these "Amazons" made upon the citizens of the empire:

. . . females were numbered among them and rode horseback in the manner of men, and they did not sit side-saddle with both legs covered by their dresses but, riding unashamedly astride and bearing lances and weapons as men do, and dressed in masculine garb, they cast about wholly warlike glances and they were more manlike than the Amazons.

After a clash with the Byzantine forces, Conrad decided to cross over to Anatolia. Because their reputation had preceded them, the inhabitants of the Byzantine cities refused to open their gates to the crusaders, nor were they willing to provide them with markets. Instead, from atop the walls the Byzantine merchants negotiated the prices for the supplies requested, and after they had first pulled up by rope the money they demanded, they would let down the agreed amount of bread and goods. Niketas Choniates admits that the merchants dealt unjustly with the Crusaders and often short-changed them in their hour of need: "They seized from their throat that which was needed for the sustenance of the body." The meanest of the merchants would take the gold and silver and then disappear without giving any provisions in return. Still worse, others put lime in with the barley-groats, thus making a fatal mixture.

Conrad and the Byzantine emperors John II and Manuel I also continued the ideological conflict over the imperial title. To cement an alliance with the Hohenstaufens against the Norman Roger of Sicily, Manuel was affianced to and later married Bertha of Sulzbach, the sister of Conrad's wife Gertrude. During the negotiations, the game of titles took place.

Otto, Bishop of Freising, records that at first Conrad assumed for himself the title of emperor of the Romans, while granting the lesser title of emperor of the Greeks to John II in defiance of Byzantine traditions. The Byzantine emperors were masters at the game, and John II replied by demoting Conrad to the lesser role of king.

Odo of Deuil emphasizes once again the Latin impatience with Byzantine etiquette and diplomatic procedures. At Ratisbon, Manuel's messengers were summoned before Louis VII:

When they had greeted the king and delivered their letters they stood to await his reply, for they would not sit unless commanded to do so; on command they arranged the chairs that they had brought with them and sat down. We saw there what we afterward learned is the Greek custom, namely, that the entire retinue remains standing while the lords are seated. One could see young men standing immobile, with heads bent and gazes directed intently and silently on their own lords, ready to obey their mere nod. They do not have cloaks, but the wealthy are clad in silken garments which are short, tight-sleeved and sewn up on all sides, so that they always move about unimpeded, as do athletes. The poor outfit themselves in garments of like cut, but cheaper sort.

When the Byzantine messengers who met Louis VII in Greece prefaced their remarks with the usually lengthy and stereotyped Byzantine expressions of affection, the irritated bishop of Langres, Godfrey, interrupted, saying: "Brothers, do not repeat 'glory,' 'majesty,' 'wisdom,' and 'piety' so often in reference to the king. He knows himself and we know him well. Just indicate your wishes more briefly and freely." The king of France was also little impressed by those Byzantine chants (*polychronioi*) in honor of secular authorities: "The king accepted, but considered of slight value, their *polychroniae* (for that is the name of the gestures of honor which they exhibit, not only toward kings, but even toward certain of their nobles, lowering the head and body humbly or kneeling on the ground or even prostrating themselves)." Thus did Western statesmen ridicule the refinements of the Byzantine court.

Odo of Deuil refers to Manuel I as Emperor of the Greeks and clearly reveals the anti-Greek sentiments of the Franks: "There were men in the assembly who said that the Greeks, as they had learned either by reading or by experience, were deceitful." To stress his point, Odo cites Vergil's verse from the *Aeneid*: "I fear the Greeks, even when they bear gifts." As a Latin cleric, Odo takes special care to cite the odious and heretical usages of the Greeks:

... if our priests celebrated mass on Greek altars, the Greeks afterwards purified them with propitiatory offerings and ablutions, as if they had been defiled. All the wealthy people have their own chapels, so adorned with paintings, marble, and lamps that each magnate might justly say, "O lord, I have cherished the beauty of Thy house." ... But, O dreadful thing! We heard of an ill usage of theirs which could be expiated by death; namely, that every time they celebrate the marriage of one of our men, if he has been baptized in the Roman way, they rebaptize him before they make the pact. We know other heresies of theirs, both concerning their treatment of the Eucharist and concerning the procession of the Holy Ghost.... Actually, it was for these reasons that the Greeks had incurred the hatred of our men, for their error had become known even among the lay people. Because of this they were judged not to be Christians, and the Franks considered killing them a matter of no importance and hence could with the more difficulty be restrained from pillage and plundering.

Once again it is forcefully brought home to us that the chasm between Greek East and Latin West was unbridgable. Greek Christians were looked upon not only as heretics but, even worse, as not even being Christian!

Yet even Odo and Louis VII were moved by the Byzantine liturgical chant, which they heard on the feast of the Athenian St. Denis (St. Dionysios the Areopagite), the patron saint of his own monastery, celebrated on October 9 in the Latin calendar and October 3 in the Greek:

> Since the Greeks celebrated this feast, the Emperor knew of it, and he sent over to the king a carefully selected group of his clergy, each of whom he had equipped with a large taper decorated elaborately with gold and a great variety of colors; and thus he increased the glory of the ceremony. These clergy certainly differed from ours as to words and order of service, but they made a favorable impression because of their sweet chanting; for the mingling of the voices, the heavier with the light, the eunuch's, namely, with the manly voice (for many of them were eunuchs), softened the hearts of the Franks. Also, they gave the onlookers pleasure by their graceful bearing and gentle clapping of hands and genuflections....

The king's chaplain might rant about the deceitful, effeminate and indolent Greeks, but he confesses that even Louis VII could not control the knights, barons and chiefs and the numerous non-combatants, and that he was forced to resort to mutilations in the vain attempt to check their vandalisms and depredations.

It was what seemed to be the incredible wealth of Byzantium, which so dazzled the Franks as it had the Normans before them, that ignited in their souls the burning passion to seize the empire by force. The conquest and rape of a Christian land was conveniently justified by Latin clerics. Godfrey, Bishop of Langres, advised the Franks to take Constantinople, declaring that it was

"Christian in name only" and that Emperor John II Komnenos had replaced the Latin bishops in Syria with Greek heretics; he disparaged Emperor Manuel I as an "idol," claiming that it was disgraceful to do homage to an "infidel." Odo of Deuil was drawn to the temperate climate and rich fertile soil of the great capital; but he, too, implied that it was too corrupt to be allowed to continue in its ways: "Contantinople is arrogant in her wealth, treacherous in her practices, corrupt in her faith; just as she fears everyone on account of her wealth, she is dreaded by everyone because of her treachery and faithlessness." Finally, the Greeks were blamed for the disastrous failure of the Franks and Germans in the Second Crusade:

> And both nations will always have something to bewail if the sons of these men do not avenge their parents' death. To us who suffered the Greeks' evil deeds, however, divine justice and the fact that our people are not accustomed to endure shameful injuries for long, give hope of vengeance. Thus we comfort our sad heart, and we shall follow the course of our misfortunes so that posterity may know about the Greeks' treacherous actions.

The partisans of Godfrey, Bishop of Langres, advised Louis VII "to seize the exceedingly rich land with its castles and cities and meanwhile to write to King Roger, who was then vigorously attacking the emperor, and, aided by his fleet, to attack Constantinople itself."

Roger II, first King of Sicily (1130–1154), at the very moment the Second Crusade was starting, dispatched a fleet from Brindisi to ravage the coasts of Greece. The beautiful island of Corfu was taken without a struggle. Penetrating into the Gulf of Corinth, Roger took Thebes and brutalized the inhabitants. Seizing as much exquisite silken cloths as he could, he also carried off "those of the women who were comely and deep-girded in form and who had bathed often in the running waters of Dirce's beautiful spring and who arranged their tresses attractively and who knew well the fine art of weaving." Corinth also fell to the Norman king, who stole the precious icon of the martyr St. Theodore Stratelates and set it up in his own chapel. The Corinthian nobility and "the fair and deep-bosomed" women of Corinth he took captive, and both the Theban and Corinthian women were put to work at the loom, weaving the much sought after "gold-embroidered garments of six strands." Otto of Freising records the importance of this abduction of Byzantine silk weavers. The Byzantine monopoly since the sixth century was now broken:

> They led away captive even the workmen who are accustomed to weave silken goods. Establishing them in Palermo, the metropolis of Sicily, Roger bade them teach his craftsmen the art of silk weaving. Thenceforth that art, previously practiced only by the Greeks among Christian nations, began to be accessible to the genius of Rome.

In 1149, Manuel called upon the Venetian fleet to assist him in retaking Corfu from the Normans. The Normans were ousted, but an incident occurred at this time which demonstrated the growing antagonism between the two allies. For some reason the Byzantines and the Venetians became embroiled in the middle of the marketplace of Corfu. Neither the Venetian magistrates nor the imperial officials could separate the two factions. Finally the Byzantine *megas domestikos* (supreme commander) managed to restrain the Byzantines, but the Venetians continued to pour out of their ships in full fury. Since the peace could not be restored otherwise, the Byzantine commander called in his bodyguard and elite troops as well as part of the regular army, who inflicted casualties on the bellicose Venetians, compelling the latter to flee to the refuge of their ships. The Venetians refused to concede that they had been bested by the Greek troops. Unable to carry the battle on dry land, the Venetians sailed out to the island of Asteris and attacked and destroyed by fire the Greek ships from Euboia that were anchored there. Next, the Venetians furtively stole the imperial ships and adorned the emperor's cabins with gold-embroidered curtains and purple tapestries. Then they set on the emperor's ship a black-skinned Ethiopian rogue, crowning him and acclaiming him Emperor of the Romans. Leading him about in a grand procession, the Venetians ridiculed the solemn imperial ceremonies and insolently mocked Emperor Manuel I, whose skin, says Niketas Choniates, was the color of the bride described in a then-popular song, "I am black and beautiful because the sun has looked upon me from the corner of his eye." Manuel, who must have been outraged by such an offensive display of bad manners, swallowed his pride; having further need of the services of the Venetian fleet, he offered the offenders full amnesty, trusting to the future the exacting of vengeance.

At the same time Manuel I infuriated the Byzantine nobility and commercial classes by showing excessive favoritism to Western knights and merchants. As a result of his Latinophile policy he alienated his own subjects. As William of Tyre put it:

> During the reign of Manuel, beloved of God, the Latins had found great favor with him—a reward well deserved because of their loyalty and valor. The emperor, a great-souled man of incomparable energy, relied so implicitly on their fidelity and ability that he passed over the Greeks as soft and effeminate and intrusted important affairs to the Latins alone. The Greek nobles, especially the near kindred of the emperor, and the rest of the people as well, naturally conceived an insatiable hatred toward us, and this was increased by the difference between our sacraments and those of their church, which furnished an additional incentive to their jealousy. For they, having separated insolently from the church of Rome, in their boundless arrogance looked upon everyone who did not follow their foolish traditions as a heretic. It was they themselves, on the contrary, who deserved the name of heretics, because they had either created or followed new and pernicious beliefs contrary to the Roman church and the faith of the apostles Peter and Paul.... For these and other reasons they had for a long time cherished this hatred in their hearts and were ever seeking an opportunity, at least after the death of the emperor, to destroy utterly the hated race of the Latins, both in the city and throughout the entire empire....

Latin mercenaries filled the ranks of the imperial army, which was divided into a western and an eastern corps. German and French knights, renegade Normans from south Italy, and Lombards predominated; Anglo-Saxons, dispossessed by the Norman conquerors in England, now filled the posts of the elite Varangian Guard. Numerous other westerners were found in the imperial court and in the imperial diplomatic service as well as in important administrative posts.

Niketas Choniates complains bitterly of these foreigners, who occupied high positions in the government and who were ignorant of Greek culture and language, the necessary attributes of the educated man. For the first time, intermarriages between the princely families of Byzantium and western nobility became common practice; the reasons, of course, were always political. Manuel's first marriage to Bertha of Sulzbach, sister-in-law of Conrad III, had as its end the alliance of the Byzantine empire with Germany against their common enemy, the Normans of south Italy. Manuel's second marriage to Maria, daughter of Raymond of Antioch, strengthened Byzantine relations with the Latin princes of Syria. In the hope of getting the French to join the Byzantine-German coalition, Manuel's son Alexios II was married to Agnes-Anna, daughter of King Louis VII of France.

Manuel also wanted to develop and strengthen his cavalry according to western patterns so that he could better counter his western opponents. His bravura in the field was chivalric, the kind of behavior expected of a western knight. He also engaged in tournaments. For example, when he came to Antioch to claim his suzerainty over the Latin principalities, he promoted a grand tournament on the plain of the Orontes River, and he himself entered the lists, along with the best lancers of his troops, unhorsing two western knights by the force of his charge.

Hatred between Greeks and Latins increased with time, however, and exploded into frequent acts of pillage and violence. In 1155 Reynald of Chatillion, Prince of Antioch, without provocation attacked the friendly Greek island of Cyprus. His forces destroyed cities and towns, wrecked the island's fortresses, looted monasteries, slaughtered without regard to age or sex and raped nuns and maidens. His ships, laden with vast stores of stolen riches and spoils, returned to Antioch.

On Christmas day, 1161, for greater political advantage, Manuel I married Maria, the daughter of Constance of Antioch, instead of Melisend, the sister of Raymond III, Count of Tripoli. Melisend had already undergone considerable expense in preparation for the nuptial celebrations. In retaliation, Raymond dispatched pirates and desperados to ravage Byzantine lands. They plundered, burned, massacred and destroyed churches and monasteries wherever they landed.

By 1170 the tension between Byzantines and Venetians became so explosive that Doge Vitale Michiele (1156–1172) advised his nationals to leave Constantinople; many of them did so. On March 16, 1171, Manuel I struck out at his erstwhile allies by ordering the arrest of all Venetians in the empire, the confiscation of their property and the seizure of their ships. Venice retaliated by attacking the Byzantine coast and by sacking the Greek islands of Chios and Lesbos. Manuel's brilliant reign, however, was doomed to end in disaster. On September 17, 1176, Manuel's army was almost annihilated by the Turkish forces of the Sultan of Ikonion at Myriokephalon in the Phrygian passes. The emperor was never to recover from this blow, and the fortunes of the empire were sealed.

Upon his death in 1180, Manuel I was succeeded by his twelve-year-old son Alexios II Komnenos (1180–1183). Alexios's mother, Maria of Antioch, assumed the regency; as was to be expected, the Westerners were even more favored by the Latin empress. This pro-Latin regency was bitterly resented by Byzantine nationals, who desired the overthrow of the hated Maria. Andronikos Komnenos, Manuel's cousin, was called upon to lead the opposition. With the support of the *megas dux*, the admiral of the navy, Andronikos entered the capital and declared himself protector of the young emperor. In response to the sentiments of the Byzantine population, Andronikos unleashed the terrible massacre of the Latins in Constantinople in May of 1182. This act of revenge, perpetrated by the citizens of the capital, together with Andronikos's troops, was the violent outcome of Manuel's Latinophile policies, which threatened, moreover, to compel the Greek church to submit to Rome.

Those Latins who had received sufficient warning escaped on forty-four galleys anchored in the harbor. The Latin quarter was put to the torch, and the aged and infirm who were unable to flee, perished in the flames. Latin monks and priests were tortured to death, and the head of the papal legate was attached to the tail of a dog and dragged through the streets. The sick found in the hospital of St. John were also put to death; and, according to William of Tyre, some four thousand survivors were sold as slaves to the Turks. Graves were desecrated and corpses exhumed. The escaping Latin galleys retaliated by sacking towns, cities and fortresses along the Hellespont and Thessaly, and by putting countless numbers to the sword.

The Republic of Venice now realized that if it was to retain the monopoly of Eastern trade and continue to profit from the fine markets in the Greek East, one course lay open: to conquer Byzantium and lay the foundations of a Venetian colonial empire upon its ruins.

Alexios II Komnenos was compelled to sign the death warrant of his own mother, the dowager Latin empress Maria. In September of 1183, Andronikos was crowned co-emperor at the insistence of clergy and court alike; not long after, the unfortunate young Alexios was strangled and dumped into the sea. Andronikos I Komnenos, now sixty-five, was sole emperor; to further his claim to legitimacy, however, he married eleven-year-old Agnes-Anna, who had been Alexios II's bride. Niketas Choniates describes this unseemly union that scandalized the Byzantine populace as follows:

And he who stank of the dark ages was not ashamed to lie unlawfully with his nephew's red-cheeked and tender spouse who had not yet completed her eleventh year; the overripe suitor embracing the unripe maiden; the dotard, the damsel with outstanding breasts; the shrivelled and languid old man, the rosy-fingered girl dripping with the dew of love.

In the face of the internal dislocation of the Byzantine empire the Norman king of Sicily, William II (1166–1189), now seized the opportunity to launch a heavy attack against Greece. Dyrrachium, which had withstood the onslaughts of Bohemond, was voluntarily surrendered by the Byzantine commander in June of 1185, while the Norman fleet easily occupied the islands of Corfu, Kephallenia and Zakynthos. No opposition was offered the Norman troops and mercenaries as they crossed from Dyrrachium to Thessalonica. The great city was besieged both by land and by sea. Poor defenses, inadequate provisions, lack of help from Constantinople, compounded by the dastardly behavior of the governor, David Komnenos, resulted in the fall of the empire's second largest city on August 15, 1185. The massacre of the Latins in Constantinople three years before was now avenged with unparalleled fury and barbarity. Niketas Choniates records the atrocities of the conquering Normans:

The evils which ensued were another succession of Trojan woes surpassing even the calamitous events of tragedy; for every house was robbed of its contents, no dwelling was spared, no narrow passageway was free of despoilers, no hiding-place was long hidden. Nor was any piteous creature shown any pity, nor was any heed paid to the entreaty, but the sword passed through all things, and the death dealing wound ended all wrath. Futile was the flight of many to the holy temples, and vain was their trust in the sacred images. For the barbarians, by confusing divine and human things, knew not how to honor the things of God nor did they grant sanctuary to those who ran to the temples; . . . Bursting in upon the sanctuaries with weapons in hand the enemy slew whoever was in the way, and as sacrificial victims mercilessly slaughtered whomever they seized. . . .

. . . they dashed the all-hallowed icons of Christ and his servants to the ground, and firmly planting their feet on them, they forcibly removed whatever precious material adorned them; then they would throw the icons out into the streets to be trampled under foot or they cast them into the fire to cook their food. Even more unholy and terrible for the faithful to hear was the fact that certain men climbing on top of the holy altar, which even the angels find hard to look upon, danced thereon deporting themselves disgracefully, and they sang certain lewd barbarian songs from their homeland; afterwards, uncovering their privy parts and letting the *membrum virile* pour forth the contents of the bladder, they urinated round about the sacred floor, performing these lustral besprinklings for the demons and improvising hot baths for the avenging spirits. . . .

But because the land which was our allotted portion to inhabit and reap the fruits thereof was openly likened to Paradise by the most accursed Latins, and longing passionately after our blessings, they were ever ill-disposed toward our race, and they are forever workers of evil deeds. And though they should dissemble friendship, submitting to the needs of the time, they despise us as their bitterest enemies; and though their speech is affable and smoother than oil flowing noiselessly, yet are they darts, and thus they are sharper than a two-edged sword. Thus between us and them the greatest gulf of disagreement has been fixed, and we are separated in purpose and diametrically opposed even though we are closely associated and frequently share the same dwelling.

Should the owner of a house which had been taken over by the Normans happen to look inside out of curiosity, he was seized immediately, flogged and compelled to reveal what monies he may have concealed. Many were tortured and maltreated; some were hung by the feet while a heap of chaff was burned beneath them, choking them with the smoke; at the same time, their mouths were besmeared with dung and their sides were pierced by arrows. Those who survived such inhuman treatment were dragged out of the house by the feet like so much garbage and cast into the open squares.

The conquerors had no pity on the citizens, who were now reduced to wearing torn garments and to using rush mats to cover their bodies. On meeting the Greeks in the street, they would grab them by their long beards and hair and poke fun at them, insisting that the hair should be clipped round about in the Western fashion. Riding through the marketplace, the knights would brandish their lances and knock over anyone in sight; if there happened to be a mud puddle or mire nearby, they would push the Greeks into it. Whenever they found Greeks partaking of whatever meager and coarse food they could gather to sustain themselves in life, the Latins would overturn their dishes and knock over their tables. Niketas Choniates continues:

> These utterly shameless buffoons, having no fear of God whatsoever, bending over, pulled up their garments, and baring their buttocks and all that men keep covered, they turned their anus on them and coming very near to their food, the fools would break wind louder than a polecat. Sometimes, by discharging the urinal content of their belly through the spout of their groin, they contaminated the cooked food, and even urinated in the faces of some. They even urinated in the wells, and, drawing up the water afterwards, they would drink it. And the very same vessel served them as both chamber pot and wine cup; without having first been cleansed, it received both the much-desired wine and water and also held the excreta pouring out of the body's nozzle.
>
> Nonetheless, they so honored the servants of God who are accounted among the firstborn and took such heed of the miracles they wrought and were so astonished at the marvelous and novel wonders by which Christ glorifies those who with their own bodies have glorified him that the unguent which exuded from the crypt of Demetrios, who was renowned in miracles and among martyrs, they would collect in jars and basins and pour over their fish dishes, and with this sweet oil they would rub their leather footgear, and they used it for all the purposes which olive oil now serves. . . .
>
> And when the time was sounded for the Romans to assemble in the temples for the singing of hymns, the boorish members of the army did not keep away even at this time, but, going inside as though to attend church services together with the Romans, offering up to God a sacrifice of praise, they did no such thing, but, babbling

among themselves and bursting forth in unintelligible shouts or violently throttling certain Romans because of some incident and causing a great disturbance, they confounded the hymn, and it was as though the chanters were singing in a strange land and not standing in the temple of God. In response to those who were praising the Lord, many would let loose with ribald songs, and, barking like dogs, they would break in upon the hymn and drown out the supplication to God.

When Constantinople received the news that Thessalonica had fallen to the Normans and that the enemy was even now advancing on the capital, the frightened populance turned against the man they had proclaimed their savior but a short while before. Andronikos had failed the empire. Isaakios II Angelos (1185–1195), grandson of Constantine Angelos and Theodora Komnena, the youngest daughter of Alexios I Komnenos, was proclaimed emperor. A description of the pitiful end of Andronikos shows that no matter how sacred the personage of the basileus might have been when he sat on the throne, the fate of a fallen emperor, who had demonstrably lost the favor of God, was terrible indeed!

He was confined in the so-called prison of Anemas with two heavy chains weighing down his proud neck, the kind of iron collars used to fetter caged lions, and his feet were painfully shackled. Appearing bound in this fashion and paraded before Emperor Isaakios, he was slapped in the face, kicked on the buttocks, his beard was torn out, his teeth pulled out, his head shorn of hair, he was made the common sport of all those who gathered, he was even battered by women who struck him in the mouth with their fists, especially by those whose husbands were either put to death or blinded by Andronikos. Afterwards, his right hand being cut off by an axe, he was cast again into the same prison, without food and drink, receiving tendance from no one.

Several days later, one of his eyes was gouged out, and, seated upon a mangy camel, he was paraded through the agora looking like a leafless and withered old stump, balder than an egg, his bare head shining before all, his body covered by meager rags, a pitiful sight evoking tears from sympathetic eyes. . . . Some struck him on the head with clubs, others befouled his nostrils with cow-dung, and still others, using sponges, poured the excretions from the bel-

lies of oxen and men over his eyes. . . . Led in this manner igno-
miniously into the theater in mock triumph, the unhappy man was
made sport of sitting on the hump of a camel, and, dismounting
therefrom, he was straightway suspended by his feet. . . . Even
after he was suspended by the feet, the foolish masses did not keep
their hands off the much-tormented Andronikos nor did they spare
his flesh, but, removing his short tunic, they assaulted his genitals.
A certain ungodly man dipped his long sword into his entrails by
way of the pharynx; certain members of the Latin race raised their
swords with both hands above his buttocks, and, standing around
him, they brought them down making trial as to whose cut was
deeper and boasting loudly in the dexterity of their hands which
resulted in such a noteworthy wound.

After so much pain and suffering, he barely snapped the thread
of life, extending his right arm in agony and then bringing it around
to his mouth in such a manner that it seemed to many that he was
sucking out the still warm blood dripping from the recent amputation.

Constantinople, as can be seen from these events, was completely
demoralized. The new emperor could not stem the inexorable flow of
impending doom. Neither the mass arrests and expulsions under Manuel nor the massacre of 1182 could daunt the Venetians. Isaakios II
agreed to compensate them by giving them more docks and wharfs
than before, as well as a heavy money indemnity.

Third Crusade

Thanks to the capable *strategos* Alexios Branas, the Normans were
defeated and forced out of Thessalonica, Dyrrachium and Corfu. But
now Frederick I Barbarossa, Holy Roman Emperor (1155–1190) and
nephew of Conrad III, conceived the idea of attacking Constantinople
and its "King of the Greeks" on the Third Crusade. In fact, he took
the Byzantine cities of Philippopolis and Adrianople and advanced on
the capital. Isaakios II Angelos was now compelled to seek a rap-
prochement; to avert a clash he agreed to transport Frederick and his
crusaders to Anatolia and to provide them with markets and cheaply
priced provisions. Unexpectedly, Barbarossa drowned trying to ford a
stream in Cilicia.

At this time the Vlachs, Peter and Asen, with the help of the Turkic

Cumans, established the Second Bulgarian Empire; Byzantine domination of the Balkans was over forever. Kalojan, also called Ioannitza (1197–1207), who succeeded Peter and Asen, proved to be an even greater threat to Byzantium. So devastating were his attacks against the Greeks that he was named *Rhomaioktonos* (Roman-slayer). To counter Byzantium, which had allied with Hungary, he turned to Pope Innocent III, accepted papal supremacy and was crowned by a cardinal in 1204. In 1202 the Serb Vukan, who came to power temporarily, also recognized the supremacy of the pope; Kulin, the ruler of Bosnia, followed suit in 1203. When the Byzantine forces suffered severe defeats at the hands of the Bulgars at the passes of the Balkan ranges, Isaakios II was deposed and blinded by his own brother, Alexios III Angelos, on April 8, 1195.

In 1194, Henry VI succeeded his father Frederick I Barbarossa as Holy Roman Emperor and King of Sicily. Henry arranged the marriage of his brother, Philip of Swabia, to Irene, daughter of the deposed Isaakios II and widow of Roger of Sicily; his purpose was to establish a legitimate claim to the Byzantine empire, which he now planned to conquer. He prepared an army to march against both Byzantium and the Holy Land. Although the papacy was claiming the Latin states in the East as vassal states, Henry VI declared that since he was the head of Christian Europe the Crusader states belonged to him alone. But before the German emperor could launch his campaign he died, and the army of the German crusade of 1197 is described as being "less like pilgrims than ravishing wolves."

Fourth Crusade

In Constantinople matters were going from bad to worse. The usurper, Alexios III, was intimidated enough by Henry VI to agree to pay a humiliating annual tribute of sixteen hundred pounds of gold. In 1198, Innocent III came to the papal throne and proved to be the most powerful pope in history. He sent two legates to the imperial capital to urge the emperor to recognize papal supremacy, thereby ending the schism, and to provide aid to the forthcoming crusade. To force the emperor's hand the ambitious pope threatened to favor Philip of Swabia's plans to attack Constantinople.

Both Isaakios II and Alexios III exacerbated the hostility of the Venetians by instigating the Pisans against them. Alexios III had refused to pay the Venetians the two hundred pounds of gold still lacking from the overall debt of fifteen hundred pounds that Emperor Manuel I had agreed to pay the Venetians as restitution for the losses suffered by them when he had ordered the confiscation of their properties in 1171. The Venetians were only awaiting the right moment to avenge themselves against the Greeks, and the opportunity was not long in coming.

For the Byzantines, the chief villain in the plot was Enrico Dandolo, Doge of Venice (1192–1205), described by Niketas Choniates in the following terms:

> The doge of Venice at that time, Enrico Dandolo, was not the least of horrors; a man maimed in sight and along in years, a creature most treacherous and extremely jealous of the Romans, a sly cheat calling himself wiser than the wise and madly thirsting after glory as no other, he preferred death to allowing the Romans to escape the penalty for their insulting treatment of his nation, all the while pondering over in his mind and enumerating how many evils the Venetians associated with the rule of the Angeloi brothers [Isaakios II and Alexios III], and of Andronikos before them and, prior to him, of Manuel who held sway over the Roman empire. Realizing that should he work some treachery against the Romans with his fellow-countrymen alone that he would bring disaster down on his own head, he schemed to include other accomplices, and to share his secret designs with those whom he knew to nurse an implacable hatred against the Romans and who looked with an envious and avaricious eye on their goods. The opportunity arose as if by chance when certain well-born lords were eager to set out for Palestine; he met with them to arrange a joint action and won them over as confederates in the military operation against the Romans. These were Marquis Boniface of Montferrat, Count Baldwin of Flanders, Count Hugh of Saint Pol and Count Louis of Blois, and many other bold warriors who were as tall as their lances were long.
>
> When within three full years one hundred and ten horse-carrying dromons and sixty long ships were built in Venice, in addition to the more than seventy huge round ships which were assembled, one of which they called *Kosmos* [Mundus] as being much larger in size than the others, one thousand cavalry clad in full armor, and thirty thousand bucklers divided mostly into heavy-armed foot-soldiers, especially those called crossbowmen, were commanded to board them.

Boniface, the leader of the Fourth Crusade, was a Ghibelline and an opponent of Pope Innocent III. Boniface also conceived the plan of destroying the Byzantine empire and substituting for it a Latin empire. The French needed the Venetians to transport them and their horses to the East, but the French knights were unable to raise the cash promised to pay for their passage.

In Constantinople in the meantime, Isaakios II, although imprisoned, managed to come into contact with many Latins who had a special antipathy toward Alexios III and who wanted him dethroned and himself restored to the throne. The Latins gladly carried letters from Isaakios to his daughter Irene, who was married, as we have seen, to Philip of Swabia. These letters asked for help to avenge her father; others were smuggled back to Isaakios advising him what he should do. He now encouraged his son Alexios to escape to the West.

The Emperor Alexios III made the mistake of taking his nephew on campaign with him; when they had camped at a place called Damokraneia, the young Alexios contacted a certain Pisan, a captain of a large round vessel, and made arrangements to be taken by boat to the captain's ship. He made good his escape by disguising himself; he cut his hair in the Latin style round about, changed into Latin dress and mixed with the milling crowd. Disembarking in Sicily in 1201, he proceeded to inform his sister and brother-in-law of his escape.

Villehardouin, Marshal of Champagne, in the *Chronicle of the Fourth Crusade and the Conquest of Constantinople* records how Alexios made his way to Ancona where he was informed of the massing of the hosts of the Fourth Crusade in Venice and advised to seek their help in recovering the throne of Byzantium for his father. The plot to divert the Fourth Crusade to Constantinople mushroomed in the West but only in secret negotiations. Emperor Alexios III learned of the conspiracy and wrote to Pope Innocent III to intervene. Although the pope officially opposed the diversion of the crusade, he insisted that the emperor agree to submit to papal supremacy. But the fortuitous combination of forces made the outcome inevitable: the designs of the young Alexios, Boniface of Montferrat, Philip of Swabia and the Venetians all coincided.

Niketas Choniates states that Alexios was given letters by both the pope and Philip of Swabia pleading his cause with the leaders of the crusade. Alexios provided the excuse needed to divert the Fourth Crusade. He was looked upon by the leaders as the source of large sums of money to satisfy their "greedy and money-loving temperament." Accordingly, the young Alexios "who was young in mind rather than in age" was taken in by the cunning chiefs of the crusade and persuaded to swear binding oaths. The Greek historian writes:

> Not only did the lad consent to their requests for seas of money, but he also agreed to assist them against the Saracens with heavy-armed Roman troops and fifty triremes. What was even worse and most reprehensible, he abjured his faith and embraced that of the Latins, and agreed to the innovation of the papal privileges and to the changing and altering of the ancient customs of the Romans.

Villehardouin, however, provides us with the details of this disastrous agreement:

> And after another fortnight came also the envoys from Germany; sent by King Philip and the heir of Constantinople. . . . And the envoys addressed them and said: . . . "And first, if God grant that you restore him to his inheritance, he will place the whole empire of Roumania [Byzantium] in obedience to Rome, from which it has long been separated. Further, he knows that you have spent of your substance, and that you are poor, and he will give you 200,000 marks of silver, and food for all those of the host, both small and great. And he, of his own person, will go with you into the land of Babylon, or, if you hold that that will be better, send thither 10,000 men, at his own charges. And this service he will perform for one year. And all the days of his life he will maintain, at his own charges, five hundred knights in the land overseas, to guard that land."

In Constantinople, Emperor Alexios III, who had been warned of the impending attack, took no heed and did nothing to prepare the city's defenses. Even more incredible, the *megas dux*, Michael Stryfnos, had emptied out every long ship in the Byzantine docks by selling the bolts, anchors, sails and halyards for gold and silver.

The crusaders who could not raise the required money for their passage had been persuaded earlier by the doge, Enrico Dandolo, to do some military service for the Venetians as compensation for their fare. They attacked and took Zara, on the Adriatic coast, from the king of Hungary; then the crusade set sail for Constantinople.

On June 23, 1203 the fleet docked at Chalcedon and the barons lodged in the palace of the emperor; after futile negotiations the fleet sailed for Galata, on the left bank of the Golden Horn. The tower of Galata, to which was attached the iron chain or boom which closed the Golden Horn to ships, was now taken by force and the chain was broken by a Venetian galley. There was a general assault on July 17, 1203; Villehardouin tells us that some twenty-five towers were seized by the crusaders, and in order to avoid being attacked by the imperial forces the Westerners "set fire to the buildings between them and the Greeks." Niketas Choniates, however, provides us with greater details. The Latins brought up their siege engines of the type called the ram and deployed their crossbowmen in many different positions; at one given signal they began the attack. The ram made an opening in the wall at that place called "the Gangway of the Emperor" but the Latins were thrown back after suffering many casualties at the hands of the Pisans and the Anglo-Saxons of the Varangian Guard. Thus Westerners were fighting Westerners!

The Latin ships next sailed up to the walls and cast anchor while the troops on board threw up scaling ladders; they engaged the Byzantines in the towers where, shooting their missiles from a higher vantage point, they easily routed the defenders. Having taken possession of the walls, the Latins scattered everywhere and set fire to the houses below.

Alexios III now lost his courage; after deciding to sally forth and attack the crusaders he became frightened and sounded the order for retreat. His cowardice and fear were such that in his haste to save himself he abandoned his whole family with the exception of his favorite daughter Irene; he stopped long enough, however, to gather a thousand pounds of gold and a great number of precious stones and magnificent translucent pearls. In the dead of night the wretched emperor deserted his people and rode on with his daughter to safety in Develtus.

Empress Euphrosyne and the members of her family were all arrested while the party of Isaakios II Angelos, with the help of the Varangian Guard, proclaimed him emperor. Isaakios immediately sent word to his son Alexios and the the crusader chiefs that Alexios III had fled. Without any formal overtures—the young Alexios had not yet discussed with his father the terms of the agreement he had made with the Latins—the crusader chiefs sent envoys to extract from Isaakios a promise that he would honor his son's pledge to them. The emperor was taken aback when he heard the terms realizing that they could not be effected, but he confirmed them nonetheless "by oath and by charters with gold seals appended." Several days later the crusader leaders and nobles presented themselves at the palace. Chairs were brought for them to use in the presence of the emperors (how times had changed!) while they were acclaimed "benefactors" and "saviors." They were then treated to all kinds of entertainment and delicacies.

Isaakios II now persuaded Euphrosyne to divulge the whereabouts of the imperial treasury and took what was left of it—some 100,000 marks —and gave it to the Latins in partial payment of the 200,000 marks promised to the crusaders.

Villehardouin records that Alexios IV admitted to Count Baldwin of Hainault and Flanders and to Dandolo, the doge of Venice, that the Greeks hated him and he convinced them to stay on to help consolidate his position so that he might fulfill his convenant with them. Accompanied by crusader forces Alexios IV subdued some twenty cities and forty castles, but he had to beat a retreat before the Bulgar Tsar, Ioannitza. In the meantime Isaakios had no more money with which to pay the crusaders who remained in the capital. Niketas Choniates describes what happened next:

> But since the recipients considered the sum to be but a drop (for there is no nation which loves money more than this race nor any more ravenous and anxious to run to a banquet) . . . [Isaakios] raided the sacred temples. It was a sight to behold not only the holy icons of Christ being consigned to the flames after being hacked to pieces with axes and cast down, and their adornments carelessly and unsparingly removed by force, but also the revered and all-hallowed vessels being seized from the churches with utter indifference and melted down and given over to the enemy troops as common silver and gold.

The common masses of Constantinople now retaliated by sweeping toward the houses owned by the Latins in the western section of the city facing the sea and proceeded to demolish and pull them down, making no distinction between friend or foe. Thus the Amalfitans and Pisans who had migrated to Constantinople and had even adopted Byzantine ways were made to suffer with the guilty. As a result some fifteen thousand Latins sailed over to the crusader camp and the Pisans were reconciled with their former enemies, the Venetians, in the face of the common danger.

Niketas Choniates provides us with a detailed description of the second fire ignited in the city on August 19, 1203, which proved to be so disastrous:

> certain Frenchmen . . . Pisans and Venetians, taking a company of men, sailed across the straits confident that the monies of the Saracens were a windfall and treasure-trove waiting to be taken. . . . This evil battalion, putting in the City on fishing boats . . . without warning fell upon the synagogue of the Agarenes called *Mitaton* in popular speech, and with drawn swords plundered it of its possessions. . . . the Saracens defended themselves by grabbing whatever weapon was at hand; aroused by the tumult the Romans came running to their assistance. . . . The [Latins] abandoning hope of resisting with weapons and having learned from experience the use of fire, proposed to resort to the means of the recent conflagration as the most effective defense and the quickest course of action to subdue the City.
>
> And, indeed, taking up positions in a goodly number of locations, they set fire to the buildings. The flames, rising unbelievably high above the ground throughout all that night, the next day, and the following evening, spread everywhere. . . . Porticoes collapsed, the elegant structures of the fora were overthrown, and huge columns went up in smoke like so much brushwood. . . . Indeed, all the buildings lying in the direction of the Arch of the Milion and adjoining the gallery of Makron, the structure also called "The Synods" came crashing to the ground. . . . The Porticoes of Domninos, as they are called, were also reduced to ashes as well as the two covered streets originating at the Milion and one of which extended to the Philadelphion. Together with these the Forum of Constantine and everything between the northern and southern extremities was destroyed. Nor was the Hippodrome spared. . . . At that time the majority of the City's inhabitants were stripped of their possessions as the flames reached out to those who were taken by surprise; . . . Woe's me! how great was the loss of the magnificent and most beautiful palaces, filled with every kind of delight, abounding in riches and envied by all!

Villehardouin adds:

> And the front of the fire, as it went flaming, was well over half a league broad. What was the damage then done, what the possessions and riches swallowed up, could no man tell—nor what the

number of men and women and children who perished—for many were burned!

Despite this catastrophe the major business of the emperors was to find money with which to pay off the crusaders. They attempted to levy taxes on the citizens, but "the people, like a vast and boundless sea lashed by a wind, displeased, were agitated toward insurrection." Next they plundered the rich "to appease the ravenous hunger of the Latins." Finally they were compelled to melt down the heavy gold furniture and silver lamps of Hagia Sophia as payment. The crusader chiefs proceeded to strip the churches, the imperial estates and the dwellings of the nobility along the Sea of Marmara and on the outskirts of the capital.

Alexios IV returned to Constantinople on November 11. Villehardouin says that he now began to act arrogantly towards the barons, neglecting to visit them in their camp and finally refusing to pay them the monies he owed them for their services. The envoy, Conon of Bethune, was dispatched to threaten Alexios IV and his father.

Robert of Clari records the following remarkable conversation between Enrico Dandolo and Alexios IV:

> "Wilt thou not," said the doge, "keep thy covenants with us . . . ?" "Nay," said the emperor, "I will not do any more than I have done." "No?" said the doge. "Wretched boy, we dragged thee out of the filth," said the doge, "and into the filth we will cast thee again. And I defy thee, and I give thee well to know that I will do thee all the harm in my power from this moment forward."

By insisting that the emperors empty out the treasury and by forcing them to melt down the chandeliers and consecrated liturgical vessels of the churches to make good Alexios's irresponsible promises, the crusaders only succeeded in undermining their own puppets and in making their position untenable.

The increasing unpopularity of the emperors sped them on the path to their inevitable downfall. As Isaakios lay mortally ill, the senate, the hierarchy and the judges gathered at Hagia Sophia to elect a new emperor. At this critical point Alexios Doukas (surnamed Mourtzouflos "from the fact that his eyebrows were joined together and hanging over his eyes") with the aid of the Varangian Guard moved to secure the crown for himself and save the state. As *protovestiarios* (chief official in charge of the imperial wardrobe), Mourtzouflos gained easy admittance to Alexios IV at dead of night. The Varangian Guard stormed the palace and, breaking into the emperor's bed-chamber, they put violent hands on Alexios and accused him of being an accomplice of the Latins. Forthwith Alexios was bound in chains, cast into a miserable dungeon and, finally, strangled. At the same time, Mourtzouflos assumed the imperial insignia. Alexios IV had reigned but six months and eight days.

Alexios V Doukas Mourtzouflos now undertook the defense of the capital against the Latins. He shored up the sea walls with beams, bricked up the gates along the land walls and rekindled the courage of the army with his own example. Clasping both sword and mace, the emperor led his army in repelling the sallies of the Latins in search of grain supplies.

Villehardouin makes it very clear that it was the clergy, including those who had special powers from Pope Innocent III, who called for an attack against the usurper Mourtzouflos and the Greeks, justifying such action on the grounds of religion:

> . . . the Greeks had withdrawn themselves from obedience to Rome. "Wherefore we tell you," said the clergy, "that this war is lawful and just, and that if you have a right intention in conquering this land, to bring it into Roman obedience, all those who die after confession shall have part in the indulgence granted by the Pope."

Robert of Clari says that the bishops preached throughout the crusader camp that the Greeks "were worse than Jews" and "enemies of God."

When Baldwin, Count of Flanders, ravaged the region of Philea outside the capital for provisions, Mourtzouflos rode out against him. The two forces engaged in battle, but the Byzantine troops were badly mauled by the outnumbered Latins and impetuously fled the field; the emperor was abandoned and very nearly captured. Ominously, the famous jewelled icon of the Mother of God, the Fellow-General of the Byzantine Emperors, was taken by the enemy together with the imperial standard and the emperor's helmet. To discredit Mourtzouflos the Latins raised the icon and standard high up on the mast of one of their galleys and sailed up and down before the city's walls.

Mourtzouflos was now taken in by the wily doge of Venice, Enrico Dandolo, who invited the emperor to enter into negotiations for a peaceful settlement of their differences. The doge's ship anchored off the coast near Kosmidion and Dandolo rode out on horseback to meet with the emperor. The crusader chiefs demanded the payment of 5000 pounds of gold; suddenly the Latin cavalry came bearing down on Mourtzouflos from the right. The emperor barely managed to escape imminent capture while some members of his retinue were, in fact, taken.

Preparation for the battle of Constantinople began on April 8, 1204, the Thursday after mid-Lent. On Friday at dawn, the assault commenced. The emperor, in the meantime, ordered the imperial scarlet pavilion set up on the slope of the Pantepoptes Monastery (All-Seeing Christ) from which vantage point he could observe the movements of the enemy ships. Silver trumpets and timbrels were sounded, announcing his presence to the enemy. The Venetian ships and galleys approached alongside the sea walls. Scaling ladders were thrown up but the attack was repulsed with heavy losses. The defenders hurled down pots full of boiling pitch and Greek fire on the enemy, and immense stones were discharged by mangonels positioned on the walls.

The weekend was spent in repairing and refitting the damaged ships. It was decided that the ships should be bound together two by two so that the individual towers could be attacked on both sides with greater effect.

The attack was resumed on Monday morning. Two ships, the *Paradise* and the *Pilgrim*, both owned by Latin bishops, managed to join on to a tower defended by English, Danes and Greeks and overcome it. Four other towers fell in quick succession, and three of the gates were broken in. Niketas Choniates relates that one of the Latin knights, a veritable giant of a man, nearly "nine fathoms tall," wearing a helmet fashioned in the shape of a towered city, managed to break through the Petrion Gate. When the Byzantine officials and troops standing with the emperor at his tent on the slope saw the incredible size of the Latin Goliath, they took off in sheer panic, a "thousand chased by one man"; fleeing to the Golden Gate of the land walls, they broke down the newly erected fortifications there and scattered in all directions. Alas! there was no Byzantine David to lay low the giant from the West. Constantinople, the Queen of Cities, fell to the Fourth Crusade on April 12, 1204, the Monday after Palm Sunday.

The crusader forces rushed about the city in disorganized fashion indiscriminately running through people of every age. The Latins were now responsible for the third fire which consumed large areas of the magnificent capital. The holocaust began in the eastern sections of the city and in the more distant region near the monastery of Christ Evergetes (Benefactor). The fire spread to the sloping areas near the sea and terminated in that part of the city where the Drungarian Gate was located. Villehardouin assures us that "more houses had been burned in the city than there are houses in any three of the greatest cities in the kindgom of France."

Mourtzouflos, in the meantime, was darting through the narrow streets of the gutted capital vainly trying to rally new forces to continue the resistance. But the populace was completely demoralized and overcome by despair. Unable to find troops to continue fighting, the emperor realized that he must flee to save his own life. Taking along his mother-in-law Empress Euphrosyne and his wife Eudokia, he escaped into Thrace. The vigorous but unpopular emperor had reigned for only two months and sixteen days.

The Latins designated the Monastery of Christ Pantepoptes as depot for the huge spoils taken from the captured imperial pavilion and palaces. The western historians were overwhelmed by the incredible wealth collected. Robert of Clari describes the scene in the following terms:

> And it was so rich, and there were so many rich vessels of gold and silver and cloth of gold and so many rich jewels, that it was a fair marvel, the great wealth that was brought there. Not since the world was made, was there ever seen or won so great a treasure or so noble or so rich, not in the time of Alexander nor in the time of Charlemagne nor before nor after. Nor do I think, myself, that in the forty richest cities of the world there had been so much wealth as was found in Constantinople. For the Greeks say that two-thirds of the wealth of this world is in Constantinople and the other third scattered throughout the world.

Villehardouin complements this picture with his own wonderment:

> The booty gained was so great that none could tell you the end of it: gold and silver, the vessels and precious stones, and samite and cloth of silk, and robes vair and grey, and ermine, and every choicest thing found upon the earth. And well does Geoffrey of Villehardouin, the Marshal of Champagne, bear witness, that never, since the world was created, had so much booty been won in any

city. . . . That which was brought to the churches was collected together and divided, in equal parts, between the Franks and the Venetians. . . . After the division had been made, [the pilgrims] paid out of their share fifty thousand marks of silver to the Venetians, and they divided at least one hundred thousand marks among themselves. . . . If it had not been for what was stolen, and for the part given to the Venetians, there would have been at least four hundred thousand marks of silver, and at least ten thousand horses.

With the flight of Alexios V Doukas Mourtzouflos two young and sober men, Constantine Doukas and Constantine Laskaris, came to the fore to vie for the abandoned crown of Byzantium. The choice was made by lot in Hagia Sophia. Although Constantine Laskaris was elected he was not officially crowned emperor and did not, therefore, assume the insignia of the imperial office. He tried to cajole everyone to put up a firm resistance, but no one, not even the Varangian Guard, responded to his pleas. It was too late! Frankish knights in armor appeared on the scene and everyone ran for his life. There was no one left to obstruct the passage of the knights. The city had capitulated and was lying still to be taken. The inhabitants lined up in the streets holding crosses and holy icons of Christ in their hands in the hope that the hearts of the conquerors would soften; but the enemy gave no sign of compassion. The Latins proceeded to plunder with impunity; they began by looting the carts of those who were now homeless. In poignant words Niketas Choniates describes the incredible calamity that had befallen the city of Constantine:

What then should I recount first and what last of those things dared at that time by these murderous men? O, the shameful dashing to earth of the venerable icons and the flinging of the relics of the saints who suffered for Christ's sake into defiled places! How horrible it was to see the divine body and blood of Christ poured out and thrown to the ground! These forerunners of antichrist and chief agents and harbingers of his anticipated ungodly deeds, seizing as plunder the precious chalices and patens, some they smashed, taking possession of the ornaments embellishing them while they set the remaining vessels on their tables to serve as bread dishes and wine goblets. . . .

   . . . The table of sacrifice, fashioned from every kind of precious material and fused by fire into one whole and blended together into a perfection of one multi-colored thing of beauty, truly extraordinary and admired by all nations, was broken into pieces and divided among the despoilers, as was the case with all the sacred church treasures, countless in number and unsurpassed in beauty.

Robert of Clari describes the holy altar of Hagia Sophia as being "fully fourteen feet long." He says that "around the altar were columns of silver supporting a canopy over the altar which was made just like a church spire, and it was all of solid silver and so rich that no one could tell the money it was worth." He also informs us that there were some one hundred chandeliers in the church and that the silver chains holding them suspended were as thick as a man's arm. In each chandelier there were twenty-five or more lamps so that each chandelier was worth at least two hundred marks of silver.

Niketas Choniates continues:

They found it fitting to bring out, as so much booty, the all-hallowed vessels and furnishings which had been wrought with incomparable elegance and craftsmanship and of rare materials; in addition, to remove the pure silver which overlay the railing of the *bema* [sanctuary], the wondrous pulpit and the gates, as well as that which covered a great many other adornments all of which were gold-plated, they led to the very sanctuary of the temple itself, mules and asses with packsaddles; some of these, unable to stand on their feet on the smoothly polished marble floors, slipped and were pierced by knives so that the excrement from the bowels and the spilt blood defiled the sacred floor. Moreover, a certain silly woman laden with sins, an attendant of the Erinyes [Furies], the handmaid of demons, the workshop of unspeakable spells and reprehensible charms, waxing wanton against Christ, sitting on the *synthronon* [patriarchal throne], intoned a song, and, whirling about, she kicked up her heels in dance.

Not long afterwards the Latins also demolished the magnificent icon-screen of Hagia Sophia "valued in tens of thousands of minas of silver, all of the purest content, and heavily plated in gold." The tombs of the deceased emperors in the Church of the Holy Apostles were also violated and plundered of their gold ornaments and precious pearls. Nor did the barbarians spare the pious maidens and nuns dedicated to God and vowed to chastity:

> there were lamentations and cries of woe and weeping in the narrow ways, wailing at the crossroads, moaning in the temples, outcries of men, screams of women, the taking of captives, and the dragging about, tearing in pieces, and raping of bodies heretofore sound and whole. They who were bashful of their sex were led about naked, and they who were venerable in their old age uttered plaintive cries, and the wealthy were despoiled of their riches. Thus it was in the squares, thus it was on the corners, thus it was in the temples, thus it was in the hiding places; for there was no place that could escape detection or that could offer asylum to those who came streaming in.
>
> O Christ, basileus, what tribulation and distress of men at that time! The roaring of the sea, the darkening and dimming of the sun, the turning of the moon into blood, the displacement of the stars —did they not foretell in this way the last evils? . . .
>
> Such then, to make a long story short, were the outrageous crimes committed by the Western armies against the inheritance of Christ. Without showing any feelings of humanity whatsoever, they exacted from all their money and chattel, dwellings and clothing, leaving to them nothing of all their goods. Thus behaved the brazen-necked, the haughty spirit, the highbrow, the ever-shaved and youthful cheek, the bloodthirsty right hand, the wrathful nostril, the disdainful eye, the insatiable jaw, the hateful heart, the piercing and running speech practically dancing over the lips; more to blame were the learned and wise men among them, they who were faithful to their oaths and loved the truth and hated evil and were both more pious and just and scrupulous in keeping the commandments of Christ than we "Greeks"; even more culpable were those who had raised the cross to their shoulders and had time and again sworn by it and the sayings of the Lord to cross over Christian lands without bloodletting, turning aside neither to the right nor inclining to the left, and to take up arms against the Saracens and to stain red their swords in their blood, they who had sacked Jerusalem, and had taken an oath not to marry or to have sexual intercourse with women as long as they carried the cross on their shoulders and were consecrated to God and commissioned to follow in his footsteps.
>
> In truth, they were exposed as frauds, and, seeking to avenge

the Holy Sepulcher, they raged openly against Christ and sinned by overturning the cross with the cross they bore on their backs, not even shuddering to trample on it for the sake of a little gold and silver. By grasping pearls they rejected Christ, the pearl of great price, scattering among the most accursed of brutes the All-Hallowed One. The sons of Ismael did not behave in this way, for when the Latins overpowered Sion they showed no compassion or kindness to their own compatriots. Neither did the Ismaelites neigh after Latin women, nor did they turn the cenotaph of Christ into a common burialplace of the fallen, nor did they transform the entranceway into the Life-bringing Tomb into a passageway leading down into Hades, nor did they replace the resurrection with the fall; allowing everyone to depart in exchange for the payment of a few gold coins, they took only the ransom money and left to them all their other possessions even though these numbered more than the grains of sand. Thus, magnanimously did the enemies of Christ deal with the Latin infidels, inflicting upon them neither sword, nor fire, nor hunger, nor persecution, nor nakedness, nor bruises, nor constraints. How differently, as we have briefly recounted, the Latins treated us who love Christ and are their fellow believers, being guiltless of any wrong against them.

O City, City, eye of all cities, universal boast, supramundane wonder, wet nurse of churches, leader of the faith, guide of Orthodoxy, beloved topic of orations, the abode of every good thing! O City, that hast drunk at the hand of the Lord the cup of his fury! . . .

O prolific City, once garbed in royal silk and purple, and now filthy and squalid and heir to many evils, having need of true children! O City, formerly enthroned on high, striding far and wide, magnificent in comeliness and more becoming in stature, and now thy luxurious garments and elegant and royal veils are rent and torn; thy flashing eye has grown dark, and thou art like unto an aged furnace-woman all covered with soot, and thy formerly glistening and delightful countenance is now furrowed by loose wrinkles.

THE TRAGIC LOSS OF RELICS AND ART TREASURES

Throughout the centuries, Constantinople had become the chief repository of the major relics of Christianity; most of the instruments of the Lord's Passion eventually reached the imperial capital where they were preserved and exhibited on special days to strengthen and inspire the devotion of the pious. In this regard, again, there was no other city in the Christian world that could vie with the Queen of Cities. The tragedy of the fall of Constantinople to the Fourth Crusade resulted in either the total loss or dispersal of these cherished relics throughout the West. One can only try to imagine the terrible frustration experienced by the inhabitants of Byzantium as a result of the wholesale theft of these precious relics.

During the reign of Heraclius the Holy Cross, the Holy Sponge and the Holy Lance were brought to Constantinople as a result of the Persian invasions. Later, the Byzantine *capella palatina*, the Church of the Theotokos of Pharos, completed in the reign of Michael III (842–867), eventually became the foremost repository of the relics of Christ and the Virgin Mary.

In 944 the famous Mandylion (towel which was believed to have the features of Christ imprinted thereon miraculously for the benefit of King Abgar of Edessa) was brought to Constantinople from Edessa. In 968 the tile, which had taken on the features of Christ when the Mandylion was hidden under it, reached the capital. In 1032 a letter, written by Christ's own hand to King Abgar, arrived completing this set of relics. Robert of Clari speaks of the "two rich vessels of gold hanging in the midst of the chapel by two heavy silver chains. In one of these vessels was a tile and in the other a cloth." In this same Church of the Theotokos of Pharos, Robert of Clari also saw "two pieces of the true Cross as large as the leg of a man and as long as half a toise [fathom]." He also saw "the iron of the lance" which had pierced the Lord's right side, and "two nails which were driven through His hands and feet." Besides these he observed "in a crystal phial quite a little of His blood," and the tunic worn by Christ and taken from Him when He was led away to be crucified. Here too was "the blessed crown with which He was crowned, and which was made of reeds of thorns as sharp as points of daggers." Emperor Manuel I Komnenos had also deposited here the stone slab on which the corpse of Christ had been laid when taken down from the Cross; it had been brought to Constantinople from Ephesus and later was placed in the Church of Christ Pantokrator in which Manuel I was sepulchred. Robert of Clari states that one could still see the tears of the Blessed Mother which had fallen upon it.

In the Church of the Theotokos of Pharos was also kept the purple fragment from the robe of the Virgin. Here too were stored the *Sou-*

darion, the famous napkin of St. Veronica with the Lord's true image, and the Sindon or grave cloths made of linen in which Jesus's corpse was wrapped for entombment. The *maphorion*, the veil or hood of the Virgin, and her girdle (zoné) were also favorite relics among the pious of Byzantium. Besides these the Greek historian Mesarites cites the reed used to quench the Lord's thirst on the Cross, the slab of stone with Christ's footprints, and the iron chain of flagellation. Robert of Clari saw in the Church of the Holy Apostles the "marble column to which Our Lord was bound, before He was put on the cross."

Besides being the repository of Christian relics, Constantinople was also the greatest museum of classical statuary in the world. The wanton destruction of the masterpieces of antiquity by the ignorant and avaricious participants of the Fourth Crusade was an unforgivable crime not only against the Byzantines but also against all mankind. And why did the Latins melt down the irreplaceable great works of art? They used the copper to mint coinage!

The bronze statue of Hera which stood in the Agora of Constantine, the figure of Paris Alexander handing to Aphrodite the golden apple of discord, the remarkable Anemodoulion (wind-servant), a bronze mechanism at whose lofty pinnacle a female figure revolved in the direction of the prevailing wind, Bellerophon mounted on Pegasus, the magnificent bronze statues of men and women and of animals of every kind decorating the stands of the hippodrome, the huge seated Herakles dressed in his lion-skin, the statues depicting the ass Nikandros and ass-driver Nikon commissioned by Augustus because their names portended his forthcoming victory over Marc Antony, the famous statue of the she-wolf suckling Romulus and Remus, representations of a man wrestling with a lion, a crocodile, an elephant waving its trunk, sphinxes, Scylla represented as a huge-breasted female, the renowned bronze eagle clutching a serpent in its claws, allegedly set up by Apollonius of Tyana to ward off a plague of snakes in Byzantium and whose wings were marked off by twelve hour-long segments to be used as a sun-dial, the delightful figure of Helen of Troy who "though fashioned of bronze . . . appeared as fresh as the morning dew," the representation of a young woman holding in the palm of her hand a man on horseback, the statues raised in honor of victorious charioteers, and finally the excellent statuary depicting the life and death struggle between a bull and a crocodile—were all cast into the smelting furnace.

We can be grateful to the Venetians, however, for not wantonly destroying their share of the immense booty as did the crude Normans and Franks who were interested only in profit. They transported the precious art treasures that fell into their hands back to Venice to adorn their Republic. Today one can still see and marvel at the superb crafts-manship of Byzantine artists who fashioned the exquisite chalices and handsome reliquaries displayed in the Treasury of San Marco. The many pieces of Byzantine cloisonné enamels, embellishing the elegant retable of San Marco's high altar, are works of unsurpassable beauty. Above the entrance of the Cathedral of San Marco, copied after the Byzantine Church of the Holy Apostles in Constantinople, the mag-nificent *Quadriga*, the four bronze chariot horses, proudly prance, reminding the spectator of the lost glories of the Queen of Cities. The treasures which flowed into *Venetia aurea* from Constantinople made that city virtually another Byzantium.

The Byzantines, who were so fond of prophecies and omens, were to witness an act of such barbarity that it seemed to recapitulate dra-matically the disastrous events of 1204. Alexios V Doukas Mourtzouflos met the fleeing Alexios III Angelos in Mosynopolis and entered into an alliance with his father-in-law; invited to dinner, the unsuspecting Mourtzouflos was suddenly seized and senselessly blinded. Later the wretched man was captured by the western knight Thierri of Loos and brought to Constantinople to be tried according to feudal law by a Latin court. Accused of having strangled his lord, Alexios IV Angelos, Mourtzouflos defended himself by saying that his victim was justly punished as a traitor to the empire. Condemned by the Latins to die on the grounds of perfidy, it was left to the imaginative doge of Venice, Enrico Dandolo, to suggest a fitting execution "for a high man high justice." The doomed former emperor was carried up to the top of the lofty column of Theodosius the Great, standing in the Forum of the Bull, and was cruelly pushed off. Robert of Clari records that in the carvings decorating the column of Theodosius there was depicted the figure of an emperor falling headlong and that the gruesome death of Mourtzouflos was the fulfillment of this prophecy.

EPILOGUE

The Latin Empire of Constantinople which replaced the Byzantine state in 1204 lasted only until 1261 when Michael VIII Palaiologos regained control of the capital and reestablished Greek rule over a greatly diminished empire. Indeed, Byzantium was only a shadow of its former self, reduced to but one of several Balkan states. At the same time, the Latins were not ousted from continental Greece and the islands. Venetians and Genoese, in fact, were to compete for the profits of Byzantine commerce, further crippling imperial attempts to make what was left of Byzantium a viable state.

Faced by a coalition of the Bulgar tsar, Serbian king and the Latin Prince of Achaia under the leadership of Charles of Anjou, who was determined to take Constantinople by assault, Emperor Michael VIII, pitched on the horns of a dilemma, decided to extricate himself by compelling the Byzantine hierarchy to submit to the church of Rome. Once again, political exigency dictated ecclesiastical policy. The union of the Latin and Greek churches was achieved at the Council of Lyons in 1274. The papal victory was complete; the Byzantine legation recognized everything that was anathema to Greek Orthodox Christians: the filioque, the azyma, and the supreme authority of the pope of Rome. The orthodox national party of Byzantium, as was to be expected, damned the Council of Lyons as a betrayal. Nonetheless Michael VIII had achieved his purpose; the imminent attack of Charles of Anjou was called off at the insistence of the papacy. This political victory, however, resulted in a disastrous schism within Byzantium between the *philenotikoi* (friends of union), the unionists who were willing to sacrifice the Greek church for political survival, and the *anthenotikoi* (anti-unionists) who refused to jeopardise their souls for the sake of the body politic. The Byzantine historian Pachymeres (1242–1310) describes the consequences of the Union of Lyons: "The church schism had reached such a point that it separates the dwellers of one house: father is opposed to son, mother to daughter, sister-in-law to mother-in-law." When Byzantine Christians began to suspect and despise one another because of pro-Latin and anti-Latin sentiments, the spiritual foundations of both church and state began visibly to crack. These two hostile factions were to remain active until the eve of the fall of Constantinople to the Ottoman Turks in 1453.

In 1281 Pope Martin IV (1281–1285) decided to reverse his predecessor's policy and to support Charles of Anjou's designs against Byzantium by excommunicating Michael VIII, the very emperor who was responsible for the submission of the Greek hierarchy to Rome. Andronikos II Palaiologos (1282–1328), who succeeded his father in 1282, publicly renounced Michael VIII's ecclesiastical policy and restored orthodoxy. Eight years after its signing, the Union of Lyons was torpedoed by both Latin pope and Byzantine emperor.

By November of 1354 when John V Palaiologos (1341–1391) had decisively defeated his rival for the throne, John VI Kantakouzenos (1347–1354), he found himself emperor of a tottering empire. Kantakouzenos's son Matthew continued the civil war; Stephen Dushan of Serbia, penetrating into Greece, assumed the title "Emperor of the Serbs and the Greeks" and was contemplating an attack on Constantinople itself; on March 2, 1354 the Ottoman Suleiman captured Gallipoli on the continent, thereby outflanking the capital. It seemed that Constantinople must inevitably fall. In the desperate hope of receiving military assistance from the West, John V made overtures to Rome for the union of the two churches. In an imperial chrysobul the emperor offered the submission of the Greek church in return for military aid. With adequate western troops at his command, he guaranteed the return of the Greeks to the Latin fold "by force" if necessary. In October of 1369, Emperor John V Palaiologos travelled to Rome, and in the Cathedral of St. Peter he solemnly read aloud the Latin confession of faith, accepted the filioque and recognized Pope Urban V (1362–1370) as the head of all Christians. But no significant help was forthcoming. The emperor had compromised himself vis-à-vis his own orthodox subjects in vain! Both emperor and pope had based their commitments on false assumptions. The emperor mistakenly thought that the pope was strong enough to force the princes of the West to send adequate troops to save the Byzantine state while the papacy believed that a converted basileus could compel the Greek church to submit to Rome.

In the meantime, Byzantium was caught in the economic vise of Genoa and Venice; like parasites they devoured the body on which they were fattened. The Genoese refused to allow the Byzantine government to refit the imperial navy and burned down the Byzantine merchantmen under construction. With anguish the Byzantine historian Nikephoros Gregoras (1295–1359) writes: "The Latins have taken possession not only of all the wealth of Byzantium and almost all the revenues from the sea, but also of all resources that replenish the sovereign's treasury."

Not only was the Byzantine government deprived of needed customs duties but as the remaining state lands were feudalized and all authority was decentralized the land tax could no longer be collected. The economic basis of the Byzantine empire had collapsed. Heavy bribes paid to Serbs and Ottoman Turks further exhausted the imperial treasury. By necessity fortresses and armaments were pared away and the army was reduced—a measure which only invited invasion and piracy. Unable to recruit a native army the emperors were compelled to hire foreign mercenary troops, who lived off the country they had been paid to protect, looting and laying waste everything before them.

The advance of the Ottoman Turks could not be stayed. They seized the last Byzantine possessions in Anatolia and occupied European Thrace. On June 15, 1389 at Kossovo, the "plain of the blackbirds," the Serbian kingdom was crushed by the Ottomans, and by 1393 the Bulgarian kingdom of Tirnovo was extinguished. In 1394 the Sultan Bayezid (1389–1402) invaded the Peloponnesus and reduced the local princes to vassaldom. Both Hungary and the Latin principalities in Greece finally realized the seriousness of the threat to their own safety posed by the Turks. A new crusade was called for by Sigismund of Hungary who was joined by the French, but when the Turkish forces were engaged at Nikopolis on September 25, 1396, the disorganized western armies were routed. The fall of Constantinople seemed imminent. But at this crucial juncture in history, the unexpected and dramatic happened. Timur, or Tamurlane, descended from the female line of the Mongol clan of Jenghiz Khan, invaded Anatolia and destroyed the forces of the Ottoman Turks at Ankara on July 25, 1402. The Byzantine state was given a breathing space of some fifty years after which, however, the Ottomans fully recovered and completed their plans of conquest. Had the European powers acted swiftly and in concert, they could have broken the Ottoman power, but the Turkish problem would have remained nonetheless.

In 1430, the Ottoman Sultan Murad II (1421–1444; 1446–1451) took Yannina in Epirus and captured Thessalonica from the Venetians who had held that city since 1423. Constantinople was an island surrounded by an Ottoman sea. In desperation, Emperor John VIII Palaiologos (1425–1448) negotiated a new Union of Churches at the Council of Ferrara-Florence in 1439. He too was willing to subject the Greek church to Rome if it meant securing western troops to fight the infidel. His father, Manuel II Palaiologos (1391–1425), who understood better the psychology of his orthodox subjects, had strongly counseled his son from ever contemplating such a measure. Ignoring this very sound advice, John VIII led a mission to Italy in person. The greek Metropolitan of Ephesos, Mark Evgenikos, a hesychast, refused to submit to imperial pressure but the other orthodox bishops were persuaded to sign a new article of union. The Byzantine historian Doukas claims that several were bribed to do so: "For there were some of the hier-archs who were saying in the act of signing 'we will not sign, unless you give us sufficient revenue.' They gave and the pen was dipped." Papal supremacy was accepted by the Greek bishops but the Greek church was allowed to retain its own distinctive ritual. The pope, however, was to decide all controversial questions.

The Union of 1439 proved to be a tragic error. The Greek Orthodox monks and populace protested with passionate fanaticism damning and rejecting the perfidious Act of Union subscribed to by emperor and hierarchy. At least Michael VIII's Union of 1274 had the practical result of staving off the impending invasion of Charles of Anjou, but the Union of 1439 was predicated on western military help against the Turks and the pope was in no position to bring this about.

In 1444 at Varna, on the western shore of the Black Sea, the com-bined forces of King Vladislav III (Ladislas) of Hungary-Poland were cut to pieces by Murad's Ottoman troops who outnumbered the Latins three to one. Vladislav and Cardinal Cesarini, the main instigator of the crusade, were both killed and with them perished the last attempt of the Latin West to stop the Turks before the fall of Constantinople in 1453.

In the meantime, the Union of Ferrara-Florence in 1439 only pre-cipitated internal dissensions within Byzantium at the very moment the doomed nation needed solidarity of purpose. The breach between unionists and anti-unionists became wider than ever. Five months before the end, the last emperor of the Byzantine empire, Constantine XI Palaiologos (1449–1453), confirmed the union of the churches by consenting to hold a combined divine liturgy in Hagia Sophia on December 12, 1452; both Italian and Greek prelates participated and the names of Pope Nicholas V (1447–1455) and of Patriarch Gregory III, exiled since 1450, were commemorated in the diptychs. The anti-unionists were outraged and flocked to the Monastery of the Panto-krator to seek the counsel of the venerable George Scholarios Gen-nadios, who became patriarch of Constantinople after the Fall. Taking pen in hand he wrote down his opinion on a piece of paper and nailed it to the door of his cell. It read:

> Wretched Romans, how you have been deceived! Trusting in the might of the Franks you have removed yourselves from the hope of God. Together with the City which will soon be destroyed, you have lost your piety. Be Thou merciful to me, O Lord. I give wit-

ness before Thee that I am innocent of this offense. Know, O wretched citizens, what you do! Captivity is about to befall you because you have lost the piety handed down to you by your fathers and you have confessed your impiety. Woe unto you in the judgment.

The orthodox party of monks, nuns, clergy and populace anathematized anew the article of union. "We have need neither of the help nor of the union of the Latins; far from us the worship of the azymites!" they cried out. Those Greek clerics who had participated in the liturgy of union of December 12, 1452 were damned as being polluted; "they are not Christians," contended the anti-unionists, and they refused to enter Hagia Sophia, considering the great church to be defiled, "a refuge of demons and a pagan altar . . . and a synagogue of Jews." The sacraments of the guilty Greek clerics were deemed invalid and whoever communicated from their hands were told that they were receiving only common bread and wine and not the body and blood of Christ.

The megas dux, Loukas Notaras, declared: "It is better to see the turban of the Turks reigning in the middle of the city than the Latin tiara." The Byzantines never forgot the catastrophe of 1204 and the atrocities of the Fourth Crusade. Thus the religious question was still burning on the lips of the Byzantines at the very moment that the political life of their state was about to go under. It was this devotion to Byzantine Christianity, in fact, that enabled the Greeks to survive four hundred years of Ottoman domination and finally, after centuries of enslavement, to create a free Greek nation.

When the end came on Tuesday, May 29, 1453 the imperial city was defended by only seven thousand troops, five thousand Greeks and two thousand westerners, Spaniards, Venetians and primarily Genoese. The enterprising young Ottoman sultan, Mehemet II (1444–1446; 1451–1481), was obsessed by the idea of taking Constantinople. Hiring a renegade Hungarian engineer by the name of Urban, he commissioned him to construct a huge cannon with a caliber of over three feet and a range of about a mile. Mehemet's army numbered some eighty thousand regulars and a horde of irregulars. The indomitable Janissaries, the converted sons of Christian parents, attacked in one wave after another. Two events doomed the city: a small sally-port known as the Kerkoporta at the corner of the Blachernae wall was left open by accident and some fifty Turks got inside. Then just before sunrise lead shot pierced the breastplate of the Genoese commander,

John Giustiniani, and he bled profusely. The emperor pleaded with him to stay at his post but Giustiniani lost his nerve; when his Genoese troops saw their chief being carried away to the ships, they rushed through the little gate abandoning the emperor and the Greek troops in the field. Constantine XI rushed to the Kerkoporta but it was too late; the Turks had taken the tower and were pouring through. The emperor fought till the very end. Doukas describes the painful scene:

> The emperor, despairing and hopeless, stood with sword and shield in hand and poignantly cried out, "Is there no one among the Christians who will take my head from me?" He was abandoned and alone. Then one of the Turks wounded him by striking him flush, and he, in turn, gave the Turk a blow. A second Turk delivered a mortal blow from behind and the emperor fell to the earth. They slew him as a common soldier and left him because they did not know he was the emperor.

Afterwards Mehemet was brought the emperor's head which was identified and then nailed to the Column of Augustus until evening. Doukas writes that "having the skin peeled off and stuffed with straw, Mehemet sent it everywhere, exhibiting the symbol of triumph to the leader of the Persians and to the ruler of the Arabs and to all the other Turks." Byzantium, which took so long in dying, had finally expired.

We shall never know the full extent of the loss to Western civilization that resulted from the disasters of 1204 and 1453. It is impossible to calculate the countless numbers of works of art, icons, mosaics, frescoes, church vessels and furniture, as well as secular *objets d'art* such as jewelry, ivories and precious fabrics which were destroyed. Moreover, the wholesale destruction of manuscripts on both occasions resulted in the loss of many priceless classical Greek, Hellenistic and Byzantine literary works which can never be recovered, studied and enjoyed as mankind's heritage. Yet some good can come out of evil circumstances. The precious and exquisite articles of Byzantine craftsmanship were scattered throughout the West profoundly influencing the techniques and styles of European artists and artisans. Silk manufacture, embroidery, glass-making, carved ivories, cloisonné enamel work, new Hellenistic and humanistic trends in religious art—all paved the way for the coming Renaissance.

To the last, Constantinople remained a center of an ardent intellectual and artistic culture. Three great Byzantine humanists travelled to the West before the destruction of 1453 and taught at major university centers contributing much to the tremendous intellectual fermentation taking place in Italy. Manuel Chrysoloras (died 1415) renewed the classical tradition in Italy by occupying a chair at the University of Florence for several years. George Gemistos Plethon (died ca. 1450) from Mistra, at the invitation of Cosimo de Medici, came to Florence where he initiated the Platonic Academy and regenerated Platonic philosophy in western Europe. Bessarion of Nicaea (died 1472), "the best Greek of the Latins and the best Latin of the Greeks," was made a cardinal of the Roman Church, and his house at Rome became a center of humanistic intercourse.

Italians also travelled to Constantinople to learn Greek and to study Greek authors. Many returned home in the possession of precious Greek manuscripts. The Sicilian, Giovanni Aurispa (died 1459), for example, amassed a library of some two hundred forty Greek manuscripts, among them rarities which are now wholly priceless. Had it not been for this indefatigable "patron saint of all bookworms" the works of Aeschylus, Plato and Plutarch may have been lost to us forever since he brought to Venice the only texts extant. In this way too, the works of the Greek fathers also found their way into the West. After the fall of Constantinople to the Turks, Doukas records that countless books were loaded up on wagons and sold throughout the East and the West. One gold coin purchased as many as ten books among which were the works of Aristotle, Plato and the Greek church fathers.

Thus Byzantium, the preserver of the miracle of classical antiquity and the creator of its own unique culture and civilization where the Christian life was lived in the most beautiful manner, continued to imbue the West and to inspire the East, even after its political demise.

It is customary at the death of a beloved and renowned parent to deliver a eulogy. With poetic anguish the historian Doukas apostrophises the fallen city of Constantine:

And the City was desolate, lying dead, naked, soundless, having neither form nor beauty.

O City, City, head of all cities! O City, City, the center of the four corners of the earth! O City, City, the boast of Christians and the ruin of barbarians! O City, City, a second Paradise planted in the West and containing within many plants, laden with spiritual fruits.

Where is your beauty, O Paradise? Where is the beneficent vigor of your spiritual graces which infuse both soul and body? Where are the bodies of the Apostles of my Lord which long ago were planted in the evergreen Paradise? Among them were the purple cloak, the lance, the sponge, the reed; when we kissed these, we imagined that we were seeing Him Who was raised on the Cross. Where are the relics of the saints and of the martyrs? Where are the remains of Constantine the great and of the other emperors? The highways, the courtyards, the crossroads, the fields, the enclosures of vineyards, all abounding with the relics of saints and with the remains of nobles, the chaste, and monks and nuns! O, the loss! . . .

O temple! O terrestrial heaven! O celestial altar! O sacred and holy shrines! O commandments, old and new! O tablets inscribed by the finger of God! O Gospels spoken by the mouth of God! O divine discourses of flesh-bearing angels! O doctrines of spirit-bearing men! O precepts of demigods and heroes! O body politic! O citizenry! O army once beyond number and now vanished like a sinking ship at sea! O dwellings and palaces of every kind and sacred walls! This day I convoke you all and as animate beings I mourn with you having Jeremias for the choral leader of this pitiful tragedy.

Appendix

CHRONOLOGICAL LIST OF COUNCILS

Ecumenical Councils

I	Nicaea (325)
II	Constantinople (381)
III	Ephesus (431)
IV	Chalcedon (451)
V	Constantinople (553)
VI	Constantinople (680–1)
	In Trullo (Quinisextum) (692)
VII	Nicaea (787)

Councils of Union

Lyons (1274)
Ferrara-Florence (1438–9)

BYZANTINE EMPERORS

324–337	Constantine I
337–361	Constantius
361–363	Julian
363–364	Jovian
364–378	Valens
379–395	Theodosius I
395–408	Arkadios
408–450	Theodosius II
450–457	Marcian
457–474	Leo I

474	Leo II
474–475	Zeno
475–476	Basiliskos
476–491	Zeno (again)
491–518	Anastasius I
518–527	Justin I
527–565	Justinian I
565–578	Justin II
578–582	Tiberius I Constantine
582–602	Maurice
602–610	Phokas
610–641	Heraclius
641	Constantine III and Heraklonas
641	Heraklonas
641–668	Constans II
668–685	Constantine IV
685–695	Justinian II
695–698	Leontios
698–705	Tiberius II
705–711	Justinian II (again)
711–713	Phillipikos
713–715	Anastasius II
715–717	Theodosius III
717–741	Leo III
741–775	Constantine V
775–780	Leo IV
780–797	Constantine VI
797–802	Irene
802–811	Nikephoros I
811	Stavrakios
811–813	Michael I Rhangabe
813–820	Leo V
820–829	Michael II
829–842	Theophilus
842–867	Michael III
867–886	Basil I
886–912	Leo VI
912–913	Alexander
913–959	Constantine VII
920–944	Romanos I Lekapenos

959–963	Romanos II
963–969	Nikephoros II Phokas
969–976	John I Tzimiskes
976–1025	Basil II
1025–1028	Constantine VIII
1028–1034	Romanos III Argyros
1034–1041	Michael IV
1041–1042	Michael V
1042	Zoe and Theodora
1042–1055	Constantine IX Monomachos
1055–1056	Theodora (again)
1056–1057	Michael VI
1057–1059	Isaakios I Komnenos
1059–1067	Constantine X Doukas
1068–1071	Romanos IV Diogenes
1071–1078	Michael VII Doukas
1078–1081	Nikephoros III Botaneiates
1081–1118	Alexios I Komnenos
1118–1143	John II Komnenos
1143–1180	Manuel I Komnenos
1180–1183	Alexios II Komnenos
1183–1185	Andronikos I Komnenos
1185–1195	Isaakios II Angelos
1195–1203	Alexios III Angelos
1203–1204	Isaakios II (again) and Alexios IV Angeloi
1204	Alexios V Mourtzouflos
1204–1222	Theodore I Laskaris
1222–1254	John III Doukas Vatatzes
1254–1258	Theodore II Laskaris
1258–1261	John IV Laskaris
1259–1282	Michael VIII Palaiologos
1282–1328	Andronikos II Palaiologos
1328–1341	Andronikos III Palaiologos
1341–1391	John V Palaiologos
1347–1354	John VI Kantakouzenos
1376–1379	Andronikos IV Palaiologos
1390	John VII Palaiologos
1391–1425	Manuel II Palaiologos
1425–1448	John VIII Palaiologos
1449–1453	Constantine XI Palaiologos

Glossary of Greek Terms

Acheiropoietai	Icons produced mechanically or by means other than human.
Azyma	The unleavened wafers used by the Latins in Holy Communion.
Basileus	Emperor.
Christotokos	She who gave birth to Christ.
Enzyma	The leavened bread used by the Greek Church in Holy Communion.
Hagia Sophia	The Church of the Holy Wisdom who is Christ. Rebuilt by Justinian I. Often referred to as St. Sophia.
Homoióusion	The term meaning that Christ is of like essence or substance with the Father.
Homoousion	The term meaning that Christ is of the very same essence or substance as the Father.
Hypostasis	The essence or substance of the Godhead.
Logos	God the Son, the Second Person of the Holy Trinity, the Word.
Megas Dux	Grand Admiral.
Ousia	The same as hypostasis. In man the essence which gives him life and being.
Physis	The nature of every being which makes it distinctive.
Proskynesis	The physical act of prostration before emperor or icon. The act of venerating the saint depicted in an icon.
Prosopon	Every being has an undivided external appearance called a prosopon. The Persons of the Holy Trinity.
Strategos	The military governor in charge of a province.
Theme	Military province governed by a strategos.
Theosis	Deification. The destiny of man is to become one with God.
Theotokos	She who gave birth to God.

Bibliography

Alexander, P. J. *The Patriarch Nicephorus of Constantinople: Ecclesiastical Policy and Image Worship in the Byzantine Empire.* Oxford, 1958.

The Alexiad of the Princess Anna Comnena, translated by Elizabeth A. S Dawes. London, 1928; reprinted in 1967. Translated by E. R. A. Sewter. Harmondsworth: Penguin Books, 1969.

Alfoldi, A. *The Conversion of Constantine and Pagan Rome,* translated by H. Mattingly. Oxford, 1948.

Anastasius Sinaites. Migne, *Patrologia Graeca.* Vol. 89, cols. 35–1180.

Atiya, A. D. *The Crusade of Nicopolis.* London, 1934.

———. *The Crusades in the Later Middle Ages.* London, 1938.

Audollent, A. *Defixionum Tabellae.* Paris, 1914.

Barker, E. *Social and Political Thought in Byzantium from Justinian I to the Last Paleologus.* Oxford, 1957.

Barlaam. Migne, *Patrologia Graeca.* Vol. 151, cols. 1249–1364.

Basil. *Ad adolescentes quomodo ex gentilium libris possint fructum capere.* Migne, *Patrologia Graeca.* Vol. 31.

Baynes, N. H. *Byzantine Studies and Other Essays.* London, 1955.

Beck, H. G. *Kirche und theologische Literatur im byzantinischen Reich.* Munich, 1959.

Bessarion. Migne, *Patrologia Graeca.* Vol. 161, cols. 11–745.

Brand, Charles M. *Byzantium Confronts the West 1180–1204.* Cambridge, Mass.: Harvard University Press, 1968.

Buckler, G. G. *Anna Comnena.* Oxford, 1929.

Bury, J. B. *History of the Eastern Roman Empire from the Fall of Irene to the Accession of Basil I (802–867).* London, 1912.

———. *History of the Later Roman Empire from Arcadius to Irene (395–800).* 2 vols. London, 1889. New edition: (395–565), 2 vols. London, 1923.

The Cambridge Medieval History, Vol. IV, Parts I and II, edited by J. M. Hussey, Cambridge University Press, 1966, 1967.

Charanis, P. *Church and State in the Later Roman Empire. The Religious Policy of Anastasius the First, 419–519.* Madison, 1939.

Choniates, Niketas. *Historia,* edited by I. Bekker, *Corpus scriptorum historiae byzantinae.* Bonn, 1835. Edited by Jan-Louis van Dieten. Berlin: Walter de Gruyter, 1975.

Cinnamus, John. *Historia,* edited by A. Meineke, *Corpus scriptorum historiae byzantinae.* Bonn, 1836. Translated by Charles M. Brand. New York: Columbia University Press, 1976.

Clement of Alexandria. *Stromata.* Migne, *Patrologia Graeca.* Vol. 8.

Constantin Porphyrogénète. *Le Livre des Cérémonies,* edited and translated by A. Vogt. 3 vols. 2nd edition. Paris: Societe d' Edition "les Belles Lettres", 1967.

Constantine Porphyrogenitus. *De administrando imperio,* edited (with English translation) by Gy. Moravcsik and R. J. H. Jenkins. 2 vols. Budapest, 1949, and London, 1962.

Cumont, F. *Oriental Religions in Roman Paganism.* New York, 1956.

The Deeds of the Franks and the other Pilgrims to Jerusalem, edited and translated by Rosalind Hill. New York: Thomas Nelson and Sons, 1962.

The Deeds of Frederick Barbarossa by Otto of Freising and His Continuator Rahewin, translated and annotated by Charles Christopher Mierow with the collaboration of Richard Emery. New York: Columbia University Press, 1953.

Demus, O. *Byzantine Mosaic Decoration,* London, 1948.

Diehl, C. *Byzantine Portraits,* translated by H. Bell. New York, 1927; reprinted in 1963.

Doukas. *Decline and Fall of Byzantium to the Ottoman Turks,* annotated and translated by Harry J. Magoulias. Detroit: Wayne State University Press, 1975.

Ducas, *Historia byzantina,* edited by I. Bekker, *Corpus scriptorum historiae byzantinae.* Bonn, 1834. Edited by V. Grecu, *Istorija turcobizantina 1341–1462.* Bucharest, 1958.

Dudden, F. *Gregory the Great: His Place in History and Thought.* London, 1905.

Dvornik, F. *Early Christian and Byzantine Political Philosophy: Origins and Background.* Dumbarton Oaks Studies IX, 1967.

———. *The Making of Central and Eastern Europe.* London, 1949.

———. *The Photian Schism.* Cambridge, 1948.

Early Travels in Palestine, edited by Thomas Wright. London, 1848.

Eusebius of Caesarea. *The Life of the Blessed Emperor Constantine,* translated by Ernest C. Richardson. A Select Library of Nicene and Post-Nicene Fathers of the Christian Church. Second Series. Vol. I. New York: The Christian Literature Company, 1890.

———. *The Oration of Eusebius Pamphilus, In Praise of the Emperor Constantine: Pronounced on the Thirtieth Anniversary of his Reign,* translated by Ernest C. Richardson. A Select Library of Nicene and Post-Nicene Fathers of the Christian Church. Second Series. Vol. I. New York: The Christian Literature Company, 1890.

Every, G. *The Byzantine Patriarchate (451–1204)*. London, 1948; 2nd ed., London, 1962.

French, R. M. *The Eastern Orthodox Church*. London, 1951.

Ganshof, F. L. *The Imperial Coronation of Charlemagne*. Glasgow, 1949.

Garsoian, Nina G. *The Paulician Heresy: A Study of the Origin and Development of Paulicianism in Armenia and the Eastern Provinces of the Byzantine Empire*. Publications in Near and Middle East Studies, Columbia University, Series A, Number 6. Paris: Mouton & Co., 1967.

Geanakoplos, D. *Emperor Michael Palaeologus and the West*. Cambridge, Mass., 1959.

Gibbon, E. *The History of the Decline and Fall of the Roman Empire*, edited by J. B. Bury. 7 vols. London, 1897–1902.

Gibbons, H. A. *The Foundation of the Ottoman Empire*. Oxford, 1916.

Gill, J. *The Council of Florence*. Cambridge, 1959.

Godfrey, John. *1204: The Unholy Crusade*. New York: Oxford University Press, 1980.

Gregoras, Nicephorus. *Historia byzantina*, edited by L. Schopen and I. Bekker. *Corpus scriptorum historiae byzantinae*. 3 vols. Bonn, 1829–55.

Gregory of Nazianzus. Migne, *Patrologia Graeca*. Vols. 35–38.

Gregory of Nyssa. *Oratio de Deitate Filii et Spiritus Sancti*. Migne, *Patrologia Graeca*. Vol. 92.

Halecki, O. *The Crusade of Varna*. New York, 1943.

———. *Un empereur de Byzance á Rome*. Warsaw, 1930.

Histoire de l'Eglise, edited by A. Fliche and V. Martin. Paris, 1934, in progress.

A History of the Crusades, edited by Kenneth Setton. 2 vols. Philadelphia, 1955–1962.

A History of Deeds Done Beyond the Sea by William Archbishop of Tyre, translated and annotated by Emily Atwater Babcock and A. C. Krey. New York: Columbia University Press, 1943.

The Itinerary of Benjamin of Tudela, critical text, translation and commentary by Marcus Nathan Adler. London, 1907.

John Climacus. *The Ladder of Divine Ascent*. Migne, *Patrologia Graeca*. Vol. 88. English translation by Archimandrite Lazarus Moore. London, 1959.

John of Damascus. *Discourses Against Those Who Reject the Holy Icons*, translated by M. H. Allies. London, 1892.

John of Damascus. Migne, *Patrologia Graeca.* Vols. 94–96.

Jones, A. H. M. *Constantine and the Conversion of Europe.* London, 1948.

Kabasilas, Nicholas. Migne, *Patrologia Graeca.* Vol. 150, cols. 368–727.

Kritovoulos, Michael. *History of Mehmed the Conqueror,* translated by Charles T. Riggs. Princeton, N.J.: Princeton University Press, 1954.

Legge, Francis. *Forerunners and Rivals of Christianity.* New York: University Books, 1965.

Mansi, J. D. *Sacrorum conciliorum nova et amplissima collectio.* 31 vols. Florence and Venice, 1759–98. Reprinted J.B. Martin and L. Petit, with continuation, vols. 32–36. 'Paris, 1901 ff., in progress.

Martin, E. J. *History of the Iconoclastic Controversy.* London, n.d. [1930].

Mathew, G. *Byzantine Aesthetics.* London, 1963.

Maximus the Confessor. Migne, *Patrologia Graeca.* Vols. 90–91.

Michel, A. *Humbert und Kerullarios.* 2 vols. Paderborn, 1925, 1930.

Obolensky, D. *The Bogomils: A Study in Balkan Neomanichaeism.* Cambridge, 1948.

Odo of Deuil. *De profectione Ludovici VII in orientem,* edited with an English translation by Virginia Gingerick Berry. New York: Columbia University Press, 1948.

Oman, C. W. C. *The Art of War in the Middle Ages A.D. 378–1515,* revised and edited by John H. Beeler. Ithaca, N.Y.: Cornell University Press, 1953.

———. *A History of the Art of War in the Middle Ages.* London, 1924.

Ostrogorsky, George. *History of the Byzantine State,* translated from the German by Joan Hussey. New Brunswick, N.J.: Rutgers University Press, 1957.

Pachymeres, George. *De Michaele et Androniko Palaeologis,* edited by I. Bekker. *Corpus scriptorum historiae byzantinae.* Bonn, 1835.

Palamas, Gregory. Migne, *Patrologia Graeca.* Vols. 150, 151.

Pears, E. *The Destruction of the Greek Empire and the Story of the Capture of Constantinople by the Turks.* London, 1903.

———. *The Fall of Constantinople, Being the Story of the Fourth Crusade.* London, 1885.

Plethon, Gemistos George. Migne, *Patrologia Graeca.* Vols. 160, 161.

Queller, Donald. *The Fourth Crusade: The Conquest of Constantinople, 1201–1204.* Philadelphia: University of Pennsylvania Press, 1977.

Robert of Clari. *La Conquête de Constantinople,* edited by P. Lauer. Paris, 1924. English translation by E. H. McNeal. New York, 1936.

Runciman, S. *The Eastern Schism: a Study of the Papacy and the Eastern Churches during the XIth and XIIth Centuries.* Oxford, 1955.

———. *The Fall of Constantinople 1453.* Cambridge, 1965.

———. *A History of the Crusades.* 3 vols. Cambridge, 1951, 1952, 1954.

———. *A History of the First Bulgarian Empire.* London, 1930.

———. *The Medieval Manichee.* 2nd edition. Cambridge, 1955.

Scriptor incertus de Leone Bardae Armenii filio, edited by I. Bekker. *Corpus scriptorum historiae byzantinae.* Bonn, 1842.

Selected Essays of J. B. Bury, edited by H. Temperley. London, 1911.

Spinka, M. *A History of Christianity in the Balkans.* Chicago, 1933.

Symeon the New Theologian. Migne, *Patrologia Graeca.* Vol. 120, cols. 321–710.

Talbot Rice, D. *The Art of Byzantium.* London, 1959.

Talbot Rice, T. *The Seljuks.* London, 1961.

Tatakis, B. *Histoire de la Philosophie: La Philosophie Byzantine.* Paris: Presse Universitaires de France, 1959.

Theodore the Studite. Migne, *Patrologia Graeca.* Vol. 99, cols. 327–1824.

Theophanes. Chronographia, edited by C. de Boor. 2 vols. Leipzig, 1883–85; reprinted, 1963.

The Third Part of the Ecclesiastical History of John Bishop of Ephesus, translated from the original Syriac by R. Payne Smith. Oxford, 1860.

Van Millingen, A. *Byzantine Churches in Constantinople.* London, 1912.

———. *Byzantine Constantinople: the Walls of the City and Adjoining Historical Sites.* London, 1899.

Villehardouin, Geoffrey of. *La Conquête de Constantinople,* edited by N. de Wailly. Paris, 1874. Edited by E. Faral, 2 vols. Paris, 1938, 1939. English translation by F. Marzials. London, 1908.

Ware, T. *The Orthodox Church.* Suffolk, 1964.

Widengren, Geo. *Mani and Manichaeism,* translated by Charles Kessler. London: Weidenfeld and Nicolson, 1965.

Wittek, P. *The Rise of the Ottoman Empire.* London, 1938.

Wolfson, H. A. *The Philosophy of the Church Fathers.* I. Cambridge, Mass., 1956.

The Works of Liudprand of Cremona, translated by F. A. Wright. London, 1930.

Zernov, N. *Eastern Christendom: a Study of the Origin and Development of the Eastern Orthodox Church.* London, 1961.

Zigabenos, Euthymius. *Panoplia dogmatica.* Migne, *Patrologia Graeca.* Vols. 128–131.

Index

Abel, 23
Abgar of Edessa, 163
Abyssinian church, 53
Acacian Schism. *See* Schisms
Acacius, 33–34
Acheiropoietai, 44, 179
Adam, 23, 54, 61–62, 74
Aeschylus, 172
Agnes-Anna of France, 141, 143
Agonia, 67
Ahriman, 54
Ahura-Mazda, 3, 54
Aistulf, 93
Aix-la-Chapelle, 98
Albigensians. *See* Cathars
Alexander (emperor), 176
Alexander of Alexandria, 21
Alexander the Great, 2–3
Alexander II (pope), 123
Alexandria, Catechetical School of,
   19; Theological School of, 19
Alexandrian Union of 633, 38
Alexios I Komnenos, 64, 118–119,
   121–122, 125–130, 146, 177
Alexios II Komnenos, 141–143, 177
Alexios III Angelos, 148–150, 151–
   152, 165, 177
Alexios IV Angelos, 150, 151, 153,
   155–156, 165, 177
Alexios V Doukas Mourtzouflos, 156–
   159, 165, 177
Allah, 2
Allegory, use of, 19, 72
Alp Arslan, 118
Amalfi, commerce of, 120
Amalfitan monks, 117
Amalfitans, 154
Ammon, 2–3
Amon-Re, 3
Anastasius I, 34, 52, 176
Anastasius II, 176
Anatolia, 122, 135, 147, 168; Loss of,
   118
Anatolios, 8
Andronikos I Komnenos, 142–143,
   146–147, 149, 177
Andronikos II Palaiologos, 82, 166,
   177

Andronikos III Palaiologos, 81, 177
Andronikos IV Palaiologos, 177
Angelos, Alexios. *See* Alexios III
   Angelos, Alexios IV Angelos
Angelos, Constantine, 146
Angelos, Isaakios. *See* Isaakios II
   Angelos
Anthenotikoi, 166
Antioch, 128, 141; County of, 131;
   See of, 132; Theological school of,
   19–21, 27
Apatheia, 70–71, 74
Apollo, 5
Appolinarianism, 24–27, 53
Appolinarius of Laodicea, 24–27, 30
Apulia, 110–112. *See also* Longo-
   bardia
Aquinas, St. Thomas, 81
Arabs, 44, 92–93, 95
Arcadius. *See* Arkadios
Architecture, of Aix-la-Chapelle, 98
Argyros, 111, 113
Argyros, Romanos. *See* Romanos III
   Argyros
Arianism, 20–24, 51, 53, 97
Aristotelian logic, 67, 69
Aristotelian Thomism, 82
Aristotle, 3, 67, 81–82, 172
Arius, 20–33
Arkadios, 175
Armenian Church, 112
Armenian religion, 52–53, 57
Armenians, 59
Arsinoe, 3
Art, Byzantine, loss of 162–165;
   Christian, 41–42
Asceticism, 50, 59, 70–74, 85
Ascidas, Theodore, 35
Ašqualun, 54
Athanasian doctrine, 21–22
Athanasius (leader of Jacobites), 36–
   37
Athenagoras, Patriarch, 116
Augustan principate, 4
Aurelian, 5
Aurilliac, Gerbert, 110
Aurispa, Giovanni, 172

187

PRINTED IN U.S.A.